Promoting Psychological Well-Being in Children with Acute and Chronic Illness

Melinda Edwards and Penny Titman

Jessica Kingsley *Publishers*
London and Philadelphia

Cover artwork kindly supplied by R.A. Harding
Figure 2.1 reprinted with permission from Kazak 2005
Figure 6.1 kindly supplied by the paediatric psychology service at Evelina Children's Hospital
(Guy's and St Thomas' NHS Foundation Trust)
Figure 9.1 reprinted with permission from Action for Sick Children
Figure 12.1 reprinted with permission from O'Curry 2009

First published in 2010
by Jessica Kingsley Publishers
116 Pentonville Road
London N1 9JB, UK
and
400 Market Street, Suite 400
Philadelphia, PA 19106, USA
www.jkp.com

Library of Congress Cataloging in Publication Data
Edwards, Melinda.
  Promoting psychological well-being in children with acute and chronic illness /
Melinda Edwards and Penny Titman.
      p. cm.
  Includes bibliographical references and index.
  ISBN 978-1-84310-967-9 (alk. paper)
  1. Chronic diseases in children--Psychological aspects. 2. Chronic diseases in children-
-Treatment. I. Titman, Penny. II. Title.
  RJ380.E334 2010
  618.92'044--dc22
                        2010006393

British Library Cataloguing in Publication Data
A CIP catalogue record for this book is available from the British Library

ISBN 978 1 84310 967 9

Printed and bound in Great Britain by
MPG Books Group

Acknowledgements

We would like to thank the families and children we have worked with over the years, who have taught and inspired us. Warmest thanks go to those who have contributed drawings for this book, including Edward, Alice, Hannah and Jemma.

Contents

LIST OF TABLES AND FIGURES

CHAPTER I

Introduction

The aim of this book is to provide a review of current research and effective clinical techniques for working with children with a medical condition or chronic illness, and their families. In bringing together some of the key themes across different medical specialities, we aim to provide a resource for psychologists working in paediatrics but also for everyone involved in the care of children with a chronic illness, including medical, nursing and allied health care professionals, as well as mental health professionals. Psychologists work alongside many other professionals in providing psychological interventions to children and families, and it is important to recognise not just the individual work a psychologist can do, but the many ways in which psychological techniques and interventions are used by other members of the multidisciplinary team.

Throughout the book we have combined a brief summary of some of the research literature and evidence base with a focus on how this is relevant for clinical practice and providing services for children and families. There has been considerable new research informing clinical practice, and the range of services provided to children has also increased. Psychological services for children have expanded in both local and specialist services and new therapeutic techniques have evolved. We hope that the themes covered in this book will be useful in helping apply the use of psychological knowledge in a wide range of clinical services.

Throughout the book, we have referred to legislation and guidance which is relevant for England and for the National Health Service (NHS) as a whole. There will be some differences in legislation affecting Scotland, Wales and other countries, and so it may be necessary to clarify local legislation and policies where necessary.

GENERAL INTRODUCTION

Psychological care is an essential component of any effective treatment regime for a chronic or life-threatening medical condition. Children who are cared for in terms of both their medical and psychological well-being are more likely to adjust positively to any challenges arising from their condition, enabling them to participate more fully in ordinary childhood activities and lead as normal a life as possible. They are more likely to feel motivated to participate in their own self-care, leading to better health outcomes, and more likely to be able to manage demanding or unpleasant treatment regimes.

Similarly, when parents feel supported and that their concerns about their children are understood, they can more easily discuss the difficulties presented by caring for a child with a chronic illness, and are more likely to be able to find within themselves the extra resources demanded of parents with a chronically ill child. As medical treatments progress and improve, expectations of what children and families can manage themselves in terms of treatment have also increased, and many parents and children have to manage complex and demanding treatment regimes at home. It is important to provide the additional input needed to support children and families who find themselves in this position, sometimes described as 'ordinary children facing extraordinary challenges' (Houghton 2005). In order to care effectively for a child with a chronic medical condition, it is essential to consider psychological well-being alongside medical care.

Research has raised awareness of the higher rates of psychological distress associated with childhood chronic illness, but the focus of psychological intervention should not just be on reducing psychological difficulties or distress associated with illness: it should also include quality indicators such as improving treatment outcomes and promoting well-being or quality of life. Although it is important to provide effective treatments for emotional and behavioural difficulties when they do arise, a further aim should be to promote resilience and positive adjustment. Providing psychological care alongside medical care makes it possible to identify potential difficulties at an earlier stage and work with the child and family to help prevent these escalating into more entrenched and difficult-to-treat problems.

It is important to remember that all members of the multidisciplinary health care team contribute to the psychological care of children with a chronic illness. Mental health professionals also contribute to psychological care for children, including psychiatrists, family therapists, psychotherapists and social workers. (In fact, only a small proportion of children affected by a chronic illness will need direct input from a psychologist (or other mental health professionals) because their needs are met by other members of the health care team.) By working with all members of the health care system, it is possible to contribute to psychological care for many more children than by just working alone, directly with individual children and families. This can be done in a variety of ways, including through joint working, psychosocial or multidisciplinary meetings, consultation with other members of the team or through supervision arrangements.

BACKGROUND: WHAT IS A CHRONIC ILLNESS?

Many children use medical services. In any year, one in eleven children will be referred to a hospital outpatient clinic and one in ten to fifteen of these will be admitted to hospital. Approximately 15–20 per cent of children have a chronic illness or medical condition that involves regular treatment or medical care (Eiser 1993) and 3 per cent of children reach the threshold for the criteria of a 'disabled' child. This is usually defined as a child experiencing significant developmental impairment or delay in one or more of the areas of sensory, social, communication, psychological or physical development. In addition, there are increasing numbers of children with severe or complex disabilities, which means that many more children survive but are reliant on complex medical management regimes.

Table 1.1 is a summary of the estimated incidence of some of the most common childhood medical conditions. These conditions vary from mild ones which have only limited impact on the child's daily life, to life limiting conditions resulting in reduced life expectancy. These rates are only estimates, and worthy of note is the fact that the pattern of childhood diseases has changed over time. For example, since the late 1990s there have been increasing numbers of children with Type 2 diabetes and obesity. Some conditions are now identified before birth or at newborn screening, and there have been some conditions where rates have reduced because of interventions in the early stages of pregnancy, as with spina bifida. There are, of course, other less common conditions not included here, and for many of these severe but rare conditions, the pattern of prevalence has changed as well, with improved medical technology leading to more children surviving, but also more children requiring intensive and demanding medical treatment.

TABLE 1.1 INCIDENCE OF CHRONIC ILLNESS AND CONDITIONS IN CHILDREN

Diagnosis	Estimated incidence per 1000 children	Notes
Asthma	90	
Eczema	120	More common in infants – rates reduce during childhood.
Diabetes	20	Rates of Type 2 diabetes have been increasing.
Cystic fibrosis	0.3–0.5	More common amongst children of Caucasian background.
Sickle cell anaemia	0.2–2.0	More common amongst children of African heritage.
Cancer	0.15	
Epilepsy	7	
Spina bifida	1	
Juvenile arthritis	1.5	
Cardiovascular	7	
Obesity	140	Rates have been increasing since the 1990s.
Cleft lip and palate	1.6	

Most childhood illnesses are treated by local services, and NHS policy has supported a general shift towards local care which is best able to provide what the child and family need with minimum disruption to their daily lives (DoH 2003a). However, some rare conditions are better treated in specialist centres where professionals can see enough children to build up expertise in managing the condition and then aim to 'share care' with local services or via managed networks of care. Psychological services have often been developed around areas of medical expertise, so there are many more psychologists working in specialist services and with rare conditions than with the more common conditions such as eczema and asthma. This may also reflect the concentration of services generally on the more severe or life-threatening conditions.

PHILOSOPHY OF HEALTH CARE PROVISION FOR CHILDREN

Within the UK, there has been a substantial shift in the focus of health care policy towards more patient-centred care since the 1990s, involving the child and family as partners in care rather than recipients of a service designed by professionals. Much of this shift does result in increased attention to psychological needs or patient-focused perspectives on health care and this is reflected in guidance papers and the content of legislation regarding the NHS. For example, the *NHS Plan* (DoH 2000) describes the changes required to ensure that the health service becomes 'patient-centred'. At the same time there has been a shift towards promoting quality and standardisation of care, partly prompted by inquiries into adverse events, such as the Kennedy report. This inquiry was set up to investigate the high level of death rates in children who received cardiac surgery at Bristol between 1984 and 1995, and recommended substantial changes in the way standards of professional care are monitored, as well as a change towards services that were more responsive to patients. Explicit and prescriptive standards of care have been introduced for many conditions via the use of National Service Frameworks (NSF) and the guidelines produced by the National Institute for Health and Clinical Excellence (NICE). These summarise the current evidence base and set down the standards of treatment expected, based on existing knowledge and good practice.

Many of these standards recognise the importance of addressing the psychological well-being of children in order to provide high quality services. For example, Standard 7 of the *NSF for Children and Young People* (DoH 2003b) states that services should 'consider the "whole child", not simply the illness being treated' and that 'attention to the mental health of the child, young person and their family should be an integral part of any children's service, and not an afterthought'. In addition, children and families 'should be encouraged to be active partners in decisions about their health and care, and, where possible, be able to exercise choice'.

This shift in emphasis also partly reflects the change in nature of the sort of work carried out by medical teams. As many more children survive with serious illnesses or with conditions that can be managed, but not necessarily cured, the focus of care has to shift to reflect this. Increasingly, research and clinical practice includes assessment of quality of life, as well as morbidity, as important indicators of treatment outcome. We are beginning to see the introduction of patient-reported outcome measures (PROMS), which are ways of measuring the impact of a treatment from the perspective of the patient, rather than biological measures of outcome. In some cases PROMS are now considered to be primary measures of outcome, because they reflect the patient's perception of the benefits of a treatment. The first example of licensing an antibiotic drug based on a PROM has recently been reported in cystic fibrosis (Retsch-Bogart *et al.* 2008).

This child-centred philosophy also extends to education, an important component of a child's daily life and one that is often affected by chronic illness. *Getting the Right Start: NSF for Children – Standard 7* for hospital services (DoH 2003b) states that 'all pupils should continue to have access to as much education as their medical condition allows so that they are able to maintain the momentum of their education and to keep up with their studies'. This is supported by legislation such as the Disability Discrimination Act 1995 and Special Educational Needs and Disability Act 2001, which require schools to put into place methods for ensuring that children with a medical condition are able to access high-quality education despite their physical difficulties. The emphasis is very much on including all children in mainstream provision whenever possible and focusing on their needs as a child, rather than focusing on their differences and difficulties.

While services should aspire to these standards, in reality these ambitious goals are not uniformly achieved at present, and it would take both greater awareness and substantial investment for this to become achievable. The reality of financial constraints within the NHS restricts these developments, and competition for resources means that psychological services are often not considered the most urgent need. Recent reviews of services demonstrate how far we currently are from achieving many of the aims or standards set. For example, *Improving Outcomes for Children and Young People with Cancer* (NICE 2005) describes the shortage of psychologists in practice. However, the existence of such standards does help provide increasing evidence for the need for psychological services and formal recognition of the part these services play in high-quality health care.

RESEARCH AND EVIDENCE BASE

All health care services have becoming increasingly conscious of the need for services to be 'evidence-based'. In order to make the best use of scarce resources there is a need to justify the treatment provided and to demonstrate efficacy and efficiency, such as cost-effectiveness of treatment. However, for many treatments, including psychological treatments, the evidence base is still evolving and the 'gold standard' of a randomised controlled trial for effective treatment is quite rare.

Nonetheless, there is a considerable amount of research about the impact of chronic illness in childhood. This research initially focused on describing or documenting the incidence and types of problems for different disease groups, for both affected children and their families (Bennett 1994; Cadman *et al.* 1987; Lavigne and Faier Routman 1992; Meltzer *et al.* 2000). These studies have consistently shown that while the majority of children with a medical condition or chronic illness do not have a psychological or psychiatric disorder, a significant minority do have some difficulties with adjustment and/or symptoms of psychological distress. Another way of describing this is that children with a chronic illness or disability are at increased risk of developing psychological difficulties when compared to healthy children.

Subsequent studies have focused on identifying risk factors that are associated with increased rates of psychological difficulties (Sloper 2000) and clarifying the nature of the difficulties these children present with. For example, there is good evidence that increased rates of 'emotional' type problems, rather than 'behavioural' problems, are seen amongst children with a chronic illness (Glazebrook *et al.* 2003). As our knowledge has increased, there has been increasing awareness of the sorts of difficulties that may be specific to certain conditions, and the sorts of difficulties that could be said to be generic, and relevant across many different illnesses and types of treatment.

Several theoretical models have been described to provide a framework for understanding the results of diverse studies and to help focus and drive forward research in this area. Wallander and Varni (1998) described a model based on a stress and coping paradigm (Lazarus and Folkman 1984), and Kazak (1989), Rolland (1987) and McDaniels, Hepworth and Doherty (1992) have described systemic models. Theoretical models can help to clarify and understand the mechanisms behind the observed increase in psychological difficulties, and effective interventions. These models have helped to identify 'risk and resilience' factors to distinguish those children and families more likely to present with difficulties. Some of these risk factors, such as social adversity and disadvantage, could be said to be general, in that they apply to all children, not just those with a medical condition. Some are specific to having a particular medical condition itself (e.g. functional disability or central nervous system (CNS) involvement), and some are specific to certain aspects of a medical condition or treatment (e.g. cranial irradiation and long-term sequelae of treatment for cancer).

Theoretical models can also guide us on how to intervene to help improve outcome most effectively. For example, psychological resources may be used in a preventative and universal way and offered to all children with a particular condition. Alternatively, they could be targeted and focus on those with one or more defined risk factors. A further option is to use a referral-based system where intervention is only offered to children with existing psychological problems.

Consistent with the move towards evidence-based practice, more recently there has been a move away from theoretical understanding towards more intervention-based research. Now the emphasis has shifted more into developing evidence-based treatment programmes for specific types of conditions, such as recurrent abdominal pain or treatment adherence (Spirito and Kazak 2006). Increasingly, treatment regimes in research studies have become more standardised or manualised as a result of a move towards evidence-based practice. In order to evaluate and compare treatment regimes there is a need to standardise them, but it often feels as if the sort of cases seen in clinical practice can be very different from those involved in research studies. For example, studies frequently exclude children and families for whom English is an additional language, and the low take-up rate of many research protocols means that only a small minority of motivated children and families engage with the treatment protocol. The sorts of children and families who have difficulties managing the child's condition and who are seen frequently within clinical services are not, therefore, represented in the research.

Within the field of paediatric psychology, there are only a few randomised controlled trials of treatment at present. Once a standardised treatment has been shown to be effective, this lends itself to training practitioners to deliver a specific intervention, as, for example, in the Improving Access to Psychological Therapies (IAPT) services where protocol-led treatments for anxiety and depression are becoming widespread. The challenge for clinicians is to support the development of evidence-based practice without losing the skill required to apply these treatments flexibly and effectively in individual cases and to ensure that they are relevant to the types of difficulties presenting in clinical practice.

Services are also required to be able to demonstrate their effectiveness through the routine use of clinical outcome measures, and to demonstrate how they are able to contribute not just to the quality of the child's care, but also to the efficiency of the service. Outcomes can be seen in quite broad terms and include a range of indices. These could include improved efficiency in operating theatres because fewer procedures are cancelled as a result of a child becoming too anxious to proceed, or fewer days of inpatient care. They might also include improved long-term outcomes in physical function as a result of rates of adherence being increased. While this is undoubtedly important in terms of maximising use of resources, it is very difficult to measure outcome in a way that accurately reflects clinical practice, and we have a long way to go to be able to use these measures routinely. It has proved difficult to develop measures that are robust and statistically sound, and also straightforward enough to be acceptable in routine clinical practice. However, this is an important area for development for the near future. (Ways of measuring outcome, quality of life and adjustment are discussed in more detail in Chapter 2.)

SERVICE DELIVERY: MENTAL HEALTH SERVICES AND PAEDIATRIC PSYCHOLOGY

There are many different ways of delivering psychological care to children affected by medical conditions or chronic illness, and there is very little evidence about the best way to deliver this input. The type of service available in any particular area is often based on historical factors, such as the individual interests of local professionals who developed services based on local service patterns and funding arrangements (Kraemer 2009).

Broadly speaking, psychology or mental health services to medical care have evolved through one of two traditions – one being 'mental health liaison' teams, and the other being what are often called 'paediatric psychology' services. The former have usually grown out of local child and adolescent mental health (CAMH) services and have reflected the need to provide mental health liaison for those children presenting with psychiatric or mental health problems but in a medical setting – for example, presenting to Accident and Emergency following an episode of deliberate self-harm. These services tend to use a mental health model of assessment and treatment and often have managerial arrangements within mental health services. They have traditionally been led by psychiatrists, but usually include a multidisciplinary group of mental health staff.

Paediatric psychology services have developed more by means of providing psychological services to work alongside or jointly with a medical team, and the focus has been much more on difficulties arising as a result of a particular condition or treatment for a condition. These services tend to use a health psychology or clinical health psychology model, and the funding usually comes as part of the medical funding for a condition. One of the clearest examples of this are services for children with a cleft lip and palate, which are organised on a regional basis using a 'hub and spokes' model, and part of the commissioning specification for regional services includes psychology sessions which are integrated into the multidisciplinary team process, alongside doctors, nurses, speech and language therapists, and orthodontists.

The number of psychological services dedicated to children with medical conditions has grown considerably since the 1990s. The Paediatric Psychology Network (PPN), a subsystem of the Faculty for Children and Young People (within the British Psychological Society), carried out a survey of services in 2008/9 and found that the majority of psychologists work within a 'paediatric psychology' context, but that there are wide variations in services across the country. Many services include only a few sessions of psychology time, which can be to generic services or to a specific clinic – for example, cystic fibrosis or diabetes. In specialist children's hospitals there can be large numbers of psychologists working together, or within multidisciplinary health teams funded to work with specific illness groups.

There are differences between the referral patterns in child and adolescent mental health services (CAMHS) and psychological services in a medical setting. Referrals in a health care setting are more likely to be for issues such as difficulties in managing adherence to treatment, or the child's adjustment to their medical condition, than problems that fit within the usual mental health diagnostic model. Working in a medical setting often means seeing children and families in a much less structured way than in a mental health setting, and fitting service provision into the existing medical framework of care. For example, children are often seen in medical outpatient clinics or at their bedside, where a quiet room free from interruptions cannot be guaranteed. This can require considerable adjustment for psychologists who have primarily been trained within a mental health setting, rather than a physical health setting, who need to learn creative ways of gaining privacy or carrying their therapeutic resources with them.

Whatever the organisation of services, in order to work effectively the most important element is to ensure good communication and a shared understanding between professionals of their roles, with respect for each other's different professional background. Given the limited amount of psychology time that is usually available, psychologists often consider that a major part of their role is consultation and working indirectly with children, by working with other members of the multidisciplinary team. Initially this may involve sitting in on medical clinics and ensuring that as a psychologist, you are both visible and available (Duff and Bryon 2005). The NSF (DoH 2003b) states: 'Good liaison depends primarily on secure relationships between staff, who can rely on a quick response when required. This happens best in the context of regular meetings, where the daily work is discussed and staff themselves can be supported.' The best way to facilitate communication is for team members to have a good understanding of the way other members work, and of how their roles differ and how they complement each other. Conflict or uncertainty about roles or a lack of interdisciplinary respect can lead to professional rivalry, which can then interfere with the delivery of services.

There is widespread acknowledgement that 'integrated' services work best for the child and family. However, services work in many different ways and can range from a loose network of professionals who coordinate their work and collaborate on some pieces of work, through to a genuinely integrated service, where psychologists are funded by and managed within the same team as the other professional groupings and all care is collaborative. However, there are many barriers to fully integrated services, including the fact that members of multidisciplinary teams are separated by coming from different professional backgrounds, bringing with them their own language and focus and differing expectations.

Services can also be very complex and include a wide variety of different professional groups. For example, within the hospital the child may meet doctors, nurses, occupational therapists, physiotherapists, speech and language therapists, dietitians and play specialists, in addition to a mental health professional. Coordinating work across all these different groups can be difficult, but is essential for the child and family. All of these professionals may be focusing on different aspects of the child's experience, and although everyone may be trying to deliver a collaborative approach, it can be difficult for families to understand the system. Families frequently report that it is very difficult for them to have to tell their story repeatedly to a range of different professionals, and that from their perspective the lack of coordination between services adds to the stress they experience (Sloper and Beresford 2006).

Social services are also an essential part of providing services for children with chronic illness. The local authority in which a hospital is located has a general duty to promote and safeguard the welfare of children in their area (Children Act 1989, section 17), including assessment using *Framework for the Assessment of Children in Need and their Families* (DoH 2000). The theme of many investigations into child deaths has been the need for good communication between professionals (e.g. the Victoria Climbié

Inquiry, Laming 2003) and particularly across different agencies. The NSF states: 'the best practice occurs when health care professionals know social services staff at a personal level, so that professional trust builds up over time.' This can be achieved in various ways. For many, the preferred option is to have a core of social service staff permanently dedicated to working with hospital services and having a base in the hospital, to enable them to provide a rapid service to children and families in hospital.

Many children and families dealing with chronic illness report that the practical problems associated with their condition contribute significantly to their stress, and that attending to these can be the most important factor for them initially. There is a significant financial cost associated with managing a chronic condition. This can be particularly difficult if the family already has social and financial difficulties. It can be difficult for health professionals to keep up to date with what families are entitled to receive, so it can be extremely helpful to have someone with expertise in this area as a member of the team – for example, a family support worker.

SUMMARY

Children with chronic health conditions are known to be at increased risk of developing psychological difficulties, and medical services need to ensure that they address these needs alongside the child's medical health care. Research studies have begun to evaluate effective interventions for children with these needs, but it is important to build on this evidence base and to ensure that it is relevant for children and families seen in clinical practice. All members of the multidisciplinary team contribute towards promoting psychological well-being in children with chronic conditions, and the psychologist's role includes providing consultation and working jointly with other members of the team, as well as working directly with children and families. While models of service vary widely, it is essential that the different members of a multidisciplinary team working with children establish effective ways of working together by ensuring sound procedures for good communication and collaboration.

CHAPTER 2

Assessment

Assessment can be carried out as part of the initial or one-off appointment, but often it is an ongoing process. With all new referrals or clinical contacts it is important to start by focusing on gathering relevant information in order to make sense of the presenting problem, to be able to develop a formulation and to identify the most appropriate intervention. There are different ways of gathering this information, and a variety of sources of information. Assessment can therefore include a range of methods, including discussing the referral with the referrer, the use of standardised assessments such as questionnaires with the child and parents, and gathering information from other important sources such as the child's teacher. It can be helpful to have an assessment framework in mind to help guide an assessment. As new information becomes available, this can be incorporated into the formulation, so that a clearer and more useful treatment plan can be developed.

It can be helpful to think of assessment in terms of different levels of need and intervention. All children and families may be at risk of developing difficulties and, ideally, it should be possible to carry out a brief screening assessment for all children with a chronic illness and their families to identify who may need further input. In practice, this is often done informally by members of the nursing or medical team, who then act as gatekeepers for referrals on to psychology or other psychosocial staff.

Some families are very resilient and have good sources of support. While they may find adjustment to their child's condition distressing, they have access to the sort of support and resources they need to be able to cope. They need general support in terms of information and general care from the medical team, but they may not need further psychological input. Others may already be experiencing higher levels of difficulty and find adjustment much more of a struggle. They may need support with practical or emotional difficulties, further interventions, and review of their needs over time. A relatively small proportion of children and families have marked psychological difficulties which need referral on to psychological or mental health services. Kazak (2006) describes a model known as the 'Pediatric Psychosocial Preventative Health Model (PPPHM)', depicting the different levels at which we can focus intervention (see Figure 2.1). This can be a helpful illustration to guide assessment and to clarify the level of support the service is aiming at.

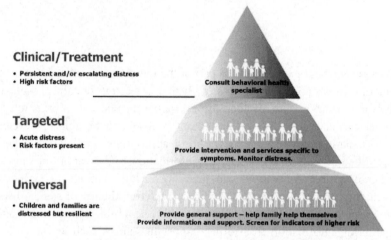

Clinical/Treatment
• Persistent and/or escalating distress
• High risk factors

Consult behavioral health specialist

Targeted
• Acute distress
• Risk factors present

Provide intervention and services specific to symptoms. Monitor distress.

Universal
• Children and families are distressed but resilient

Provide general support – help family help themselves
Provide information and support. Screen for indicators of higher risk

Figure 2.1 Pediatric Preventative Psychosocial Health Model (PPPHM)
Source: Kazak 2005

UNIVERSAL/PREVENTATIVE APPROACHES AND PROTOCOL-BASED ASSESSMENT

Since we know that caring for a chronically ill child is very stressful and can lead to increased risk of psychological difficulties, it is important to consider whether it is possible to prevent or reduce the psychological difficulties frequently described. In children's cancer services, social workers are often employed on this basis to provide accessible practical and emotional support via the Cancer and Leukaemia in Children (CLIC) Sargent charity, and they meet with all newly diagnosed children.

In some specialist paediatric settings, a routine or protocol-driven psychological assessment is offered to all children as part of the management of their health condition. Ideally, this should be developed in conjunction with the medical team and be guided by knowledge of important features or milestones in the treatment of a child. This could be prior to a new major phase of treatment or at key transitions (e.g. when starting school or moving to secondary school). Given that we know that there is a higher rate of psychological difficulties in children who have a chronic illness, compared to healthy children, it does makes sense to screen for known risk factors and try to identify children and families more likely to develop difficulties at an early stage, before the problems have developed. However, this does have resource implications because it can be time-consuming to carry out routine assessments, and this can only be justified if it is likely that there will be some possibility of improving outcome as a result.

Research studies which have attempted to evaluate proactive or preventative approaches by providing universal support have not always shown them to be effective, and as they are quite costly in terms of resources they have also not been seen to represent the most efficient use of resources. For example, one large randomised controlled study which tested an intervention delivered by hospital social workers to all newly diagnosed families found no benefits of this type of universal intervention, compared to conventional treatment (Nolan, Zvagulis and Pless 1987). It has also proved very difficult to carry out large-scale universal treatment trials in the more rigorous form of randomised controlled intervention trials, with even some of the most highly developed centres reporting only small proportions of families participating in such interventions (Stehl et al. 2009).

The outcomes of a universal or protocol-based service are quite difficult to quantify and there are a variety of different ways in which outcome may be improved. For example, this could include preventing a difficulty arising, or in increasing ability to provide effective input once a problem arises. One additional benefit of routine screening is that it can also help normalise psychological input as part of the routine care of the child, so that psychological factors are seen as an important part of treatment process and outcome. This often results in better uptake of psychological input later on if a problem does arise.

- Children being considered for a cochlear implant will be assessed by a psychologist as part of a wider multidisciplinary protocol for assessing whether the child is physically able to have this procedure and will be able to benefit from the implant. The wider assessment involves an ENT surgeon, an audiologist and a speech and language therapist. The purpose of psychological assessment is to provide a developmental screening to identify children with profound or pervasive developmental problems which might prevent the child being able to learn to use and benefit from the implants. Another key role is to assess parental and child expectations for the cochlear implant, to ensure they are realistic. A third aim is to identify any areas of practical or emotional support the family may require during the implant process, including management of emotional or behavioural problems, to enable the child to cope with surgery and the process of learning to use the implant most successfully.

- Bone marrow transplant is an intensive treatment for some types of cancer, immunological and metabolic conditions, which requires six to eight weeks' hospital admission in an isolation cubicle. There is an existing evidence base about the experience of children and parents during transplant (Phipps *et al.* 2002a, 2002b, 2005), which has described the patterns of psychological distress and has helped to identify children at risk for higher levels of distress during transplant. In many treatment centres, all children referred for a bone marrow transplant are now offered a psychological assessment as part of their preparation for transplant. The assessment includes an explanation of the role of psychology and how to access psychological support during admission, screening for any pre-existing difficulties in either child or parents which may affect their response to the stresses during admission, and developing a plan for any treatment-related concerns the child or family has in preparation for the hospital stay.

TARGETED APPROACHES

Where it is not possible or considered effective to offer a universal service, it may be possible to provide a targeted service which relies on having a system to identify families who are more likely to be at increased risk. This is often done via consultation to staff who are involved with all children affected by a condition – for example, a clinical nurse specialist. Providing regular consultation to another member of the health care team can ensure that any concerns regarding psychological difficulties can be identified and prioritised so that good use is made of limited specialist psychology or mental health time. In addition, over time the team can become more effective at identifying the children and families who need further specialist input, and develop their understanding of each other's work at the same time. Some services may do this using standardised measures, but these need to be simple and brief enough to be used in routine clinical practice, for example the 'distress thermometer' (Gessler *et al.* 2008).

REFERRALS FOR PSYCHOLOGICAL CARE

Most referrals for psychological assessments occur once a concern or problem has been identified. Whenever a referral is made, it can be helpful first to consider the context in which the referral arose – in other words, to assess the referral before you assess the referred problem. Different organisations and teams have different systems for accepting referrals. These can include informal ('corridor') referrals, referrals arising following discussion about a child and family with another colleague (e.g. during a psychosocial meeting), and more formal written referrals. In many contexts where an outpatient service is provided, written referrals are more common and services may specify the types of information they require. This is particularly important when there may not be direct contact with the referrer themselves and when the service operates through specific referral criteria, in order to ensure that there is enough information to determine whether the referral is appropriate for that service or not.

However, if the psychologist is working as part of the medical team or closely with the team, they may have more opportunity to be directly involved in the referral process (and may already have had some initial discussion about the nature of the referral). The advantage of this is that, over time, the team gains expertise about which types of difficulties are appropriate for referral and what the psychologist can and (equally important) what they cannot do. Many services have developed regular psychosocial or multidisciplinary meetings which provide the opportunity to discuss a child's care from a psychosocial rather than a medical perspective, and these meetings can provide a forum for referrals (other than urgent referrals) where it is possible to discuss the case initially (Duff and Bryon 2005).

WHO IS REFERRING TO YOU AND WHY?

It can be helpful to consider first why the referral is being made now, and to consider the child or family's perception of the referral. Seeking or accepting a referral usually indicates that the problem has reached a point where a family feels they need some help to address it because it interferes in their life (Reder and Fredman 1996). They may not know or understand what sort of help is available or would be helpful to them, but they know they want to address it. Within a child medical health setting, the family may not necessarily have sought a referral to a mental health service, and they may not be clear about the role of psychology alongside the medical team.

Many families of children with a physical health difficulty feel wary of a referral to psychology and this can be for a number of different reasons. For example, there is still considerable stigma associated with seeking help for psychological concerns. Some families fear that a referral for psychological help minimises the child's physical difficulties and even suggests that the child's physical symptoms are not 'real', but are 'all in the child's mind'. The family can also feel blamed, or feel this suggests some failure on their part because they have not been able to cope with the child's difficulties. It can also make them feel overwhelmed – not only does their child have a physical problem, but now, apparently, they have a mental health problem too. In addition, many families are fearful that talking may not help things get better, and may in fact make the situation worse. If they see the problem as directly related to a physical problem, which talking is unlikely to change, then they may not feel that talking will improve the situation. Other families may feel uncomfortable talking about their difficulties, for fear that it may just force them to address issues which they feel are better kept below the surface because they do not currently have the resilience to manage the emotional upheaval that facing them would involve.

These difficulties can act as barriers to working successfully with a family, so it can be helpful to bring some of them into the open so that they can be explored or addressed. For example, it can be helpful to begin the assessment by asking the child or members of the family who suggested they come to the appointment, and why, and what their thoughts were when coming to the appointment. For example, if the family feels that the child's physical problem is being dismissed by the medical team because their difficulties are 'all in the mind', it can be helpful to have a discussion about these concerns with the family and to help them understand the role of the psychologist who works alongside the medical team. It is usually only possible to help a family once a shared understanding of why psychological input may be relevant has been reached.

> A three-year-old child and his family were referred to the ward psychologist because the nurses were concerned about the child having frequent and distressing temper tantrums, including biting and hitting his mother, who was pregnant. Both parents were reluctant to meet the psychologist and it emerged during the first assessment interview that they felt embarrassed and self-conscious about managing these tantrums in the public ward area, and felt they were referred because they had been shown to be inadequate parents. They explained that their son's tantrums had got a lot worse since being in hospital but they also felt guilty about disciplining him when he was so unwell. The beginning of the first session was spent acknowledging the difficulties of being in such a public situation with an irritable and unwell child, and working to a point where the family was able to see the referral as a helpful and positive attempt to provide help, rather than a judgement of them as parents.

Just as families are not always clear what a referral to a psychologist will involve, it can be difficult for other members of the health care team to know or understand what a psychologist does. While there are now increasing numbers of psychologists working within physical health settings, it is still unusual to have the experience of working alongside one. In order to develop a good understanding of psychological input, joint work with a number of children and families can help to demystify what happens during sessions. Meetings such as psychosocial or multidisciplinary team meetings where referrals and difficulties can be discussed jointly also help members of the team to understand the sorts of work that can be usefully done, as well as those which are not appropriate. While written communication with referrers is essential and it is always good practice to write to referrers and inform them of work with the child and family, it is often the informal conversations or shared pieces of work that enhance understanding of each other's work, and this in turn influences the nature of future referrals.

Sometimes referrals are made to psychology when the medical team themselves feel very frustrated, or feel they have reached an impasse with a child or family, often in the context of non-adherence to treatment (see Chapter 7). Sometimes this process can be seen as a useful way of containing the levels of emotional distress, in order to enable the medical team to continue managing the child's physical condition. However, it can also lead to frustrations among team members if they have very different views about how to manage the problem, and may lead to the teams 'taking sides', or result in the patient 'splitting the team'.

> A 14-year-old boy with HIV infection was referred because nursing staff were concerned that he was not taking his medication regularly and that this was affecting the control of his medical condition. They also wondered if he might be depressed. After an initial assessment, the psychologist fed back to the team that the boy did not have any mental health problems and was not depressed, but that he was ambivalent about whether the medication made any difference.
>
> The psychologist normalised the adolescent's difficulty with taking medication, but the medical team felt frustrated that she was somewhat critical of their attempts to confront the boy directly and that she was more sympathetic to his difficulties. A joint meeting with the professionals involved was organised before the next clinic appointment, and the psychologist and medical team were able to discuss ways of working together. Their joint aims were to reinforce the message that the medication was essential, and that, although they could understand the boy's frustration with the treatment regime, they needed to help him find other ways of managing it that did not affect

his treatment plan. By working together, the psychologist and medical team were able to work more cooperatively with the young man to engage him with them in maximising his treatment.

WHAT IS THE BEST WAY OF DOING AN ASSESSMENT OF THE CONCERNS RAISED?

Many referrals are made on the assumption that the first step will be to offer the child and family an appointment to carry out an assessment with them directly. However, this is not always the most effective response, and sometimes it is more appropriate to find out more from others first – for example, by talking to the referrer or other staff involved. It can be really helpful to know the other team members well enough to have a discussion about the reason for referral, and to gather information that is already known in preparation for seeing the family. Many other members of the team may also know the child and family, and it is important for working productively as a team to understand what each member is able to contribute, and to respect the boundaries of each other's expertise.

With complex cases it is often the case that the child is referred to several different people with overlapping skills. For example, a child may be assessed by speech and language therapy, and occupational therapy, and be well known by the play specialist, before being referred to psychology. Rather than starting again from the beginning, it is important to gather information from all these sources in order to make the most of information already available and to understand what the other professionals' goals are for working with the child.

Depending on the situation, it may be appropriate to see the child and family together, or to see the parents separately and also to see the child on his or her own. While most medical consultations are usually held with the child and accompanying parent together, it can be difficult for parents and children to talk honestly and openly about their concerns in front of each other. For example, if parents are protective of the child and do not want the child to hear all their concerns, they may feel unable to discuss them fully with the child present. This can be particularly important if there are issues regarding long-term health concerns which the parents are aware of but of which the child may have a more limited understanding. If there are wider family issues or relationship issues between the parents, it may be appropriate to maintain the hierarchy between the parents and the children and see them separately. Parents do sometimes need to be able to talk about some difficulties without their child present.

There are also times when it is easier to have an open discussion with children and young people on their own. Adolescents are often unforthcoming in front of their parents and it is important to give them the chance to talk alone, particularly about their mood, in order to get a more accurate assessment of their mental state. This becomes increasingly important as the young person takes on more responsibility for their own care and as they approach transition to adult services (see Chapter 10, 'Transition to Adult Services').

It is not always possible to carry out a formal, traditional assessment with a child and family in a paediatric context. It may be difficult to find a private room and follow a structure in the way that may be standard in a mental health setting. It is often necessary to use clinic space which has been set up for a medical consultation, to interview by the bedside and to adapt as necessary. This can feel very uncomfortable at first because it breaks down the usual boundaries that help to maintain a professional distance from a child or family. It is also very difficult to ensure privacy in a medical setting. It is normal practice in medical settings for appointments to be interrupted by nurses or other members of the medical team, and clinics are often very busy, so the provision of a quiet uninterrupted space cannot be guaranteed. A consequence of these differences is often that assessments are more informal and may take several sessions to complete.

ASSESSMENT AND OUTCOME MEASURES

In clinical practice, psychologists in paediatric settings often choose not to use standardised assessment measures. They may not seem meaningful in a clinical context and can be time-consuming to administer and score up. In some situations, for example when working during an acute exacerbation of an illness, introducing a questionnaire can interfere with developing a therapeutic alliance, and it can be much more important to engage the family and gather similar information verbally. It is important to engage the child and family during the assessment, and if the process is seen as too formulaic, some families find this difficult, and it can also seem irrelevant to their individual concerns. However, standardised measures can be useful at times and can also help to document change or record outcomes. Given the emphasis on demonstrating effectiveness of our work and on patient reported outcome measures (PROMS), it is becoming increasingly important to be able to show that our interventions have had a beneficial impact for the child and family, and quantitative data can be important at a service level to demonstrate the effectiveness of psychology and to support service development.

It is, however, not a simple task to develop outcome measures which are practical enough to be used routinely and accurately reflect complex clinical work. First, psychologists work with a wide variety of different physical conditions, all of which have slightly different effects, and it is unlikely that any single measure can adequately reflect the impact of these varied conditions. Most measures in child psychology were developed for children presenting with mental health difficulties, but children with medical conditions often present with difficulties which do not easily fit into mental health categories. For example, assessing a 12-year-old with difficulties with adherence using just a routine screening questionnaire such as the Strengths and Difficulties Questionnaire (SDQ) (Goodman 1997) may not pick up any differences pre- and post-treatment, despite the child or family finding the work very helpful. A lot of work in this field involves brief interventions but these may be interspersed with long periods of no interventions being necessary. It is then hard to identify appropriate 'pre' and 'post' treatment periods. There are also many conditions where the child's mood varies according to their physical health status, and even in situations where the child or family has found it very beneficial to have psychological help, the child's mood may actually worsen – for example during an acute exacerbation of illness. The challenge is to find a measure which is sensitive enough to pick up changes in the problems presented by the child and family, and flexible enough to be used in different conditions, and even for very brief interventions.

One of the most helpful tools is to use an individualised rating scale based on the main concerns identified in the initial assessment. This involves asking the child and the parent each to identify their main concern and to come up with a simple description of it, and then to rate its severity on a scale of 1–10 using a visual analogue-type scale. The strength of this approach is that the child or family can generate their own 'categories' of concern using their own vocabulary, rather than having to fit in with a pre-existing construct such as depression or anxiety. The process of eliciting these descriptions and the joint process of clarifying exactly what the child or family means can be a very useful therapeutic process in itself for establishing joint treatment goals for the intervention. If appropriate, parent and child can then identify a second and third concern, and rate these as well. At each subsequent session and at the completion of the intervention, the nominated concerns can be reviewed and rated using the same format, and this gives a simple numerical record of progress. These provide individually relevant goals which are relevant to the assessment process and also give easy to score pre–post measures.

Another example of a generic measure which is a useful screening device is the 'distress thermometer' (Gessler *et al.* 2008) which is now used widely in adult services for people with cancer and is being piloted with children. One of the benefits of this sort of generic assessment is that it can be used by other members of staff (especially nurses) to identify children and families at an increased level of risk and who may benefit from psychological input. Being brief, it can be used on several occasions and not seem burdensome to families.

STANDARDISED ASSESSMENT MEASURES

There are a large number of standardised measures which have been developed in paediatrics and while some of these are generic, many are specific to a particular condition. It is beyond the scope of this book to cover all these measures – however, a recent special edition of the *Journal of Pediatric Psychology* (Cohen *et al.* 2008) contains a review of evidence-based assessment measures.

It is important to consider to what extent you want to use assessment measures that have been developed as mental health assessment tools, and to what extent it is more informative to use specific child health tools. Generic mental health measures such as the SDQ (Goodman 1997) are well established and have the advantage of extensive normative values for comparison. However, they are not always appropriate in a paediatric health care setting because they are not necessarily sensitive to the sorts of problems which are commonly referred and therefore may not be able to demonstrate change following an intervention. Some clinical areas have well developed specific measures (e.g. for cystic fibrosis, diabetes, asthma, pain), but with rarer conditions it may not be possible to find an appropriate specific measure.

An alternative to using measures of psychological difficulties or distress is to use a measure of quality of life (QoL). There is now a range of QoL measures to choose from. (For a recent review of QoL measures see Palermo *et al.* 2008, or Eiser and Jenney 2007.) Some of these are specific to a particular condition or type of condition, for example Children's Dermatology Life Quality Index (CDLQI – Lewis-Jones and Finlay 1995) or the Cystic Fibrosis Questionnaire (CFQ-R – Quittner *et al.* 2005). Others are more generic, but have additional modules for different medical conditions – for example the PedsQL (Varni *et al.* 2001). Generic QoL measures are more useful for comparisons across conditions, but specific measures have the advantage of being more sensitive to changes in clinical outcome because they are able to capture the main difficulties encountered in that condition. However, developing a specific QoL measure requires considerable research in order to standardise the measure, and this may not be possible for some of the rarer conditions.

For some conditions, it can be useful to carry out an assessment of the child's cognitive ability or their developmental level. Some medical conditions are known to have an impact on the child's developing central nervous system, and it can be useful to get an accurate assessment of the child's level of ability to inform treatment options and to track progress, or to provide information for educational assessment. The standardised cognitive assessments such as the Wechsler Preschool and Primary Scale of Intelligence (WPPSI – Wechsler 2003) or the Wechsler Intelligence Scale for Children (WISC IV – Wechsler 2004) are frequently used, but it is important to remember that the norms for these assessments have been based on a sample of children who broadly represent the UK population, but who do not have sensory or physical difficulties. In addition, they may not fully represent all ethnic groups, particularly when the child has English as an additional language, and this may affect the accuracy of the results. More specific assessments of specific cognitive skills such as executive function, memory or concentration or attention can also be helpful for some children.

FORMULATING A PROBLEM IN PAEDIATRIC PSYCHOLOGY

An assessment guideline can help both with carrying out the assessment and with formulating the problem. The assessment framework described below consists of three stages and is broadly a systemic/cognitive behavioural model (see Figure 2.2).

Stage 1: Identifying pre-existing contextual or risk and resilience factors which may be relevant to the development of the problem

It is important to first set the problem in context by considering any pre-existing factors that are likely to have an impact on the child and family.

These can be general factors such as social deprivation, which are known to influence both child and parental well-being for all children, whether or not they have a medical diagnosis. The family's social circumstances and cultural background are important influences on the child and the family and it is important to remember this, since these may outweigh factors related to the illness itself. Examples of these could include housing difficulties, recent immigration, or English being an additional language for the family.

There are also some contextual factors related to the specific illness which may be known to be associated with outcome. By way of example, conditions affecting cognitive development and function are known substantially to increase the risk of developing psychological difficulties. There may also be illness-specific factors which have been identified from previous research which are known to affect outcome, for example age or diagnostic category.

There could also be factors to do with the developmental stage of the child or family which have a significant influence on the identified concern. This might include a recent transition such as a move to secondary school, or it could include important tasks associated with the child's development, such as considering the increasing need for independence for adolescents and the parallel process of helping parents to allow a young person to take more responsibility.

Stage 2: Assessment of the important psychological factors from the child, parent and family perspective

Whether this is done formally using standardised measures or as part of an interview, this is the core part of assessment. The aim is to develop an understanding of the key psychological processes and factors that underpin the presenting difficulty. While some psychologists work solely within one theoretical model, predominantly a cognitive behavioural model, it is possible to take a more eclectic theoretical approach and consider alternative formulations depending on the model used. For example, while we may develop a cognitive behavioural model to explain a child's anxiety about medical procedures, it may also be relevant to consider the family process – for example, the mother's behaviour which is due to her own difficulty in accepting the child's diagnosis.

These aspects are covered in detail in Chapters 3 and 4. Chapter 3 deals with the child's understanding and beliefs about illness, and Chapter 4 considers the other members of the family, including siblings.

Stage 3: Identifying the most appropriate target outcome for intervention

The aim of the intervention and the main outcome goal may vary according to the presenting problem. The intervention may target mental health difficulties, physical symptoms, quality of life, adjustment or well-being or adherence to treatment. For example, if a child is experiencing high levels of pain and has reduced mobility, the most important goals may be managing the pain (physical symptoms) and improving their quality of life. However, if the child's main difficulty is post-traumatic stress symptoms, then reducing the child's psychological distress will be the main treatment goal.

If using outcome measures, it is important to ensure that these measure the target outcome, or they will not be sensitive to change. For example, it may be possible to help improve a child's well-being or level of distress, even if it is not possible to change their physical symptoms. In order to demonstrate the effectiveness of the intervention, it would be important to measure psychological distress in this instance, in order to determine whether this aim has been successful.

There are a few areas now where there is good evidence for a particular therapeutic approach, for example Cognitive Behavioural Therapy (CBT) for headache or abdominal pain (Spirito and Kazak 2006). However, there are still only a small number of areas where specific therapeutic techniques have been tested against credible alternative treatments in an unbiased way. As in all areas of psychology, there are real difficulties in collecting large enough numbers of children with a similar type of problem, and then randomly allocating them to treatment alternatives is also very hard. There is the additional problem of generalising from interventions that have been shown to be effective in one setting, to another setting. For example, while parenting programmes have been shown to be effective for parents of healthy children with behaviour problems, they may have to be adapted to be useful to parents of children with a serious medical illness, in order to take into account the different challenges that these parents encounter.

Summary

A good assessment of the psychological concerns presented by a child with a chronic condition is essential to develop a good formulation of the difficulties and develop an appropriate treatment plan. However, there are many different ways in which children may be identified as having psychological needs and therefore the context of the referral, and the child and family's role in this, is also important information in the assessment process. Assessment can include a variety of methods, ranging from formal psychometric tools to interviews with the child and/or family, or gathering information from other sources, such as the school. The use of an assessment framework can help guide the process and identify the most appropriate goals for outcome.

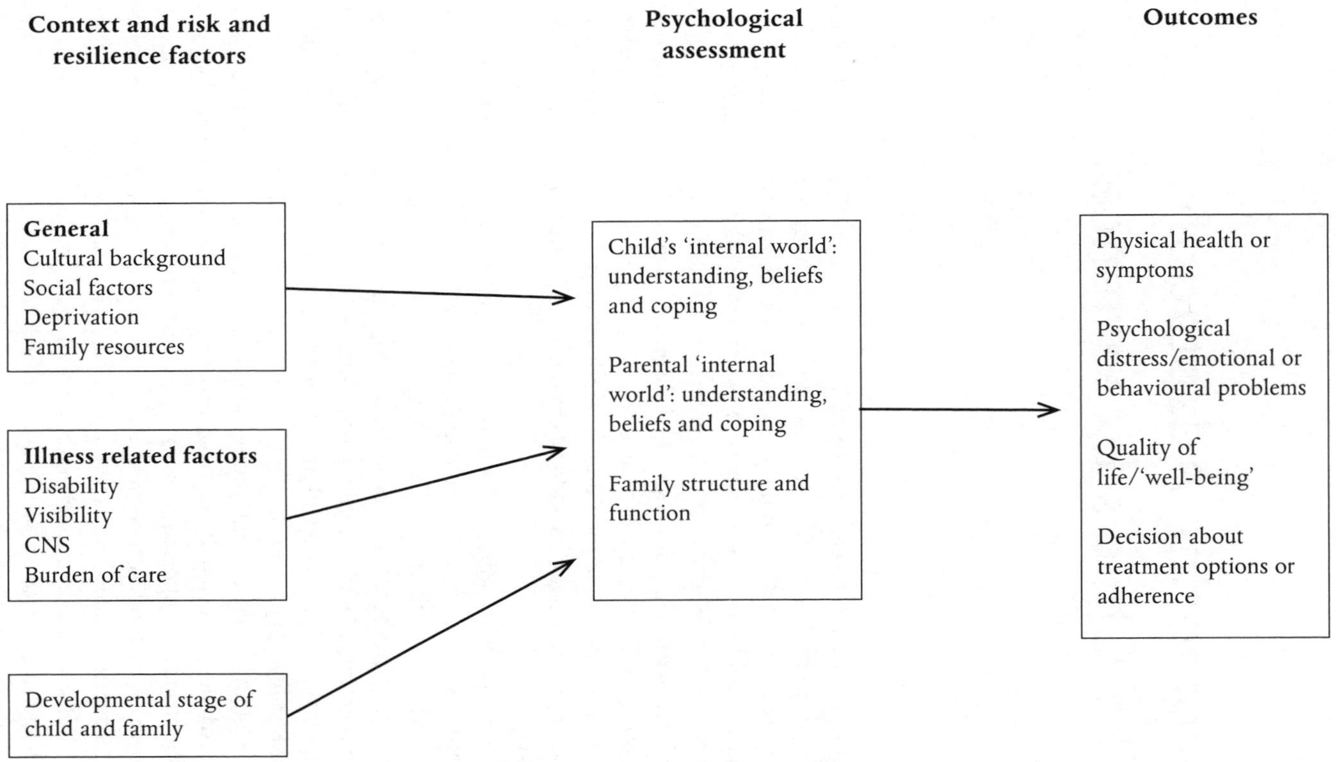

Context and risk and resilience factors

General
Cultural background
Social factors
Deprivation
Family resources

Illness related factors
Disability
Visibility
CNS
Burden of care

Developmental stage of
child and family

Psychological assessment

Child's 'internal world':
understanding, beliefs
and coping

Parental 'internal
world': understanding,
beliefs and coping

Family structure and
function

Outcomes

Physical health or
symptoms

Psychological
distress/emotional or
behavioural problems

Quality of
life/'well-being'

Decision about
treatment options or
adherence

Figure 2.2 Framework for assessment

CHAPTER 3

Promoting Adaptation: The Child's Experience

While many children can be very resilient and cope well with the demands of a physical illness, children with a chronic illness are known to be at increased risk of developing psychological problems when compared to healthy children, with estimates of psychological difficulty ranging from 10 per cent to 37 per cent (Glazebrook *et al.* 2003; Meltzer *et al.* 2000). Children with neurodevelopmental disorders such as epilepsy have been reported as having up to five times as many problems as the general population and more than double the level of difficulty of children with conditions that do not affect the central nervous system (Austin and Caplan 2007).

Our understanding of adjustment or adaptation of children and families is based on stress and coping models (Wallander and Varni 1998). In recent years there has been a greater emphasis on identifying and promoting resilience and promoting adaptation. In Chapter 4 we look at promoting adaptation in parents, siblings and the wider family. In this chapter we will focus on children themselves, with the implicit assumption that families play a central role in all aspects of the child's life.

Helping children and young people is a process, and underpinning this whole process is being able to engage and develop a relationship with them. An important aim is to understand their experience and the impact of the condition on their lives. A further aim is to come to a shared understanding about what would be helpful and to make an agreed plan for change. In this chapter we will start by looking at children's understanding of their bodies and medical treatment, and then consider studies which indicate the impact of specific challenges they face. In the final section we will look at strategies for helping young people, including giving information to children, and reviewing some resources available in this work.

CHILDREN'S UNDERSTANDING OF THEIR BODY, CONDITION AND TREATMENT

Children acquire information about their bodies and how they work in the same way as they learn about any other part of the world around them. Their understanding develops as a combination of cognitive development, direct and indirect experience, and the social and cultural context of their lives, rather than along predetermined developmental stages (Eiser 1989). Cognitive thinking develops from pre-logical, 'magical' and phenomenological thinking to logical thinking. Logical thinking is initially based on limited concepts, in terms of being concrete, literal and based on objects and problem solving in the here and now, to children being able to generalise between one experience and another and developing increasingly sophisticated, abstract and multifaceted thinking.

Many experiences will impact on a child's developing concepts and so it is important not to make assumptions about what children know based on their age. Children may be at different levels in terms of their understanding of different concepts or areas. For example, children may acquire particular knowledge about the part of their body affected by their condition through their own direct experiences, but this will not necessarily generalise to advances in knowledge about other parts of their body or treatment.

Young infants are generally very curious and will explore their bodies with intense interest. As their vocabulary develops, they will take great delight in first pointing to and then naming eyes, nose, mouth and other body parts, both on themselves and others. Children have to develop a concept of 'inside' for any understanding of what is inside their body and how it works. As their knowledge increases, children are able to appreciate that food and drink goes inside their body and that their wee and poo comes out of their body, but may not necessarily link together these functions. Young children may initially be aware of blood being something that is inside their body and be concerned about blood loss because of this. One young boy was particularly upset after grazing his knee, exclaiming to his mother, 'My blood is falling out of me!' It may be for the same reason that some children can be very upset by having 'holes' in their body, for example, from a cannula.

As children continue to develop their knowledge, through direct experience, or through information they are told or acquire from books, they are able to name further body parts (see Figure 3.1). The heart, lungs and brain are often amongst the first organs to be named, although children may not be sure exactly what they do. One six-year-old child described the brain's function as being to tell the arms and legs to move, another child described it as thinking, and another as being brainy! One

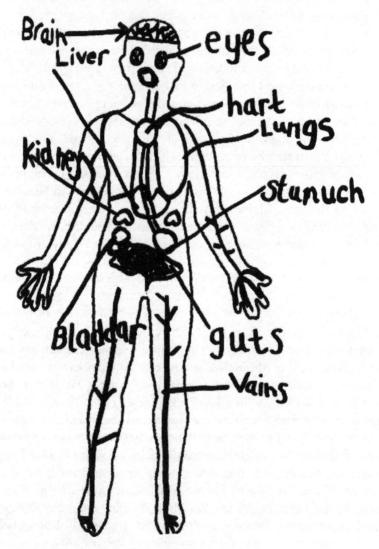

Figure 3.1 Child's drawing with names of body parts

child reported that the job of the lungs was to go in and out, and another, who was recovering from pneumonia, was very matter-of-fact, saying that her lungs were broken. Many children think the heart is for loving (and most children will draw a 'love-heart'), and some for beating. One child who was waiting for a heart transplant was worried that if she had a new heart it might not love the people her own heart loved.

Children are likely to acquire knowledge of the parts of their body and bodily functions which are relevant to them first. Figure 3.2 shows a drawing from a child asked to draw what was inside his body. He had a keen interest in bones, having recently broken his arm, and had learned all about healthy eating for healthy bones. From our clinical experiences we have observed that, generally, very few children spontaneously draw their

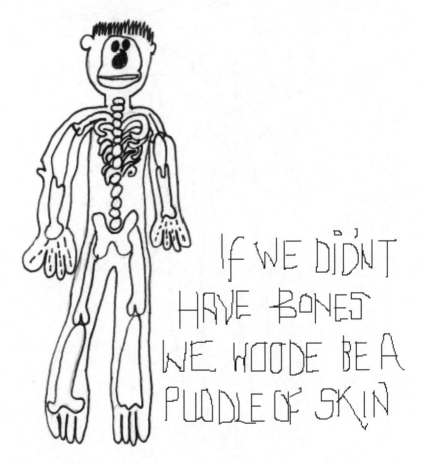

Figure 3.2 Child's drawing: Inside the body

rib cage. (The rib cage 'holds everything in' according to one seven-year-old child.) However, children with cardiac conditions were more likely to draw in their rib cage and to mention its function of protecting the heart. Children with continence issues may be very aware of having a bladder or bowel in their body, but have less well advanced understanding of other organs or body function. Figure 3.3 was drawn by a six-year-old boy, who was able to demonstrate his knowledge of a drinks tube and food

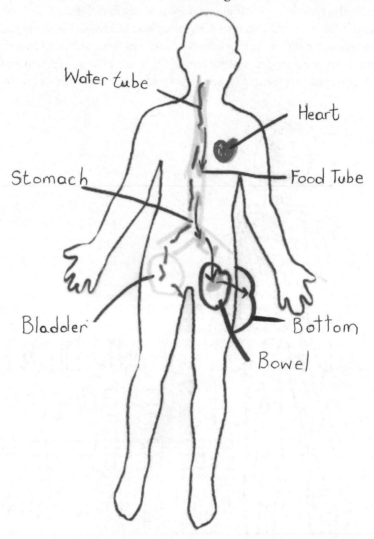

Figure 3.3 Child's drawing of body, showing tubes connecting with bladder and bowel

tube leading to his bladder and bowel. This young man had difficulties emptying his bowel and had learned from his doctors that when the bowel got very full, it pushed on his bladder and made him wet as well. Older children can have an impressive understanding of their bodies, which may be advanced by work covered at school in biology lessons. Adolescents may include sexual organs in their diagrams, which are unlikely to be drawn by younger children.

It can be very interesting and helpful to use pictures as a way of exploring what children understand and misunderstand about their bodies. In addition, many children enjoy filling in a body outline as an introductory task, and this can be used as a reference point on which to base explanations of the body.

It is helpful to frame children's understanding of their illness and treatment within a developmental context. Very young children will have little or no comprehension of their condition, and will be dependent on a parent or carer's cuddle for comfort or to 'rub it better'. Young children may be aware of having a 'tummy ache' and communicate that they have a 'tummy ache' in their head, or any other part of their body that hurts. Before children have acquired more logical thinking ability, their understanding may present as more magical, or based on what can seem rather arbitrary links. For example, some children are adamant that only pink and nice-tasting medicine works, since that has been their experience so far. Children can also be engaged in the 'magical' properties of topical anaesthetics such as Emla (the tradename for a widely used topical anaesthesia, known by many children as 'magic cream'), but may also expect other medicines to work straight away, like magic, and be very frustrated when this is not the case. Some children may also believe that they have become unwell due to some 'external force' such as catching a cold from the wind, or being punished for doing something wrong.

As logical thinking develops, children are initially likely to be quite concrete and literal in their understanding. For example, it can be perplexing for children to feel so poorly after surgery when they have come into hospital to 'get better'. Clinicians often use analogies with everyday objects in an attempt to help children understand complex medical terms or procedures. However, it is helpful to check what sense children have made of any analogy used.

> One eight-year-old child, who was awaiting surgery for a shunt, was told that the function of the shunt was like that of a tap, to take fluid away. This child was very upset at the idea of having a tap on the outside of his head. Another child was prepared for his MRI scan by

being told it was like being in a washing machine, as the scanner would go round his body. As well as assuming he would be going round at high speed, this young man was very unhappy about the idea of being submerged in water.

Children will learn from adults that it is important to wash their hands in order to remove germs. As they understand contagion as a possible means of catching illness from other people, young children may overgeneralise this concept and believe that eczema, cancer or broken legs can also be caught. Clearly, any information given to children will need to take account of their level of understanding and how they might interpret and use this information.

As children develop their knowledge of the body and organs, they will understand that illness or disability may be due to an organ not working properly inside their body, and become increasingly aware of the impact of this. For example, the following responses were gained when asking children with cardiac problems why their lips are sometimes blue. A young primary-school-aged child said it was 'because it was cold', an older child answered that it was 'because of my heart, I just get cold more quickly and easily,' and a young adolescent was able to say that his heart was not able to pump the blood (and oxygen) around his body so well, and so his lips turned blue at times, which was a sign of less oxygen in them. A mature understanding will involve knowledge of multiple causation of illness, including an interaction between environmental factors, germs, individual susceptibility and psychological factors.

It is important to recognise that having the cognitive skills to understand illness and treatment does not necessarily mean children will be interested or able to acquire this knowledge. Children who are very anxious or overwhelmed by what is happening to them may be so preoccupied with the prospect of having a procedure, or be so worried about what they hear that they selectively or erroneously focus their attention, like the 11-year-old girl who understood her doctor to say she might 'die' from her 'betes'. Others demonstrate considerable ambivalence or denial regarding their situation:

One 17-year-old reported that he frequently 'shut off' when the doctors spoke about his condition, as it scared him. Over many years he had avoided listening to or being part of any discussions with doctors, allowing his mother to do all the talking. He felt he could only cope with his fears, and the reality of treatment and numerous surgeries, by just believing and hoping the doctors would make him better, and that was all he wanted to know. This young man was not able to name either his condition or the medication he was taking.

CHALLENGES AND IMPACT OF THE CONDITION AND TREATMENT

Children react in a range of ways to having a chronic illness, and research has tried to identify why some children develop difficulties and others are resilient. There are some features of a chronic illness that can increase the risk of psychological difficulties for the child, but there is still a lot of individual variation. For example, it has often been assumed that children who have more severe life-threatening illnesses (like cancer or cystic fibrosis) would have greater levels of difficulty than children with milder problems (such as eczema or obesity). However, this is not necessarily the case. There are different ways in which a condition is 'severe' and any measure of severity will depend on the individual's perception of how the condition impacts on their life. Some conditions are severe in the sense of being life-threatening, but from day to day do not cause pain or restrictions for a child. Other conditions may cause daily pain and discomfort, and involve tedious treatment routines, and yet not be 'serious' in the sense of posing a threat to life.

Variables that have been suggested as important risk factors are pain, cognitive difficulties, visibility and appearance-related factors, and the interference or impact any of these might have on daily life. Some of these variables will be considered in subsequent chapters. (See Chapter 6 on chronic pain, and Chapter 8, which looks in more detail at the cognitive and educational challenges for young people.) Central to any discussion of the challenges posed will be the child's own perception in terms of what they consider to be a difficulty, and the perceived and actual support resources available to them. Many parents try to ensure that despite the child's medical condition, he or she is able to lead as normal a life as possible, and some children respond to this by developing a strong sense of resilience and ability to cope. The impact of parental and family coping is discussed in the next chapter (Chapter 4).

In this section, we will look at two particular challenges for young people: visibility and appearance factors, and the impact of trauma.

Visibility and appearance

Research indicates particular challenges both for conditions in which the child is visibly different, but also for those which entail an 'invisible difference'. In terms of the latter, Pless (1984) suggests that invisible differences may create specific difficulties and confusion around self-identity, with young people sometimes investing considerable energy in their effort to conceal their 'difference' from peers and appear 'normal', but with considerable shame and fear of being found out.

> Sally, an adolescent with spina bifida, went to great lengths to conceal her wasted calf muscle and abnormally shaped foot from her friends. She managed to wear thick tights and clothes which covered these areas and always wore boots, even in the hottest summer weather. She would make excuses why she could not go swimming and join her friends in trying on clothes when they went shopping together, to avoid her body being seen by others. She was terrified that if her friends found out she was 'disabled', this would adversely affect her friendships.

Infants and young children are gloriously disinhibited about revealing their bodies and even when they show curiosity about body differences, they are usually non-judgemental about these differences. Young children can also be very inquisitive but accepting of naso-gastric tubes or scars, wearing special shoes or splints, using a buggy or wheelchair, or having no hair following chemotherapy. It is only when children develop a sense of self-identity and become more aware that they are different from other children, or when other children demonstrate negative attention to this aspect of their body, that emotional difficulties may arise. For some children these visible differences may be transitory, but for others this may be a constant feature and may become part of their image of themselves, having a significant impact on confidence and self-esteem. (See Figure 3.4 for a picture drawn by an adolescent distressed by her physical appearance and identity following an illness in which she required surgery to her head.) Common physical differences arising from medical conditions include scars, changes in skin colouring, facial differences, unusual body movements and restricted growth.

Differences related to physical appearance have been linked with peer relationship difficulties (Vannatta *et al.* 2009). It is also well established that children who are visibly different are likely to experience frequent bullying, name calling and teasing, and that there is considerable stigma associated with perceived disfigurement (Rumsey and Harcourt 2007).

Figure 3.4 Adolescent's drawing of her reflection in a mirror

Therefore many children who are visibly different find it hard to feel confident about their appearance, and this can affect their overall self-esteem and cause mood difficulties. This can also be exacerbated by other people's reactions to them, because if other people constantly react to the child as 'not normal' it is harder for the child to maintain a sense of normality. School is an area which can be particularly difficult for young people, but, with appropriate support, there are also opportunities for young people to have positive experiences which enable them to manage and adapt to their visible differences (see Chapter 8).

Trauma and post-traumatic stress

Following diagnosis of a serious medical illness, or as part of the treatment for an illness, both children and their parents are exposed to potentially traumatic experiences, and may develop acute symptoms of anxiety or stress. This may apply particularly to treatments involving more frequent and invasive procedures (Rennick *et al.* 2002), and when children are younger and more severely ill.

In the longer term, both children and parents can go on to develop symptoms similar to those seen in post-traumatic stress disorder (PTSD) following an episode of illness or treatment, or as a consequence of a traumatic experience during medical treatment. These symptoms include re-experiencing the event, including flashbacks and intrusive thoughts about the event, avoidance of reminders of the event, and hypervigilance or hyperarousal. These symptoms can be severe, can cause considerable distress for the child or parent, and can evolve into PTSD. However, they can also occur in a milder form which would not meet the diagnostic criteria for PTSD, and which is sometimes referred to as post-traumatic stress symptomatology (PTSS). The term 'paediatric medical traumatic stress' has also been used to describe these types of difficulty and is defined as 'a set of psychological and physiological responses of children and their families to pain, injury, serious illness, medical procedures and invasive or frightening treatment experiences' (Kazak, Schneider and Assam-Adams 2009).

It can be difficult to assess symptoms of traumatic stress in children and, as in some studies of PTSD in children, parents are sometimes unaware of the extent of their child's symptoms and tend to under report them. Parents themselves can also be traumatised by their experience, and therefore it is important to ask the parents and the child separately about symptoms, or to use both child and parent report symptom questionnaires. It is important to be aware and assess the impact of potentially traumatic experiences for children and their parents, since, if these are undetected and unresolved, they can continue to impact on children's quality of life and their ability to cope with aspects of their condition and treatment. (See Chapter 7 on adherence to treatment.)

> Inga suffered complications following abdominal surgery and required emergency surgery. Her mother had left the hospital for a short time, during which Inga's condition deteriorated and required urgent action. With her mother absent, feeling very unwell and with little or no opportunity to prepare for surgery, which she always dreaded, Inga was extremely frightened and distressed, believing she might die.

Following this trauma she found it difficult to return to hospital for any clinic appointments and also found it very difficult to be apart from her mother or to sleep at night, as she was worried she might dream and find herself back in the situation in hospital. Her fears and exhaustion from not sleeping had a profound impact on her mood, school attendance and ability to participate in any social activities.

THE HELPING PROCESS

There are different theoretical models which can be used to formulate and provide psychological help, including cognitive behavioural, behavioural, systemic, solution-focused therapies and acceptance and commitment therapy. Each model has its own framework for understanding difficulties and formulating a treatment plan. In this section we will look at engaging children, listening effectively, and formulating a shared plan of work with them. In the last section we will look at two strategies for helping, focusing on effective information giving and utilising group work and peer networks.

Engaging children

Introductions are very important for ensuring that the child and family know who you are and what you do, and also learning if there is a name by which the child would like to be called rather than the one written on their medical notes. The child may use an abbreviated version of their name, only being called by their formal first name when they are in trouble, and so it is helpful to address the child by the name which feels most comfortable to them.

The child may have decided independently that he or she wants some help, or their family or the professionals caring for them may have decided that it is important for them to have help to support them emotionally or to change some aspect of their behaviour. It is very helpful to establish with the child or young person what their understanding is of being referred for help, exploring what they feel would be important for them and also what others (such as family members or professionals) would be wanting to be different for them. It may be helpful to ask children what would make their appointment helpful, or what they might like to be different by the end of the appointment.

Children may be very unfamiliar with talking with professionals, and may also be highly anxious about what will be asked or said. It is important to be aware of the family's cultural beliefs about health care and seeking help, as well as the child's own expectations or perceptions. An initial aim is to help the child relax and feel comfortable before focusing on more emotive or problem areas. Engaging the child in conversation about neutral subjects such as their journey to the hospital, or finding out about their hobbies or special interests, can show them that you are interested in them and not just their problem, and can help them feel more comfortable to engage in a conversation.

Listening and valuing children's experience

Actively listening to a child's experiences helps them to feel that these have been validated and have meaning. This may be particularly relevant when others have dismissed their negative experiences, suggesting the child should just consider how lucky he or she is and not complain, or when very positive parents convey an attitude of 'just get on with it' without providing a space to let the child experience or say what this really feels like. Many children are extremely resilient, and have learned skills and coping strategies for managing very complex aspects of their medical condition. However, when they are stuck or overwhelmed in one particular area, they can easily feel undermined and see themselves as not coping. Talking and reflecting on their experiences can help children recognise the many skills that they do have, and also to recognise how they succeeded in overcoming previous difficulties, so as to be able to cope again in the present context.

> Ravi was continuing to feel fatigued many months after surgery, when the doctors believed he should be coping better and feeling better. Ravi had felt very frustrated with himself for 'not coping' and had been unsuccessfully trying to push himself to do more. During an exploration of his experience, it became clear that Ravi had been very successful in managing his post-operative recovery. He had learned a new treatment regime, including taking medications, and had engaged well in regular physiotherapy sessions. He was committed to taking his examinations at the end of the year, despite having missed several weeks from school. It was clearly an empowering experience for Ravi to appreciate what he had achieved and how pacing himself had been a useful way of coping, and this helped him to evaluate his current difficulties more objectively within this context.

Formulating a shared plan of work

The aim should be to reach a shared understanding and to be collaborative with children in drawing up a plan of work. The plan of work may involve further exploration or monitoring of what is happening, learning information or skills for managing situations more effectively, or identifying and communicating more effectively with others involved in the child's care so that they can adapt or change things accordingly. The plan of work may include identifying people who might be most able to contribute in some way to a successful plan. This might include family members, friends, teachers or anyone the child considers a potential support or help in their plan.

Further monitoring may involve the child keeping charts or diaries of their symptoms and feelings, or activities they have been able to carry out. A good example of this is the 'Day by Day by Me' seizure chart (see National Centre for Young People with Epilepsy in Appendix 1 for details). Through careful monitoring it can be possible to gain a greater understanding of the possible triggers of symptoms or the impact of symptoms on daily life and work towards gaining more control over them. It is helpful to work with children in drawing up a chart or diary in a form which is most meaningful, relevant and personalised for them. They may, for example, prefer to invent their own computerised form or to communicate their results using their computer. There is also increasing use of hand-held computer monitors or mobile phones to capture specific information.

Skill acquisition could involve areas such as developing social confidence and overcoming negative feelings and fears, learning to adopt routines to take medications, developing pain management strategies, and learning more about their condition or illness. Framing work as a learning opportunity and building on children's knowledge, experience and growing expertise can be a more positive and empowering experience for children than work that is more problem-focused or directive about what the child has to do. One of the possible outcomes of learning more about their condition and coping strategies might be for the child to develop an information leaflet which could be shown to the health care team and also shared with school staff and friends. Children can feel very proud of their information booklets, and these can significantly improve communication with others about the challenges of the condition, and also about how people can be helpful in supporting the child to manage.

> One young man with a chronic pain condition used his leaflet to inform others about the different sorts of 'pain days' that he had and what assistance would be helpful for him on each sort of day. For example, on any day it was helpful if his friends did not walk too fast, as it was difficult for him to keep up. On a day when he was in more pain, it was helpful for him if his friends would carry his bag between lessons, and on days when he was in even greater pain it was helpful for him if they would understand that he needed to use his wheelchair, without being surprised or challenging him as to why he only used it on some days.

Techniques associated with motivational interviewing can be effective in establishing the child's likely motivation for change, as well as for exploring and resolving ambivalence to change, rather than making assumptions about what needs to done (including simply focusing on the referral problem as stated by the person making the referral). For example, a child who experiences pain and fatigue may work more effectively towards the goal of being able to get out of their wheelchair to join their friends at the cinema, than towards that of getting to school for a whole day. (See Chapter 7 for more information on motivational interviewing.)

The overall aim is to work and monitor with the child how things are going. 'Therapeutic letters' to children, summarising what has been discussed and planned in sessions, can be a helpful way of checking and reinforcing plans, and also for linking with children in between appointments, especially if these cannot occur regularly. Children rarely receive letters addressed to them, and these clinical letters can help engender feelings of being valued, special and respected.

STRATEGIES FOR HELPING

Giving children information about their condition or treatment

This is often a time when good communication and collaboration with parents is important, as parents will know best what their child might know, or want to know, and how the child might respond to the information – as well as being able to give feedback as to how the child has reacted. The child is likely to ask the parents questions, once away from a clinic appointment, and therefore it is important to help parents develop their own understanding, and also their understanding of what the child needs to know.

Effective information-giving is an interactive and a skilled process, including establishing what the child already knows, as well as what he or she may want or need to know, providing information and checking the child's interpretations. It involves more than giving out leaflets or information DVDs, or just telling the child information. Providing children with information involves consideration of the content, format and timing of information, as well as the role of individual differences (such as age, cognitive abilities, emotional state and preferred learning style). Jaaniste, Hayes and Von Bayer (2007) provide an overview of the evidence base for each of these aspects, which we will look at later in this section. In addition, providing information should include a wider consideration of the impact of this knowledge for the young person and family.

In Chapter 5 we look at preparation for procedures as one aspect of providing information to children. There is evidence that both sensory and procedural information needs to be given, with a suggestion that procedural information on its own has limited effectiveness (Suls and Wan 1989 in Jaaniste et al. 2007). Procedural information needs to be specific, rather than general (i.e. information about what the child will see, feel and hear, rather than saying the nurse or doctor is going to look at their tummy, for example).

When presenting information to children, the use of illustrations alongside text has been shown to be effective for a number of reasons. It can make the information more appealing and engaging, improves comprehension and also improves retention of information. There is less clear evidence as to whether photographs or drawings are most effective, although there is some suggestion that children prefer brightly coloured, cartoon-like pictures (Andrews, Scharff and Moses 2002). However, it is likely that for children whose mode of understanding is more concrete, and particularly for children with social communication difficulties, it is helpful for the pictures to be as true to life as possible. It is also useful to consider that younger children may engage better with information provided in a social story format (rather than just factual information sheets) where they have some connection to the character (in terms of age, sex or cultural background).

A selection of books which may be useful resources for children are referenced in Appendix 2, and also a list of websites which can be helpful in providing information to children. Some of the most effective websites are interactive and tailored to children of different ages. A Canadian study of children's books representing information about illness and health found that most books depicted animal or human characters that were familiar to children, as these were most attractive for them (Turner 2006). Furthermore, most children's books easily accessible to families (i.e. through libraries and bookshops) focused more on the social aspects of care when unwell, rather than on causes of illness, and largely had a positive tone, where the illness gets better. The study concludes that the positive messages in these books might make them a good resource for young children, and also highlights a role for health professionals in creating more helpful books which are more relevant and realistic in terms of the kind of care children may receive. Scope (a national charity supporting people with cerebral palsy) has recently initiated a project to include children with disabilities in children's stories ('Childreninthepicture'). A selection of their books can be found on their website (see Appendix 1) and a further selection of books featuring storylines that include children with a disability can be found in Appendix 2.

The timing of information is also important, but in many ways dependent on the individual needs of the child and the nature of the procedure. Generally, younger children should be prepared nearer to the event than older children. If possible, it is useful to ask children how much preparation time they would like to have, and to plan with them how to make best use of this time. If children are prepared too far in advance, this may increase their anticipatory anxiety, with some children experiencing nightmares and feeling preoccupied with their worries. Younger children have little concept of time, and so being told something will happen in 'a few weeks or months time' may not be helpful, as they may be constantly thinking it is about to happen. However, if information is given too near the event, the child may not have an opportunity to process and work through how they are going to manage. If children are anxious, as the procedure is imminent, they may be less able to take in information. Blount, Piira and Cohen (2003) recommend that procedural information is given in the lead up to the procedure, but that new information should not be introduced just before or during the procedure, as this is a time for prompting the child in the use of coping strategies (such as distraction).

It is important for doctors and families to have some shared vocabulary with which to communicate about the condition. However, many conditions have extremely complex names, sometimes being named after the person who discovered them. These can be difficult for children to remember or pronounce, and this can be undermining for a child who may need to communicate to others about his or her condition. It can be helpful to develop a more meaningful word, using acronyms or simplifying the name in some other way. For example, one young man decided to call his (metabolic) condition 'hippo' as the condition particularly affected his hips and mobility. He described that his movement on dry land was cumbersome, but in water he was able to move as well as any one else, which is why he felt 'hippo' was so appropriate. He felt confident to tell friends and the medical team that he had named his condition 'hippo', and why.

GROUP APPROACHES TO HELPING CHILDREN

Most direct work involving young people is done in the context of their family, and may involve some individual time for both the young person and the parents. Working with groups of parents and/or young people can provide an extremely valuable way of sharing and discussing information and helpful strategies for normalising experiences and developing peer support networks. Group interventions require considerable preparation and organisation, particularly when young people are unwell and visiting the hospital has to be juggled between other commitments, such as school. However, group interventions can provide a very different and often very normalising and positive experience for children.

Plante, Lobato and Engel (2001) reviewed 125 studies of group interventions and concluded that these were effective in a number of areas: increasing knowledge, providing information, increasing adaptation and reducing physical symptoms. The supportive aspect of group interventions in terms of reducing social isolation and increasing social support has also been recognised (Curle *et al.* 2005).

The importance of peer relationships in developing a social identity, and the importance of this in developing independence, is well recognised. Chronic illness can impinge on the social opportunities available for adolescents, and also on their confidence and sense of being part of a social network, since illness often disrupts time with peers, both at school and socially out of school. However, there are few studies which have looked at providing social support for adolescents with chronic illness, with most group interventions being illness-specific, time-limited and focused on some aspect of managing or living with the condition. In a qualitative study of a social support group for adolescents with chronic illness, Deiros-Collado (2010) carried out focus groups with adolescents to explore the meaning and benefits of group participation. Themes of belonging, collective empowerment and being able to build new identities emerged. One outcome was that the group became a supportive place to construct an identity: focusing on friendship and relationships with other group members, rather than around their condition. Young people began to shape a new self-concept that placed their talents, skills and abilities in the foreground, and chronic illness in the background. Although young people's experiences of medical care were not the focus of the group, another outcome was that young people feel less hopeless and more confident, looking forward to what was possible, rather than feeling limited and more hopeless about their condition. When working with young people to promote adaptation to their condition, it is important to keep a focus on the family and social context of their lives, and the interaction between these.

SUMMARY

Children and young people with chronic illness may experience a range of challenges associated with their condition and treatment. Adaptation to illness is conceptualised as a model of risk and resiliency, and clinical research has indicated many areas in which coping and resiliency can be promoted. Helping children involves knowledge of their beliefs, understanding and experiences, and ability to engage and work collaboratively with them to develop their knowledge and skills to meet existing challenges.

Two specific examples of helping have been discussed:

1. Providing information to children is a way of preparing them for medical procedures and supporting them to feel more confident in aspects of their condition, including communicating about it to other people.

2. Providing group interventions for young people is a means of attending to the social needs of adolescents and developing a supportive peer network.

CHAPTER 4

Promoting Adaptation: The Experience of Parents, Siblings and Families

This chapter focuses on the experience of the whole family when a child has a chronic illness. It will outline the different areas of research and then investigate common themes that arise when working with a family of a child with a chronic illness.

We know that the long-term process of adapting to a chronic illness in a child and managing the demands of the child's condition can present a challenge for any family. There has been considerable research describing this process in terms of the psychological impact on different members of the family: mothers, fathers or healthy siblings, for example. Some theoretical models have been developed to explain which factors may be seen as increasing the likelihood of difficulties (risk factors) and which factors are likely to be associated with better adaptation (resilience factors). In terms of interventions, a few studies have tried to evaluate the benefits of systematic interventions, either on a universal or on a targeted basis. The aim of research in this area is to find ways of promoting adaptation, so that we can help reduce the difficulties and improve the resilience of all members of the family.

DIAGNOSIS AND EARLY STAGES

The early stages of diagnosis and 'breaking bad news' are crucial because many families' experiences are subsequently affected by this early stage, which can be very traumatic. The charity Scope has done a lot of the pioneering work in this area and has produced guidelines which have been agreed by professionals and parents and now form part of the Department of Health guidelines *Together From The Start – Practical Guidance for Professionals Working with Disabled Children and Their Families* (DfES 2002; Scope 1994). Although the focus of this guidance is on young disabled children, the principles are applicable in many other circumstances. The following extract from the guidelines summarises the important features of the advice, and the role of professionals in ensuring that the diagnosis stage is managed well:

- listen to parents and share information sensitively and honestly

- allocate time for individual and team preparation prior to specific interviews/consultations

- evidence shows that parents, wherever possible, prefer to hear the news together and always in private

- parents' reactions vary enormously and cannot be predicted, so professionals need to be well prepared and confident to share the news while flexible enough to respond to parents' needs.

Some services are able to offer a screening assessment following diagnosis to pick up on any immediate concerns of the child and family. For example, Cancer and Leukaemia in Children (CLIC) Sargent social workers meet with all families of children newly diagnosed with cancer and are able to offer both practical and emotional support. It is important to recognise that high levels of anxiety and uncertainty are normal at this early time, and it is essential to develop a level of confidence in dealing with these high levels of emotion but also to identify when these are so debilitating that they are likely to affect the family's ability to care for the child.

> A mother was referred by nursing staff on the ward following her child's admission for investigation and after she had just been given the diagnosis of her child's rare condition. Staff were concerned about her difficulty managing the baby's usual care, such as bathing and changing his nappies, and felt that she was not bonding with her baby. When the psychologist talked to the mother at the baby's bedside, the mother was standing by the cot but not playing with the baby, who was happily murmuring in his cot. She talked about the shock of the diagnosis and the fear that her child would not survive. As this was her first child, she felt lacking in confidence about how to manage her baby and preferred to let the nurses do as much as possible – as she put it, 'so she could learn from the experts'. She also spoke about the fear of losing her

baby and was very tearful. Over the next two weeks she gradually became more confident, was able to ask for the information she needed and, although still very upset at times, became more hopeful about the treatment plan.

The following description of adaptation is by a parent, who describes her adjustment in terms of a journey to a country that she had not planned to go to.

> What do you mean, Holland?? I signed up for Italy! All my life I've dreamed of going to Italy… But they've taken you to Holland. It's slower paced than Italy, less flashy than Italy. But after you've been there for a while…you begin to notice that Holland has windmills… and Holland has tulips. Holland even has Rembrandts. But everyone you know is busy coming and going from Italy. And for the rest of your life, you will say, 'Yes, that's where I was supposed to go. That's what I had planned.' And the pain of that will never, ever, ever, ever go away… because the loss of that dream is a very very significant loss. But…if you spend your life mourning the fact that you didn't get to Italy, you may never be free to enjoy the very special, the very lovely things… about Holland. (Kingsley 1981)

Even when the diagnosis stage is handled well, it can take a while for families to understand the implications of a child's condition, and the process of adaptation to a child's illness is a gradual one. Most families experience many different stages or phases of adaptation. These may be partly influenced by psychological factors, such as the parents' beliefs or emotional reaction, but they will also be determined by the developmental stage of the child and the variation in the illness itself. While there have been attempts to describe and classify the stages a family may go through, there are great individual variations, and there is no series of feelings or stages that a family 'has' to go through in any particular sequence in order to adapt.

Also, while it is important to acknowledge that everyone in the child's family will be affected in some way, the way that different members of the family adapt will vary, partly depending on their role within the family and their relationship with the affected child, as well as their own personality. Since this is a process rather than a single event, it can be impossible to simplify into a 'cause and effect' relationship and there will always be interaction between the different parts of the system. Many research studies have tried to find associations between specific family styles and psychological outcomes in children, but these are difficult to interpret because of the cross-sectional nature of most studies and the interaction between family functioning and the well-being of the child. If the child is coping well, managing their treatment demands and thriving, this is likely to have a positive influence on other members of the family. However, if the family is already struggling with high levels of conflict within itself, then this will affect how well it manages any difficulties experienced by the child, and the child will find it harder to cope.

As well as factors that are associated with the child's medical condition, families will also be influenced by all the factors that are important predictors of adjustment or stressors for all families – for example poverty, pre-existing mental health problems or single parenthood (Brown *et al.* 2008). Many children live all or part of their childhood in single-parent families or step-families, and many children lose contact with their father following separation. Families of children with a chronic illness still have to deal with all the other normal stresses of day-to-day family life, as well as those associated with their child's illness. For this reason, families greatly value practical as well as emotional support, and practical interventions, such as sorting out housing or accommodation difficulties, can have a positive impact on emotional well-being too.

Clinical experience shows that there is huge variation in how different families manage and adapt to having a child with a chronic illness. In any clinic, it is possible to see families who are coping impressively with an array of complex difficulties, and doing so with humour and grace, and it is also possible to see families worn down by the constant demands of the child's condition and the pressures on them as a family. It is also clear that adaptation varies over time, so the same family might sail through some difficult episodes, only to struggle when it appears from the outside that many difficulties have reduced. Therefore it is important not to make assumptions about how a family is managing at any one time, or that there is a 'right' way of coping with chronic illness.

> Sarah is an eight-year-old girl with multiple health problems, including cerebral palsy and profound delay. She has no language and is unable to feed herself, is in nappies and in a wheelchair. However, she is a contented girl and most of the time is peaceful, and often smiling. Her mother has two other children as well. Whenever Sarah and her mother come to clinic, her mother is organised and calm and is able to see positive changes in Sarah. She is very affectionate towards her and always fully participates in any treatment plans. Every time she comes, staff comment on how 'amazing' Sarah's mother is. Within the framework used by the staff, they would see the outcome of Sarah's

condition as a 'failure' in that she is left with profound difficulties. However, her mother is very accepting of Sarah's condition, grateful she is alive, and currently supported by services well enough to be able to manage her condition positively.

THEORETICAL MODELS

Various theoretical models have been used to describe adjusting to having a child with a chronic illness. Within psychology, the predominant model has been based on a stress and coping framework and understanding parents' experiences in terms of the additional stressors entailed in caring for a child with a chronic illness, such as attending hospital appointments, or managing their child's distress, and the ability to manage these stressors by using coping strategies (Wallander and Varni 1998).

The way in which a family adapts is going to depend to a large extent on how they make sense of their experience, and this will often be influenced by their religious or spiritual beliefs. This is especially true where the child's condition is life-limiting, because this raises fundamental questions for any family. Making sense of this experience or finding some meaning in serious illness in a child is a challenge for any belief system, but is also fundamental to adaptation. For professionals working with families it can be difficult to discuss these spiritual beliefs, either because of the similarities or because of the differences between our own beliefs and those of the family. It is often at these sorts of times that the family does draw on its existing supports in the community, such as spiritual or religious leaders who can help with this, particularly from within the particular religion or beliefs of the family. Hospital-based religious and spiritual leaders can also be very helpful to families, and provide them with the opportunity to raise some of their questions or doubts with someone who is familiar with their cultural beliefs and rituals. While chaplaincy services may not be able to provide services for families of all different religious groups, as well as those who do not follow any specific religion, they can be very useful for some families and for supporting staff.

WHAT IS ADAPTATION AND HOW IS IT MEASURED?

In terms of adaptation, most research used to be restricted to measuring psychological difficulties or symptoms such as anxiety, depression, or post-traumatic stress symptoms. However, 'adaptation' is much more than just the presence or absence of a 'disorder'. While the literature in this area does acknowledge the limitations of these types of measures, it is surprisingly hard to measure 'adaptation' in a positive sense. Health-related quality of life measures (HRQoL) do provide a broader measure, and there are now many forms of generic QoL measures, as well as specific measures for capturing the difficulties associated with a particular condition or treatment. (See Chapter 2 on assessment for more discussion of how to measure adaptation.)

IMPACT ON MOTHERS

Research has shown that mothers of children with a chronic illness do report higher levels of anxiety and more symptoms of depression than mothers of healthy children, particularly at or immediately after diagnosis (Barrera, Chung and Fleming 2004; Glasscoe *et al.* 2007; Sloper 2000; Vrijmoet-Wiersma *et al.* 2008). This can partly be explained by the additional number of stressors that the mother and child experience, as well as the process that takes place as the parent gradually makes sense of the implications of the child's condition itself.

Other researchers have described the impact on mothers in terms of post-traumatic stress – either in terms of the disorder itself, or in terms of symptoms, for example flashbacks, re-experiencing or avoidance. The term 'paediatric medical traumatic stress (PMTS)' is increasingly used to specifically refer to post-traumatic symptoms associated with a child's medical treatment (Kazak *et al.* 2006).

However, much of the research that is carried out in this area is somewhat limited from a methodological point of view. Adjustment is a gradual process, and most research is cross-sectional, therefore it is hard to capture the process involved and to take into account changes that have already occurred and been assimilated. So, if a mother is asked about the impact of her child's illness on herself, she may already have adjusted her expectations and be using a completely different 'contextual frame' for her judgements, compared to a mother of a healthy child. This is something mothers often comment on because they find themselves coping with and managing situations that would have seemed impossible to them before their child became ill, but 'they cope because they have to – there is no alternative'. It is a familiar pattern that mothers and families manage to cope during an acute phase (e.g. of hospitalisation or treatment) and then find it harder some time later, when the demands may appear less, but the parent is able to think over and process some of the difficulties that they and their child have experienced.

The demands of caring for a child with an illness can make it much harder for the child's main carer to maintain an independent role in the way they used to, or would ideally like to (Quittner *et al.* 1998). Mothers who were previously employed outside the home can find it difficult to continue with this because of the extra demands of caring for a child with an illness, which are often not easily compatible with working. Many employers are not willing, or not able, to allow time off, but parents need time off for planned appointments or admissions, and also for all the unplanned or unpredictable episodes that may arise. Only 11–16 per cent of mothers with a disabled child work outside the home, compared to 61 per cent of mothers with healthy children (Russell 2003). As a consequence, the 'traditional' family set-up, with the father holding responsibility for supporting the family financially, and the mother taking responsibility for caring for the children and home, is more common amongst parents of children with a chronic illness. This can lead to some role restrictions, such that the main carer may feel that they do not have their own independent life and have become exclusively their child's carer. In addition, fathers become more aware of financial demands on them.

Many treatment regimes for chronic illness are very demanding and require considerable time and effort. Increasingly, families are expected to take on complex medical treatment regimes such as administering intravenous medication themselves at home. In some ways this can help reduce the impact of the treatment on the child, because they do not need to go to hospital for treatment, which can be very disruptive. However, it does require the parent (often the mother) to take on a nursing role as well as a parental role. Some mothers adapt to this and enjoy the extra responsibility and expertise. However, for others it can be extremely daunting. There is some evidence that the burden of care required by the condition is an important risk factor in parental adjustment (Stoneman and Gavidia-Payne 2006). Those conditions that include a high burden of care (e.g. regular, distressing treatment regimes), and where children are physically disabled, have a more marked effect on maternal and paternal adjustment.

For some mothers, the additional expertise and knowledge they acquire through this process can have some rewards and offer some small amount of positive experience when offset against the many difficulties encountered in caring for their child. For example, Barakat, Alderfer and Kazak (2006) found that 90 per cent of mothers of adolescent survivors of cancer were able to identity at least one positive outcome of their experience of their child's illness, but this is much more common when there has been successful treatment or outcome. It is often felt that acknowledging these positive aspects can result in 'belittling' the negative impact, but in fact both the negative and the positive can co-exist. For a long time research has struggled with how to measure adjustment or adaptation other than in a negative way, but positive psychology approaches have become increasingly popular and there are several measures of post-traumatic growth for parents. The Posttraumatic Growth Inventory (Tedeschi and Calhoun 1996) is the most widely used and has been adapted for use by older children and adolescents (Clay, Knibbs and Joseph 2009).

IMPACT ON FATHERS

There have been fewer studies looking at the impact on fathers of caring for a chronically ill child, mainly because it is much harder to include them in research as they are less often present at outpatient appointments. Some research has suggested that the impact on fathers may be very different to the impact on mothers (e.g. Holmbeck *et al.* 1997; Sloper 2000) partly because of the difference in roles. For example, fathers may feel more responsible for ensuring the financial security of the family, particularly if the mother is not able to take up employment. It is also possible that fathers tend to feel less comfortable reporting psychological distress. However, it is important not to assume that fathers are less affected, and to include them as much as possible in discussions. Often, if allowed time and opportunity to reflect on the impact on themselves, fathers do report psychological difficulties.

It is well established that additional financial costs are involved in caring for a child with a chronic illness or disability (Beresford 1994). While families may be entitled to some help with additional costs, the system is very complex, so that many families do not manage to claim for all that they are entitled to (and find the process of claiming demanding in itself). For this reason, families greatly appreciate the help of people with expertise in both statutory and charity funding applications, who are able to help them navigate through the system – such as family support workers and social workers.

While most services aim to be helpful to parents and to reduce any difficulties, some parents do find that lack of flexibility and rigidity of services can actually make the situation more stressful for them. One of the stressors that many families report is the lack of coordination between services, or the lack of clarity about who is responsible for what. It can be difficult enough for professionals to understand the different referral criteria or roles for different services, but this is even harder for parents.

TREATING PARENTS' MENTAL HEALTH DIFFICULTIES

Given the evidence that parents do often experience psychological distress, it is important to consider this possibility in any assessment with a child and family, and it can be helpful to normalise the parent's experience – for example, by helping them to understand that this a common response to this sort of stress, and not a result of failure or inadequacy on their part. Some parents find it particularly helpful to be able to meet other families who have had a similar experience, via condition-specific groups; and many use blogs or websites set up for the purpose of connecting people in similar situations. These sites are often originally set up by parents who find themselves with few others who really understand, and as a result are the 'experts by experience'. While these facilities can be very useful to parents, they can also be overwhelming on occasions when many parents with high levels of distress or need dominate the discussions.

For a parent with high levels of anxiety or depression, it may be appropriate to manage this as part of managing the child's condition, but sometimes it is important to refer the parent on for help in their own right. There is a substantial evidence base about the best ways of treating anxiety and depression, and an increase in resources to help with these conditions in the community. Usually the parent's GP will be able to refer on for psychological help. Many parents have found medication helpful as well, particularly in situations where they have to continue to manage the demands of the child's illness and would find it difficult to access regular therapeutic support for themselves, for example during a relapse or inpatient stay.

IMPACT ON PARENTS' RELATIONSHIP

Most parents with healthy children report that becoming parents has a significant impact on their relationship as a couple. This is likely to be much more marked when the child has an ongoing illness or medical condition. It can be hard to give priority to the parental relationship when both parents are struggling with the additional demands and anxieties of looking after an ill child. Studies have not convincingly demonstrated that there is an increase in marital breakdown, but there is no doubt that there are changes in the relationship (Berge, Patterson and Reuter 2006; Sabbeth and Leventhal 1984).

Many parents report high levels of fatigue and difficulties with sleeping, and this in itself can affect normal intimacy and sexual relationships. Parents of children with a chronic illness do have more disrupted sleep due to the demands of night-time caregiving and monitoring symptoms, as well as to the effect of stress on sleep (Meltzer and Moore 2008). This can lead to symptoms of anxiety and depression, and if couples are not able to find other people who can share the caregiving burden (such as friends, grandparents or aunts, etc.) then this is also going to have a big impact on the energy and time they have for each other. However, relationship difficulties can be very hard to address directly and this may sometimes be seen as too intrusive in the context of the child's health care needs, particularly during acute treatment. In some circumstances it can be better to refer parents to organisations such as Relate for specific help, or to a counselling or therapy service specifically for adults (see Appendix 1).

Relationship difficulties can be exacerbated if the parents feel guilty about transmitting their child's condition and having burdened their child with it. In some cases the child's condition may be directly linked to one parent or the other (e.g. in some X-linked genetic conditions). In other cases, the guilt takes the form of a sense of having jointly created a child with something wrong. Underlying guilt can interfere with the parents' management of their child's condition, and therefore is worth exploring and taking the opportunity to see how this may be influencing the way they respond to their child's difficulties.

In families where parents are separated or divorced, there are sometimes difficulties for the health care team to ensure that communication works as well as possible, especially when there are difficult decisions to be made. It can be difficult to know how far to involve the parent (usually the father) who is not the main carer, and it is important to check whether or not he does have parental responsibility, which gives him the legal right to make medical decisions on behalf of the child. Fathers who are married to the child's mother automatically have parental responsibility for the child, but if the couple are unmarried the father needs to be named on the birth certificate (if the child was born in 2003 or later), or to have obtained parental responsibility via a court order or agreement. Fathers are easily excluded by the system, and, as we know, many fathers lose contact with their children following separation and divorce. It is easy for fathers to get inadvertently excluded, as well, if they do not have the expertise or experience of managing their child's condition. It quickly becomes the mother who takes over the care, and then the father may feel increasingly uncomfortable, and the child may also insist that care is only done by one parent. If there is already conflict between the mother and the father, this becomes justification for excluding him, and then the situation becomes even more difficult.

However, fathers are central to decision making and it is important to include their views. In a recent study of parents who cared for their child during bone-marrow transplant (BMT), where fathers do often have to become carers because of the long-term hospital admission required, fathers all reported that the experience of caring for their child during such an intense phase of illness was a very beneficial one and had enabled them to become much closer to their child (McDowell, Davidson and Titman 2010).

IMPACT ON PARENTING

The usual tasks of parenting can be affected by chronic illness in a child. It can be very difficult for parents to know to what extent they should make allowances for the fact that their child is feeling unwell, and to what extent they should enforce boundaries and rules as they would with a healthy child. It is easy for 'normal', run-of-the-mill parenting activities to become more difficult when children are unwell. In addition, chronic illness often has a direct impact on those activities which are commonly a source of parenting difficulties with young children – for example, eating and sleeping.

It can help to discuss this dilemma with parents and help them to reflect on whether they are getting the balance right between treating the child as 'special' and allowing him or her to lead as 'normal' a life as possible. Just as with other parents, these sorts of discussions often reveal differences between the parenting styles of parents, and lead to discussions of how they themselves were parented and what they consider 'normal' or optimal parenting. While there has been a substantial increase in parenting programmes or interventions offered to parents of healthy children, there are few programmes specifically for parents of chronically ill children.

General parenting programmes such as The Incredible Years (Webster-Stratton 2005) or Triple P (Sanders 1999) can be useful for families, as they do help parents become more aware of the ways in which their own behaviour can reinforce or reduce their child's behaviours. Although it can be very difficult in practice, it is important that parents feel able to set consistent boundaries and work out what sanctions or consequences they can use effectively with their child. However, some parents feel that the experience of having a child who is unwell makes this particularly hard for them, and this in itself needs to be explored before parenting programmes can be useful to them. While group parenting programmes have a substantial evidence base, there are some parents who find the group experience or the didactic style of these programmes difficult to engage with. For example, Curle *et al.* (2005) describe a parents' group run concurrently with a group for children with chronic illness, but evaluation by that group strongly suggested that parents preferred to use it as a non-structured support group, rather than as a group covering specific topics and parenting techniques.

IMPACT ON SIBLINGS

Research on the impact of chronic illness on siblings has been less extensive, and the results are less clear than the impact on the affected child or mother. Siblings not only have to witness the impact of the condition itself on their brother or sister, they also have to cope with all the changes which occur within the family as a result of their sibling's condition. This will include both the direct impact of the additional demands on their parents' time and attention, as well as the indirect impact on their parents' emotional resources.

While some studies do demonstrate higher levels of difficulties and higher rates of post-traumatic symptoms in siblings of a child with a chronic illness, this has to be viewed in the light of findings that there may also be some positive impact on siblings. A meta-analysis carried out by Sharpe and Rossiter (2002) demonstrated a small increase in psychological difficulties in siblings of a child with a chronic illness (effect size 0.20). The magnitude of this effect was larger for parents' ratings than for children's own ratings, smaller for studies that used a control group rather than using normative values, and greater for internalising problems compared to externalising problems. The researchers also claim that there was a greater effect when the condition had a significant impact on day-to-day functioning or required a greater burden of care.

However, many studies also report a possible positive impact on siblings who can become more 'compliant', more helpful and more 'mature' as a result of the change in their circumstances. This can be seen as beneficial, but at other times it is the result of having grown up accepting that in the family their needs are secondary, and may actually indicate that the sibling is not able to express the difficulties they themselves feel.

In the case of bone-marrow or stem-cell transplant, siblings are often the preferred donor for the ill child, and the Human Tissue Act 2006 now requires that all child donors are assessed prior to transplant in order to ensure that they have an age-appropriate understanding of the donation process and that their views are taken into consideration. Although the donor's parents still technically give consent for the donation to take place, this cannot be done without the cooperation and agreement of the sibling. The existing literature and clinical experience show how being a bone-marrow donor can be stressful, but also a positive experience for siblings (Macleod *et al.* 2003; Packman 1999). When a transplant is successful, this can be a very positive experience for the donor sibling, who has been able to help their brother or sister; however, if the transplant is not successful, it can have the opposite effect, leaving them feeling partly responsible for the failure of the transplant. Sibling donor assessments often reveal the intense nature of sibling relationships and are a way of acknowledging the contribution of the sibling in quite a formal way, even though there is usually little doubt about the sibling agreeing to donate stem cells.

In clinical practice it can be difficult to include siblings in any intervention plan because they are usually not present at clinic visits, and it is often more important for them to have the possibility of some normality – for example attending school and activities rather than coming to hospital. However, it is important to acknowledge and use opportunities when they are present to think of the effect on them. Some services arrange sibling days or sibling groups as part of their clinical service and include both educational and therapeutic activities. There are also some helpful websites which are designed for child and adult siblings of children with disabilities, chronic illness or life-limiting conditions (see Appendix 1).

SUMMARY

All members of the family can be affected by a child's illness, and are at increased risk of developing psychological difficulties as a consequence. However, there is a lot of variation in how families adapt, and it is important not to make assumptions or to assume that there is a 'right way' of adapting or coping. Assessment should include considering the impact of the child's illness on all members of the family, and whenever possible, treatment plans should include them too.

CHAPTER 5

Managing Procedural Distress

In this chapter we will outline the factors which may impact on a child's experience and response to medical procedures, and describe good practice in preparing and supporting children through procedures. All children will benefit from psychological approaches to support them through potentially distressing events, and these strategies should be incorporated by front-line staff such as doctors, nurses and phlebotomists in their routine clinical practice (Duff 2003). Play specialists have considerable expertise in this area and are the first line of support for children who have difficulty in coping with routine procedures. Referral on to clinical psychology services is only necessary when difficulties are more severe or persisting.

Children with acute and chronic medical conditions are likely to require a number of medical procedures, investigations and tests during their hospital careers. Venepunctures, intravenous catheters, lumbar punctures, chest tube insertions and dressing changes are just a few examples of procedures which we would anticipate being painful for children. There are other examples of procedures which we might not consider painful and might therefore assume to be less distressing (such as having an MRI scan, taking oral medicine, or having a cast made or removed), which children can still find very upsetting and difficult to cooperate with. Therefore the guidelines in this chapter relate to any procedure which could be potentially distressing, however 'trivial' or innocuous it might appear to adults.

Although many children show remarkable resilience, studies indicate that children still experience procedures and associated anticipatory anxiety as the most fearful and distressing aspect of their condition or hospitalisation (Broome *et al.* 1994; Schechter *et al.* 1997). The invasive nature of many of the procedures can also heighten children's sense of vulnerability, particularly if the procedure is unknown or unfamiliar. For some children there may be additional anxiety relating to the results of the tests, which may bring upsetting news about how their body is functioning and the possible need for further tests or treatment.

Providing the highest possible quality of health care for children requires improving children's experience of procedures, promoting effective coping strategies and reducing the risk of post-procedural emotional and behavioural disturbance. This is particularly important for children who require repeated procedures or treatment over prolonged periods of time. There is a clear risk for children if they are repeatedly exposed to distressing situations, as this may increasingly sensitise them to difficult aspects of the procedure and even become traumatic for them. This can set off a spiralling negative chain of responses to treatments in both the short and long term, with implications for health care and well-being.

Reducing children's distress can also reduce stress for parents and professionals. Parents can feel totally helpless and undermined when seeing their child upset during procedures. Children may react angrily to parents for allowing medical staff to 'hurt' them, and parents may feel the impact of this on their relationship with their child, and their ability to support the child at subsequent hospital appointments. Professionals also report high levels of stress when carrying out procedures on very distressed children, which can impact negatively on the way they interact with children, making them more hesitant or, conversely, more impatient to finish the procedure. It may also undermine their confidence and lead to avoidance of carrying out particular procedures.

There is also a cost benefit to enabling children to manage procedures more effectively. Considerable time can be spent trying to carry out a procedure with a distressed and uncooperative child, and the outcome of this might be a need for sedation, or even having to abandon the procedure altogether. Promoting coping may help to reduce the clinical time needed for the procedure. It may also reduce the number of procedures which need to be rescheduled, with cost implications for professional time, as well the additional time and costs incurred by the family in travelling to the hospital for further appointments.

> A recent study carried out by the MRI department at the Evelina Hospital (Guy's and St Thomas' Foundation Trust) showed that when children were appropriately prepared for MRI scan (in a play preparation session with a play specialist), a significantly higher proportion of children were able to lie still for the scan and achieve good quality pictures without using a general anaesthetic. An improvement of 42 per cent was reported in terms of picture

quality, which reduced the need for repeating the scan using a general anaesthetic. (Moon and Stachini 2009)

FACTORS ASSOCIATED WITH COPING WITH MEDICAL PROCEDURES

Children and their families will have a unique set of characteristics which will interplay to determine a child's reaction and coping with medical procedures. These include characteristics of the child, parental attitudes and behaviour, the context of the procedure and the child's previous experience of hospital and tests.

Characteristics of the child

The age and temperament of the child may affect coping style. Younger children are likely to report greater pain and show more behavioural distress than older children (Goodenough *et al*. 1999; Kleiber *et al*. 2007). Children with a temperament characterised by low adaptability, low mood and high emotionality are likely to show higher levels of distress (Ranger and Campbell-Yeo 2008).

Parental factors

A systematic review of studies of the impact of parental presence during medical procedures concluded that there was limited evidence of the relationship between parental presence and the levels of distress shown by children, but indicated potential advantages for parents in being present (Piira *et al*. 2005). Most parents do prefer to be present during venepuncture (Bauchner, Vinci and Waring 1989), and an increase in parental satisfaction with care was reported when a parent was present (Kain *et al*. 2000). Other studies have indicated that most children prefer their parents to be present and experience less distress when parents take on appropriate active roles during the procedure (Waseem and Ryan 2003; Woolfram, Turner and Philpur 1997). A possible exception to parents being present is if parents are extremely anxious themselves, or if they are conveying negative expectations about pain during the procedure, as this can impact negatively on children's experience of pain and behaviour (Hirschfield *et al*. 1992; Lansdown and Sokel 1993; Liossi *et al*. 2007). The value of psychological intervention with parents, helping them to focus positively on the forthcoming procedure and training them to be most effective in supporting and distracting their child, has been highlighted by Liossi *et al.* (2007).

Previous experience

There is no documented relationship between the number of procedures experienced by a child and levels of distress. However, the more negative the experience of procedures (in terms of pain or distress), the greater the subsequent anxiety and difficulty in managing future procedures (Dahlquist *et al.* 1986; Weisman, Bernstein and Schechter 1998). Many children who are extremely anxious about having a procedure can recall a traumatic or upsetting previous experience in hospital. This may have included being restrained or held down, being hurt or being in pain. Some children feel strongly they were not listened to, particularly when they asked for the procedure to stop, or remember feeling humiliated when told off by cross parents or frustrated staff. Examples include being told by professionals that 'even little children don't make so much fuss', and to 'stop being such a baby', parents threatening to leave them on their own in hospital if they did not cooperate, and feeling scared as they did not know what was happening or what was going to happen next.

The implications of negative experiences can be seen in both the short and long term. In a retrospective study of young adults, their childhood memories of procedural fears and pain was predictive of their current self-reported levels of pain and fear as an adult (Pate *et al.* 1996). Aversive childhood experiences were also predictive of avoidance of medical situations such as clinic appointments as adults, with clear implications for appropriate health seeking and optimum health care as adults.

Situational factors

Children who present as acutely unwell and those who are less familiar with being in hospital have been shown to find needle insertion more distressing than children who have more experience with hospitals (Bauchner, Vinci and May 1994). This may be due to having fewer pre-existing coping strategies, less time available for preparation due to the urgency of procedures, and added anxiety about unfamiliar hospital staff and procedures.

Prolonged exposure to anxiety-provoking cues (particularly if the child is already sensitised and anxious) for venepuncture can also increase fear (Duff and Bliss 2005). Anxiety-provoking cues can include seeing medical equipment or even having Emla (the tradename for a widely used topical anaesthesia) cream patches applied, which must be done an hour before a blood test.

PREPARATION

The NSF (DoH 2003b) recommends that children need access to 'accurate information that is valid, relevant, up-to-date, timely, understandable and developmentally, ethically and culturally appropriate'. Good preparation for children addresses both the sensory and affective experience of medical procedures. It can help to mobilise coping thoughts and responses prior to the event and enable mental rehearsal (the 'work of worrying') to occur. It can also help children and parents correctly anticipate what the procedure entails. Preparation can help enhance children's sense of control in a situation which can feel overwhelming, and can improve self-esteem. (See Figure 5.1. This picture was drawn by a seven-year-old girl, who was pleased with how well she coped with her blood test.)

Figure 5.1 Child's drawing of a medical procedure

The Paediatric Psychology Network (PPN), a subsystem of the Faculty for Children and Young People within the British Psychological Society, has produced a set of good practice guidelines on managing procedural distress (PPN 2010). It provides both a theoretical framework and a practical process for supporting children through procedures.

The following are general points for good practice in preparation for medical procedures:

1. *Establish a good rapport with the child/young person and their family.* A positive and effective relationship underpins all work that can be carried out with the child.

2. *Assess the child's developmental level, understanding of the procedure to be carried out and prior experience of procedures.* It is important not to make assumptions about what a child knows or might find difficult. If the child has already experienced this or a similar procedure, it is helpful to clarify their understanding of the event so as to be aware of any misconceptions which might undermine coping. It is particularly good to know what, if anything, has previously been helpful. This might include who was present, what distraction techniques were used, and the most helpful topical anaesthetic used. Talking with children about previous success and positive aspects of their prior experience can help build on resiliency and reinforce the skills already used.

3. *Ensure that the parents are well prepared and can work with the health care team in preparing their child most effectively.* For younger children, much of the information about their experiences of previous procedures will be given by parents. It is important to ensure that parents are aware of the processes involved in carrying out the procedure, and to formulate a plan with them about the best way of supporting their child, including what role they themselves would be comfortable to take in the room. Parents can be guided as to how they might be most effective in supporting their child – for example by providing distraction or positive reinforcement for their child's coping behaviours. It may be helpful if some of these discussions are not held in the child's presence.

4. *Allow sufficient time for the preparation to take place.* For older children, information and preparation may be helpful some time in advance, but for younger children, preparation much closer to the event is thought to be more helpful. Younger children may have a poor concept of time and might inadvertently be put on a permanent

state of readiness and anxiety waiting for the procedure to happen, which may counteract any positive effect of the preparation.

5. *Give the child appropriate information about the procedure.* Information needs to be honest, but framed in such a way as to be as containing and reassuring as possible. Children need to be told what is to be done and why, sensory information about the process (what they will see, hear, smell and feel), how long the process will take (e.g. a few minutes or as long as it takes to sing a particular song), and how they will feel afterwards. The framing of sensations in a meaningful and safe way for children is important. For example, the gentle, whirring sound of a machine can be likened to the wings of a butterfly, whereas a louder sound (such as that of the saw for removing plaster casts) can be likened to a motorbike. An ultrasound is often referred to as 'jelly on the belly', as the lubricating gel used is cold and slippery, like jelly. When giving any information to children about procedures, it is also helpful to let them know what they can do that will help. This might include holding their arm still (for a blood test) or curling into a ball (for a lumbar puncture). It might be helpful to focus on the most important things that the child can do to help, and not give too many instructions, which could feel overwhelming. It is also helpful to frame all instructions positively ('Hold your arm as still as you can' rather than 'Do not move your arm'). It can also be helpful to let children know that it is alright to make a noise during the test. Children do not have to be silent for the test to be successfully carried out, even though it does make parents and health professionals feel better if they do not cry out! Some children respond very positively to the suggestion of making a more interesting noise during the procedure, such as singing the highest musical note that they know, or roaring like a lion! It is important not to give false reassurances to children (such as 'You won't feel a thing'), as this will quickly prove not to be true and will only serve to undermine confidence in what they are told on future occasions.

6. *Plan and rehearse helpful strategies.* This might involve giving the child and family the opportunity to familiarise themselves with the equipment (such as looking at the cannula). Children may also find it helpful to role-play the situation, including walking into the treatment room and finding the most comfortable way

of sitting on the chair or resting on the couch, and holding their arm still.

7. *Acknowledge and praise the child's efforts, skills and development of skills to help them manage the procedure.* Children can be praised for their ideas about what will help during the procedure, and this can be made more concrete by writing or drawing out a plan for their doctors and nurses to follow. Children can also be rewarded for practising any of the skills that have been identified for them to use, such as sitting still or looking away from what is happening. Some children may choose to help during the procedure by bringing together the equipment that will be used, and can be praised for their expertise in knowing what to get ready.

8. *Prepare the environment.* It is helpful to consider carefully the most appropriate place for carrying out the procedure. It is usually best for this to be in a treatment room, and to avoid 'safe' places, such as a play area or the child's bedside, so that the child knows, when they leave the treatment room, that the procedure is over and they can relax and not worry about anything else happening to them. It is also important to decide who needs to be in the room, and the role that each person will have. It is helpful to be clear who is leading during the procedure, and to assign one person to engage with and talk to the child. It can be confusing and chaotic if members of the team have not coordinated their approach, with conflicting plans and conversations taking place in the room as one person tries to distract the child while another is giving the child instructions about the procedure. It is helpful to keep the number of people to a minimum, especially if the child is likely to be anxious. It is best to prepare medical equipment before the child enters the treatment room and to keep it out of sight until it is needed, so as to minimise the child's exposure to potentially anxiety-provoking stimuli. To provide the most appropriate environment for the child in the treatment room, it is useful to get the advice of a play specialist, who will be skilled in advising on appropriate distraction and toys to have in the treatment room to draw the child's gaze to something pleasant instead of just medical equipment in the room.

RESOURCES FOR PREPARATION

Many hospitals have their own leaflets and resources to prepare children and their parents for procedures. Some of these can be accessed through the hospital's own website. Other materials can be accessed through Action for Sick Children (see Appendix 1). As a general principle, preparation material should be specific rather than general. There is good evidence that watching a film of another child undergoing the procedure while using a coping model strategy (where the child model displays some anxiety but overcomes this and demonstrates coping skills to get through the procedure successfully) is effective (Melamed and Siegal 1975). Preparation involving skill development (such as relaxation training) is particularly effective. Information may also be given in preparation booklets (see Appendix 2), and through preparatory play sessions with play specialists. If children are likely to be anxious during a procedure, it is very helpful to involve a play specialist prior to the procedure taking place. Clearly, once a procedure has been attempted and the child is distressed, it is much more difficult for a play specialist to succeed in distracting and reassuring the child.

SUPPORTING CHILDREN TO PROMOTE COPING DURING PROCEDURES

Psychological interventions for managing pain and distress in children are primarily based on Cognitive Behavioural Therapy (CBT). Cognitive interventions are those which identify and alter negative thinking styles (in this context, specifically those which relate to anxiety about the procedure) and replace them with more positive beliefs and attitudes to support a more adaptive behaviour and way of coping. A range of cognitive behavioural interventions may be utilised, including distraction, guided imagery, relaxation training, graded exposure and reinforcement scheduling. Christie and Wilson (2005) carried out a systematic review of practice-based evidence and concluded that CBT was successful in the alleviation of procedurally related distress. A meta-analysis of cognitive behavioural strategies has supported their efficacy in interventions with children and adolescents to manage or reduce pain and distress associated with needle procedures. The largest effect sizes for alleviating pain were found for distraction, a combination of distraction and suggestion, and hypnosis for self-reported pain, and for combined CBT interventions for observer-reported distress and behavioural measures of distress (Uman *et al.* 2008).

One of the main aims of any intervention is to help children feel more in control of their feelings and what is happening. There are ways of helping children feel more in control that offer them appropriate (and suitably limited) choices. When children are very anxious, they may try to take on more control and use this to delay or even prevent the feared event from happening.

> Asha, a seven-year-old girl, was very anxious about having regular blood tests, and had reacted by organising people in the room and telling them how she wanted things to be done. In an attempt to help Asha feel less anxious, staff were eager to follow her lead. Unfortunately, the outcome of this 'free hand' was that Asha wanted first to sit on her mum's lap, then her grandmother's lap, and then to have the play specialist, then her nurse, to hold her hand. Then she wanted one doctor, then another, and then her nurse to do the blood test, and continued with these demands, until considerable time had passed and the test had still not been done, with Asha becoming increasingly agitated and distressed.

Clearly, in this example, the child was procrastinating and becoming more anxious as time passed. Children can still be given control, but it is best if the preparation and planning is carried out and agreed in advance, with children's choices being limited appropriately in the treatment room.

Distraction

The aim of distraction during procedures is to help the child shift attention away from distressing aspects of the procedure to something more pleasant and positive. Distraction can have sensory, physical and cognitive domains. In order to be most effective, distraction techniques or resources need to be interactive and varied, and require active participation from the child (Dahlquist *et al.* 2002). They also need to be developmentally appropriate.

Infants can be distracted and soothed with stroking or nursery rhymes, and young children may engage well with action toys, pop-up or musical books, party blowers, interactive hand puppets and blowing bubbles.

> Jamie, aged 16 months, was just in the process of letting out a cry following an injection when he was presented with an action toy which moved when pressed, and let out a cry of delight instead!

There are a variety of distractions suitable for older children, and it can be helpful to tailor these to the interests of the child. For example, children may be well engaged by competitive games against another person in the room, such as card games ('Snap') or being challenged by verbal sums, such as times tables or counting backwards in multiples of threes. Children can often be well engaged in spotting 'deliberate' mistakes of an adult reciting tables or singing a song, which can be a useful strategy if the child is less willing to participate directly in distraction techniques. Children might also participate well in non-medical talk such as telling jokes, singing, or engaging in fantasy/superhero stories. Lansdown and Sokel (1993) suggest a way of enhancing coping strategies using storytelling, and give an example of a story in which the child meets their hero, who tells them about an invisible 'magic glove'. When they put the glove on, any sensations of pain are greatly reduced. The child can then be helped to participate in the rest of the story by trying out the glove during the procedure.

It can be helpful to plan with children what they would find the most positive distraction for them. An excellent idea from one young person involved crunching on a mint sweet (that he was normally told off for crunching!) at the exact moment he sensed the needle going in, in order for the full explosion of mint taste to distract him away from any pain.

There may be a need to have a variety of distraction materials or strategies available, in order to occupy the child both prior to the procedure (as when waiting for the topical anaesthesia to take effect) and during the procedure itself. It may be more useful to keep the most active and engaging strategies for the actual procedure itself. It is also likely that the novelty factor of some distraction techniques may wane over time and therefore not engage the child.

Dahlquist *et al.* (2002) have noted some promising results showing the long-term effects of distraction for children needing repeated procedures, following a standardised nine-session coaching of their parents on distraction techniques. However, many other situational factors will impact on the effectiveness of distraction, including the length of the procedure and the level of discomfort, as well as the child's response to the particular distraction technique.

Breathing techniques

Taking controlled and slightly deeper breaths has been shown to be very useful in attaining a relaxed physical state. Children can be instructed to inhale up to a count of three and exhale through their mouths for a slow count of three. Younger children may benefit from more concrete ways of learning to control their breathing: they could be asked to pretend they are blowing out the candles on a birthday cake when exhaling, or blowing a 'magic feather' on their hand, hard enough to make the feather 'dance' on their hand, but not so hard that it falls off!

Relaxation

Relaxation helps reduce physiological arousal by breathing slowly and releasing muscle tension. Progressive muscle relaxation techniques are often used, where muscle groups are tensed and then relaxed around the body. Many procedures will feel less uncomfortable for children if they are more relaxed, such as the insertion of a catheter. If muscles are tense, it is much more difficult to ease the catheter through to the bladder. Relaxation is a skill which takes time to learn and requires practice before the child is able to apply this skill in a situation where he or she may feel tense. There are helpful resources, such as relaxation tapes, available to help children learn relaxation skills that can be practised at home (see Appendix 1). Some clinicians prefer to make their own recording of the relaxation session, so that the pacing and words used are familiar and meaningful for the child.

Hypnosis

There does not seem to be a universally accepted definition of hypnosis. Some suggest that it is really deep relaxation and guided imagery, and others believe that it is an altered state of consciousness. As a result, the evidence base for hypnosis is equivocal. Clinically, staff trained in hypnosis are able to offer this treatment, and some children and families do report finding this helpful, although it is difficult to know which element of the hypnosis has been effective. (For example, it could be either the deep relaxation or the power of suggestion.)

Topical anaesthesia

Emla and Ametop are topical anaesthetic creams which are widely used in paediatric practice, providing a non-invasive and painless way of delivering local anaesthetic. They need to be left on the skin for at least 30 minutes (Ametop) and 60 minutes (Emla) to be effective. It is most helpful for the person who is going to carry out the blood test to apply the cream, or someone knowledgeable about the most likely sites on the child's body for the test, otherwise the child might end up with multiple sites covered in cream, but end up needing the test carried out on a different site, which is very distressing for the child. Although many children are very reassured about using this 'magic cream', for others it can serve as a trigger for pre-procedural anxiety and heighten their distress, and so may not be useful. An alternative to cream for older children is a 'cold spray' (a preparation of ethyl chloride), which numbs the skin and is used directly before the procedure. The extreme coldness of the spray can be quite a shock if this experience is not expected, with the sensation interpreted as painful by some. It is useful to let the child try out the spray before using it during the procedure, to familiarise them with the resulting sensations.

Studies have compared psychological preparation to the use of topical anaesthesia such as Emla or Ametop cream, with psychological preparation being as effective, or more effective, than Emla (Cohen *et al.* 1999). Emla can serve as both a local anaesthetic and a mediating factor in reducing distress, with children anticipating being in less pain due to their belief in the effectiveness of Emla. A combination of psychological intervention and pharmacological treatment is seen to be the most effective approach (Kazak *et al.* 1996). Sedation may be required when the procedure is more complex or painful. A good review of this area has been carried out by Harvey and Morton (2007).

For young infants under the age of 12 months, sucrose solution is recommended as the most effective pain relief, in combination with a trusted adult providing physical containment and distraction.

POST-PROCEDURAL EVALUATION AND FEEDBACK

Following the procedure, it is helpful to spend a little time talking with children about their experience, both in terms of the difference between what they had expected and what their actual experience was, and also in thinking about what helped most, or anything specific they did which contributed to their success. This stage is often neglected, as people are often just pleased (or relieved) to have finished the procedure and quickly move on to the next thing, and so the opportunity to acknowledge and make a note of what helped and needs to be in place the following time may be lost. Also, if children have not been able to process what was helpful, they may not be any better prepared the next time they have this procedure, and may go away with the belief that they were lucky to have got through the procedure, but could never do it again.

WAYS OF HELPING DURING A PROCEDURE WHEN PREPARATION HAS NOT BEEN SUCCESSFUL

When problems arise during the procedure, such as the child becoming very distressed and unable to cooperate, it is helpful to have an agreed plan about how to manage this situation as effectively as possible. Such a plan will focus around the best interest of the child, with the child's safety being paramount, and with sensitivity to preserving a positive relationship with the child and promoting the child's self-esteem and dignity.

A main consideration will be whether it is imperative for the procedure to be carried out at that specific time, or whether it is possible to delay it. If the procedure needs to take place, the second consideration might be whether there is sufficient time to take a rest and re-introduce the procedure, maybe allowing for the child to leave the room and do something distracting for a while before inviting them back into the room to try again. If the child is unable to cooperate with the procedure after a break, and/or there is an urgency which prevents any opportunity to reschedule, then options such as sedating the child should be considered. If there are no other options available, then skilled restraint of the child may be the next step. Restraint is described as 'the positive application of force with the intention of overpowering the child' (DoH 1993), and by definition is carried out without the child's consent. Guidelines from the Royal College of Nursing are clear that restraint should only be carried out in a safe and controlled way by appropriately trained staff. The rationale for needing to use restraint should be communicated effectively to the parent and child. A parent may wish to be directly involved and to restrain their child, but this should be carefully considered in terms of the impact on the parent's relationship with the child and whether the parent can be taught to restrain effectively and safely within the necessary time frame. Following the procedure, it is important to talk through what has happened with both the child and parent.

It can involve considerable amounts of clinical time to try and carry out a procedure with a distressed and uncooperative child, and can feel extremely frustrating for the child, family and professional when it has not been successful. Sometimes there is pressure to continue trying to carry out a procedure, from a parent who is frustrated or embarrassed because their child has not 'behaved' or cooperated, or from a health care professional who has been instructed to carry out the procedure and wants to achieve this for the child (or wants the child to achieve this after trying so hard). However, unless there is a strong clinical need for the procedure to be carried out, a decision to stop and set another time for it should be made. In this instance, it can be very helpful to end the session in the most positive way possible, thinking through with the child what has been achieved or learned from the experience, and even to start to make a plan as to what can be different next time, or what needs to be in place before attempting the procedure again. It can be helpful to acknowledge that sometimes children find these procedures difficult and that other professionals (such as play specialists or clinical psychologists) have expertise in helping young people overcome these difficulties. It would not be helpful for children to leave their appointment feeling they have just been 'naughty' and experience having to come back for the procedure to be done as a form of punishment, without opportunity to develop additional coping skills.

SUPPORTING CHILDREN WITH SPECIAL NEEDS

In addition to all the general preparation strategies already discussed, children with learning difficulties and sensory impairment may need some additional care. It is important to learn as much as possible about the unique needs of each and every child from their carers and from previous experiences. It can be extremely important for carers to be present during procedures to understand and interpret the child's responses to what is happening, and to be able to support and reassure the child.

The National Autistic Society (NAS) provides some useful recommendations on its website (see Appendix 1) about supporting children with autistic spectrum disorders (ASD) in undergoing procedures. They suggest placing the child either first or last on the clinic list, and allocating additional time for the procedure. Also, wherever possible, provide a quiet and calming space rather than a busy and over-stimulating waiting area prior to the procedure taking place.

For children with sensory impairment, in addition to all the good practice guidelines already discussed, it is important to be aware of the child's unique experience of the procedure, and to adapt practice accordingly. For example, for children with hearing impairment, it is first important to ensure that you have their attention, and then to continue to maintain good eye contact in order to check that the child is following what you are doing or saying. Speaking using normal speech rhythms, mime, gestures and clear facial expressions will allow better understanding. It can also be important to keep background noise to a minimum, and for one person to be clearly identified as the one to talk to the child (rather than several people talking together, or talking to the child). The National Deaf Children's Society has some helpful strategies for supporting children, including a list of British Sign Language for use in hospital (see Appendix 1).

PREPARATION FOR SURGERY

Preparation for surgery will require all of the good practice guidelines previously discussed, but may require further time and planning due to complexities of the process preceding surgery, and the medical care likely to be required afterwards. If children are not well prepared and become distressed following surgery, this may impact on their willingness to cooperate with necessary rehabilitation treatments (such as physiotherapy) or further medical treatments. Surgery is often just one part of the treatment process, and children who undergo surgery but do not carry out the appropriate self-care following surgery could well be at risk of undermining any positive effects of surgery, or even of being in a more compromised situation. For example, children with neuropathic bladder may have surgery to enlarge their bladder as part of the treatment to improve bladder capacity and continence. They will then need to catheterise to ensure that it empties properly. If children do not catheterise afterwards, they are at risk of damaging their bladder by retention of urine.

It is important for children to be informed of how they might feel after surgery, where they will be when they wake up, and what medical equipment, lines or tubes may be in their body. If they are likely to receive post-operative care in an intensive care environment, it can be helpful for them to have a preparatory visit to gain a sense of where they will be, and to make a positive link with a member of the nursing staff who will be caring for them. On waking in an intensive care unit, children may have a very limited view of their surroundings, as they may need to lie flat, or medical equipment may block their view, and they may just be aware of noises and activity from machines behind them. It can be helpful to have a perspective on the environment beforehand, as this may reduce anxiety later.

Children may have particular fears about surgery which are important to address. One common fear is whether they will wake up after surgery. Some children who have been told they will be having a 'magic sleep' during their operation may also have been told by others in the past that when someone dies it is a 'magic sleep', and so this term is best avoided. Other children may be fearful of waking up during surgery. It can be helpful to tell children that there is a special doctor (the anaesthetist) who will give them a special medicine to make them fall asleep and will monitor them to make sure they stay asleep until the operation is over and it is time for them to wake up.

Preparation for surgery will also include preparation for coming into hospital, as the child will have to cope with being in a different environment with different routines. Many children will find it helpful to make their own plan for coming into hospital. This might include what toys or activities they would like to have with them and an idea of who they would like to visit them. 'Hospital passports', which give details about children and the most helpful ways of communicating with them and caring for them, are considered good practice for children with special needs, such as communication or learning disabilities. If a child uses a communication board or other assisted communication, it is helpful for a team of professionals caring for the child to familiarise themselves with the preferred mode of communication, and to consider how best to communicate with the child around the time of surgery if it is not possible to use these methods at that time. Passports are potentially useful for all children, if appropriately used (which includes staff making time to read through the information on the passport).

Play specialists have considerable expertise in preparing children for surgery, and are highly skilled at using play as a medium for preparing younger children and exploring their fears. Video and DVDs are increasingly being used to show older children information about surgery, using peers modelling their experiences. Many preparation books are written by staff for children attending a particular hospital, or having a specific procedure, as this enables the information to be more factually accurate and tailored to what the child will experience. A good example of a more general preparation booklet for families with a child having a cardiac procedure is published by the charity Little Hearts Matter (see Appendix 1). General story books preparing children for their hospital stay are available at bookshops and a list of these is given in Appendix 2. Children may also want to draw or write their own book about their surgery, and can add photographs of key staff or events which happen during their hospital stay. This book can be a helpful way for children to share their experiences with peers or teachers at school, and can also be a good resource to support children who may require further treatment later on, as they can refer back to previous positive and coping experiences.

Some hospitals also operate a 'buddy system' in which children who have already successfully had surgery can meet with children and families who are awaiting it. From our clinical experience, this appears to be more helpful for parents than for children. Children may not relate to or even like the child who has agreed to be their 'buddy', which can make communication less effective. Also, care must be taken so that knowledge that might be imparted from child to child about a procedure does not heighten anxiety or raise new anxieties.

Even with preparation and support, some children will refuse to have surgery, and some will even get as far as the anaesthetic room and then become too distressed to continue. Although there are likely to have been times when the procedure has gone ahead regardless, unless the child is in a life-threatening situation the child's wishes need to be respected and surgery postponed. Referral for psychological help and preparation is more likely in this situation, to explore previous experiences, including preparation for surgery, and to determine what further areas need to be addressed.

> Jamie, an eleven-year-old girl, had reluctantly agreed to have surgery, but once in the anaesthetic room she became highly distressed and refused to lie on the trolley. Surgery was postponed. In discussion with Jamie it became clear that she had tried her best to stay calm for surgery, but had become increasingly anxious while waiting her turn on the morning of surgery. She had been told to stay on her bed and had seen other children returning to the ward following their surgery. Some of them had been sleeping, but she had heard moaning and crying, and thought they were upset. In working with Jamie to create a new plan for helping her manage surgery, she was clear that keeping busy and not waiting around before surgery were key aspects. Time was booked with the play specialist to plan some distracting activities she could do, and a plan was arranged for Jamie to be as early on the next surgery list as possible. With this plan in mind, some strategies for positive thinking, including being able to refer to her plan, and reminding herself of all the things she had managed before, were incorporated into her plan. Good communication of this plan to the ward and surgery team was a key component in Jamie being able to implement her plan successfully.

SUMMARY

Children with illness and chronic conditions are likely to require multiple procedures as part of the process of diagnosis, monitoring or treatment of their conditions. To improve children's experience of health care and living with their condition, it is important to promote acquisition of skills for coping with medical procedures. Procedural distress and the factors which impact on children's experiences and behaviour are well understood. Effective preparation can decrease anxiety, increase cooperation and engender a sense of mastery in coping with the procedure. This has implications for developing trust with health care professionals and for children's longer term emotional well being. Good practice guidelines (Paediatric Psychology Network 2010) are useful for informing and training health professionals in effective management of procedural distress.

CHAPTER 6

Assessing and Treating Chronic Pain and Medically Unexplained Symptoms

Effective pain management is a key quality indicator in health care, because pain has a significant impact on all aspects of a child's life, and treatment of pain involves a significant cost in terms of health care resources. Pain occurs in a wide variety of forms, including acute pain due to injuries and medical events or procedures, and recurrent or chronic pain. Acute pain is typically brief, ending around the time of healing of the injury. Chronic pain has been defined as 'a pain that persists or recurs for three months or longer' (Eccleston *et al.* 2002). It does not necessarily correlate with nerve or tissue damage, and may or may not be symptomatic of underlying chronic disease.

There have been significant advances in understanding pain in recent years, with a greater appreciation of pain experiences, particularly for those who are unable to communicate about their pain, such as neonates and children with cognitive impairment. There have also been both medical and psychological advances, with a strong evidence base for the effectiveness of Cognitive Behavioural Therapy (CBT) for chronic pain. Newer techniques, such as mindfulness, and acceptance and commitment therapy (ACT) have been piloted successfully at the Bath Centre for Pain Services within a multidisciplinary programme of chronic pain management. This may prove to be an effective and viable alternative to the more established cognitive behavioural approaches for certain pain conditions. Medically, a greater range of drugs is available, with some able to target specific types of pain more effectively, as well as an emerging range of complementary therapies.

In this chapter we will look at assessment and treatment of both acute and chronic pain. A comprehensive and holistic assessment underpins any effective treatment. Given the highly subjective nature of pain, it is imperative that children and parents feel listened to in order for their experience of pain to be properly understood and respected in the context of their values and their lives, before it is possible to embark on any collaborative pain management programme. This is particularly true for conditions known as medically unexplained symptoms (MUS) which have no apparent physical cause, or where the severity of the impact of the condition on the child is beyond that which would be expected for the medical condition. The management of MUS, which often include pain, is discussed in the second part of this chapter.

HOW DO WE UNDERSTAND PAIN?

Pain is a highly personal and multifaceted experience consisting of physiological, behavioural, emotional, developmental and sociocultural components (McGrath et al. 1993).

The gate control theory of pain

The influence of psychological factors on pain experience can be explained using the 'gate control' theory (Melzack and Wall 1965, 1982). This theory proposes that sensations of pain are modulated by both physiological and psychological processes. Input from receptors in the nervous system is assumed to pass through a neural 'gate' in the spinal cord before being passed to the brain. The degree to which the gate is open is determined by activity in different parts of the nervous system, and controls the amount of pain that is felt. Figure 6.1 is an illustration of how the gate control theory of pain can be used to help children understand how other factors can affect their experience of pain.

Although new models of pain have been developed, the concepts of 'gate control' have remained central to our understanding of pain and how mood, focus of attention and expectation of pain influence pain perception.

Other models of pain

The biobehavioural model of pain (Varni et al. 1996) provides a comprehensive model of the variables which influence pain perception and pain behaviour. In this model, pain experience is modulated by a range of intervening

What opens the pain gate?

These are some of the things Candy finds open his pain gate really wide and let big pain messages through

Figure 6.1 Child's version of pain gate model

variables including temperament, age, gender, cognitive appraisal, coping strategies, perceived social support and family environment (such as family functioning and family pain models). Pain experience affects, and is affected by, functional status, which includes activities of daily living, school attendance, mental health and interpersonal relations.

THE MEANING OF PAIN FOR CHILDREN

Pain is not a unitary experience, and can mean different things for a child and family. Children may cry out 'in pain' when they see or hear frightening equipment being used on them (such as a drill in dentistry, or the saw used to remove plaster casts). Conversely, children sometimes deny high levels of pain if they are fearful of the consequences, such as having to go to hospital. Pain is usually seen as being a bad thing, with some children becoming furious with a doctor who has 'hurt' them. Pain may signify a deterioration or worrying change in a condition or a recurrence of a problem. It can be interpreted as a warning of further or more intense pain unless rest and appropriate treatment is initiated immediately, or it can be viewed as something that will pass in time.

Pain can also be seen more positively – for example as the expected feeling associated with recovery and healing following successful surgery, such as following a kidney transplant, or the return of sensation and movement following temporary paralysis and lack of sensation in conditions such as Guillain-Barré. Pain can also be within the 'normal' range of pain experienced by anybody, such as muscle aches, twinges, menstrual pains and occasional headaches. However, the meaning ascribed to these by children and parents may vary depending on the level of anxiety and the context of their presentation.

The consequences of pain may also vary considerably. Some children may receive positive attention, comfort and treats as a consequence being in pain. It may also result in them avoiding activities or chores they are not keen to do. For other children, it can make them fearful of attempting anything which might trigger pain, and they may become fearful of separation from parents or other key adults who they believe can keep them safe and pain-free.

DEVELOPMENTAL UNDERSTANDING AND COMMUNICATION OF PAIN

Children's understanding of pain follows a similar developmental progression to their understanding of illness and other concepts. Younger children do not possess the vocabulary for describing pain and may not be able to give a reason why pain hurts or what their pain feels like. As they develop skills in this area, they will tend to verbalise a general, external cause for their pain. There is also some suggestion that younger children associate pain with punishment (Gaffney and Dunne 1986). Older children are more able to consider multiple causes of pain, including physiological and psychological factors, and understand that there may be a protective element in pain. Younger children are more likely to focus on the immediate and aversive nature of pain, being preoccupied by their current sensory experience, whereas older children may be able to communicate cognitive aspects, including feelings of helplessness, and anxiety about the direction of pain and about its significance (Gaffney and Dunne 1986).

Younger children are much less likely to have had the opportunity to develop self-initiated coping strategies, and are therefore much more dependent on others for help (Jay *et al.* 1983), whereas older children might be more active in their self-care skills, having learned these from experience – for example rubbing the affected part or resting.

It is helpful to know how children understand their pain, in order to be able to give them information to help them make sense of their experiences. For example, it can make little sense to a child to have a painkilling injection in their arm when it is their leg that hurts. Children may also believe that only 'pink' medicine will make them better, or that nasty-tasting medicine will not help (Beales *et al.* 1983). Children with social communication difficulties may respond differently to pain. It may not be clear from their behaviour that they are in pain, as they may not seek care and comfort from others.

ASSESSMENT OF PAIN

There is an extensive range of pain assessment tools available, and excellent reviews of both chronic and acute pain measures can be found in Cohen *et al.* (2008) and the Royal College of Nursing (RCN) guidelines (2009). Cohen reviewed seventeen pain measures and classified these in terms of how well established they were found to be clinically, finding eleven measures 'well established' and the remaining six measures 'approaching well established'. In their review of acute pain measures, the RCN (2009) found thirty-one measures which met high standards for reliability and validity for children and infants (with a further eight measures in neonates).

Both reviews conclude that there is no single tool which can be recommended for pain assessment in all children and in all pain situations, and each measure needs to be considered in terms of the purpose and context for the assessment. The RCN review also emphasises that pain should be measured routinely in all situations considered to be potentially painful for neonates and children, and that this should be reviewed regularly. Generally, acute pain measures focus on pain intensity, location and effect, whereas chronic and recurrent pain measures also address the frequency, duration and impact of pain on daily life. There is also agreement that the 'gold standard' for assessment of pain is the use of self-report measures, with behavioural assessments and physiological assessments being used to supplement or replace self-report if a child does not have the cognitive maturity or communication skills required for self-report measures. For example, most self-report measures are unlikely to be helpful for children younger than three years of age, due to their cognitive and language skills.

Self-report measures

Visual analogue scales are extremely well validated as tools for measuring pain in children, correlating well with both parents' and medical professionals' ratings of pain. One example is a horizontal line with developmentally appropriate descriptors of pain intensity along the scale (such as 'not hurting' or 'no pain' to 'hurting a lot' or 'very severe pain'). The child is asked to make a mark on the line to indicate how much pain he or she feels. Scales using a series of faces depicting different levels of pain, such as the Oucher faces pain scales, and Wong and Baker Faces (Wong and Baker 1988) are also widely used. Although these scales are simple and quick to use, it is very important that enough time is given to explain the scales to the child and family, as the scale is not always self-explanatory to a child. For example, it would be helpful to explain that the first face represents 'no pain' and the last face represents the 'worst pain ever'. Without this information, children may believe they have to choose the face with exactly the same expression as themselves, rather than the one that represents the level of pain they are experiencing, which may be confusing if the child is not smiling (as this represents 'no pain' in the Wong and Baker Faces scale) or not crying (as the crying face represents the most pain).

Figure 6.2 Child's drawing of his headache

Using body outlines

Children can be invited to draw their pain on an age-appropriate body outline, or may chose to draw their own outline, or indeed, to draw around themselves. Using a body outline can help the child communicate the location of their pain and also the intensity, using a range of colours to represent different levels of pain severity.

The Varni–Thompson Pediatric Pain Questionnaire (PPQ), a widely used and well evaluated pain measure, incorporates a visual analogue scale and body outline, and a list of descriptive words to help the child describe their pain. Versions of the PPQ for children, adolescents and parents are available.

Diaries are commonly used to record chronic pain. These can be used to monitor both pain and the impact of pain on daily activities, which is important because there are few pain measures focusing on the impact of pain on the child's daily life (Eccleston *et al.* 2006). Electronic diaries may be more appealing to young people than written ones, enabling a more acceptable, portable and accessible form of recording information.

Children can also be asked to draw or describe their pain. Figure 6.2 shows one child's drawing of his headache, which he described as being like a number of elephants in his head. For this young man, his most severe pain was accompanied by a 'whooshing' sensation, which he likened to the elephant squirting water from its trunk!

Behavioural observations

Behavioural assessment tools are non-obtrusive and do not rely on the child's ability or willingness to cooperate. These tools assess particular behaviours which are indicative of pain, such as crying, facial expression, motor responses, body posture, activity and appearance. However, a number of these behaviours can indicate other forms of distress and are not solely associated with pain. Therefore, it is recommended that behavioural observations are not relied on as the sole source of information, but rather used in conjunction with self-report measures wherever possible.

Physiological measurements

These measurements are based on physiological changes associated with pain, such as increased heart and respiratory rate, raised blood pressure, oxygen saturation, and palmar sweating. However, these physiological changes are shown not only in the presence of pain, and can also indicate stress, fear or anxiety; therefore it is important to take into account the context of the assessment as well. These measures may still be important to use in situations where the child is unconscious, or unable to communicate their pain, for example when intubated and ventilated. Reaney (2007a, 2007b) reinforces the general principle that it is important to anticipate or assume that there will be some pain in situations known to cause pain.

ASSESSMENT OF PAIN IN CHILDREN WITH COGNITIVE IMPAIRMENT

The National Service Framework (DoH 2003) makes specific reference to the need for assessing and managing pain in children with cognitive impairment who are unable to communicate their pain experience verbally. Breau, Camfield and McGrath (2003) reported that cognitively impaired children experienced pain more often than unimpaired children, and viewed them as a population particularly vulnerable to pain experiences due to the higher number of medical interventions they experience. It has been widely acknowledged that pain relief for children who have cognitive impairment and limited verbal skills has often been inadequate, due to the challenges of assessing their experience, or difficulties identifying consistent presentations of being in pain. The RCN guidelines (2009), however, report that cognitively impaired and nonverbal children display predictable, observable behaviours, which lend themselves to observable behavioural measures. These measures are based on the principle that children in pain are likely to show changes in their behaviour, appearance, activity levels and vital signs, and that these signs will be particularly noted by carers, who should be respected for their skills in interpreting and understanding the child's behaviour. The RCN guidelines recommend three measures:

1. The 'Face, Legs, Activity, Cry, Consolability' tool (FLACC) (Voepel-Lewis *et al.* 2002), which rates the child's behaviour on each to the five listed areas.

2. The Paediatric Pain Profile (PPP) (Hunt *et al.* 2002), which uses a four-point scale to record the extent to which each of 20 behaviours occurs within a given time period.

3. The Non-communicating Children's Pain Checklist – revised (NCCPC) (McGrath *et al.* 1998), a 30-item checklist in which the observer rates if particular behaviours are present or not, and which has been shown to have good psychometric properties (Breau *et al.* 2002). (There is also a post-operative version of this test (NCCPC-PV), which excludes items on eating and sleeping as these behaviours might be heavily influenced by the effects of sedation or the surgery.)

Stallard (2002a) cautions that some measures we use to identify pain might also be indicative of more global distress, making it important to be sensitive to the context and the child's unique way of communicating. He also points out that it is more difficult to assess chronic pain, as any behavioural changes may be more subtle over time (e.g. decreased activity and being more subdued).

THE CHALLENGE OF CHRONIC PAIN

Twenty-five to thirty per cent of the general school population report chronic or recurrent pain (Perquin *et al.* 2001). Thirty per cent of these visit their general practitioner and ten per cent are seen by a specialist. The most prevalent chronic pain sites are headaches, abdominal pain, back pain and limb pain. The impact of chronic pain is considerable in terms of daily living, with very poor attendance at school and consequent lower academic achievement reported in many studies of young people with chronic pain. Emotional distress, particularly depressive symptomatology, is also common and the impact on family life can be profound.

COST OF PAIN

Pain has an impact on all areas of a child's and family's life, including an economic cost. Sleed *et al.* (2005) calculated that the mean cost per adolescent with chronic pain was £8,000, which equated to a national economic burden of adolescent pain of approximately £3,840 million in one year. This data was collected from 52 families of adolescents with chronic pain, and extrapolated to the population statistics of adolescent chronic pain in the UK. This figure included direct and indirect costs, including service use (the number of inpatient and outpatient episodes), home tutor sessions, lost employment, informal care given as a result of the adolescent's pain, and 'out-of-pocket' costs for families.

Within many areas in the UK, hospital admissions are calculated on a tariff system, and the local primary care trust (PCT) is charged for an 'average' amount of days per admission, for each child admitted. Uncontrolled pain is one of the main reasons why a child remains longer in hospital, with clear cost implications for any hospital trust.

It can be more difficult to measure and evaluate chronic pain, and it is very difficult to be objective about a sensation or experience which has lasted for several months or years.

> One 16-year-old girl reported severe headaches for nearly 18 months. She rated her pain as being a constant background pain with frequent peaks of higher intensity, and rated it as being 'off the scale' when presented with a visual analogue scale. She gained A grades in all of her GCSE examinations, despite experiencing this intensity of pain.

MANAGEMENT OF CHRONIC PAIN AND PAIN MANAGEMENT STRATEGIES

Because assessing and understanding chronic pain presentations is so challenging for medical professionals, children and families may feel that they are not believed or taken seriously, and are often frustrated by ineffective treatments. Families may continue to believe that their doctors may have missed something, and may find it difficult to accept that further tests or medication cannot control and cure this pain. As a result, some families may feel ambivalent about accepting or exploring psychological strategies for helping.

In Chapter 3 we discussed ways of engaging and developing a shared focus of work with children, and these are all-important in clinical work with children experiencing pain. It is important for the family and child to feel that their pain has been properly assessed, and the impact on their lives explored and taken seriously. It is important to develop a shared language with the child which describes or represents their pain, and to use these terms. It is also helpful to maintain the positive outlook that there is always some way of improving an aspect of the child's experience, even if the pain remains the same. Pain management strategies may involve any of the following.

1. Goal-setting

The goals for managing chronic pain have a wider focus than being pain-free, or even pain relief. A more central aim is to optimise function across all domains, socially, physically, and academically, and enable fuller activity and participation. The aim is to be collaborative with children and young people in setting goals which are meaningful and achievable for them.

2. Relaxation

Relaxation is a skill which needs to be practised and developed. It can be helpful to carry out relaxation sessions directly with children in order to tailor the relaxation strategies for their individual needs. For example, children who have difficulties controlling their bodies due to muscle spasms, or who are not able to move some parts of their bodies, may need a more tailored set of exercises. It can also be important to adapt relaxation training according to the age and maturity of the child. Some children are overwhelmed with mirth at the idea of tensing and relaxing their 'buttocks' or bottom, for example!

There are a number of useful resources, including websites to use with children and families to help them acquire relaxation skills, with a range of relaxation CDs using progressive muscle relaxation and guided imagery techniques (see 'Relaxation' in Appendix 1). It is also possible to download leaflets and relaxation scripts for young people about relaxation (see Appendix 1). Young people might be interested to download their relaxation and guided imagery sessions on to their MP3 players, to have a mobile resource available to them.

3. Relaxation and imagery

The imagery used to complement relaxation exercises needs to be meaningful, positive and conducive to a relaxing and non-painful state for the child. Although some children may enjoy a peaceful scene, such as relaxing on a beach, other children may prefer a more entertaining and 'active' scene, such as going on exciting rides at a funfair, or having a party. It is therefore important to take the lead from children with regard to what would be a special and positive place for them. Imagery can also be introduced that directly focuses on changing an experience or perception of pain. One example of this is visualising a block of ice as a concrete image of pain, and transforming it through relaxation and positive thoughts into a smaller, melting piece of ice. Another image might be of dials or switches that the child can control in their imagination to 'turn down' their sensation of pain.

4. Cognitive behavioural strategies

Strategies derived from Cognitive Behavioural Therapy (CBT) form the most robust evidence base for managing pain, particularly headaches (Eccleston 2006). The goal is to decrease the unpleasant sensations or feelings associated with pain. Strategies like relaxation and guided imagery, distraction and positive self-talk are among the components that can be used. Please refer to Stallard (2002b) for a review of CBT.

CBT techniques have been utilised in computer-based therapy programmes. Connelly *et al.* (2006) have evaluated a pilot project with Headstrong, a CD-ROM programme based on psychoeducation and cognitive behavioural strategies (guided imagery, relaxation, problem solving and thought changing) that was used at home by children. Results showed significant improvement in headache activity when compared to a control group receiving medical care. Connelly *et al.* suggest that CD-ROMs could be used effectively as an adjunct to other treatment for headaches and other pain conditions.

The challenge of using CBT is that children and young people may continue to experience pain symptoms, regardless of medical help or CBT programmes, and this can undermine their confidence in the psychological treatment they are receiving. For example, some children who try relaxation for pain control may find it difficult due to discomfort, or may give up on relaxation skills as they are still in pain, both during and afterwards.

CBT can be helpful for children in cases where pain has a strong emotional association, for example for tension headaches, and for dealing with the emotional consequences of pain, including low mood (which may need treatment in its own right). As discussed in Chapter 5, CBT can be very successful in managing both distress and pain in acute situations such as procedural distress.

5. ACT and mindfulness

Acceptance and commitment therapy (ACT) and mindfulness techniques have been shown to be an effective and a positive approach, especially where other interventions have not been effective (Currie 2006). The approach is firmly based on the values that the person holds and cares for in life, and the idea that they can meet these values in spite of being in pain. The focus is on reducing the disabling impact of pain and distress, rather than the pain itself. An example that is given to convey this principle to children is to imagine being out in the rain without an umbrella, and without any cover, and to imagine how they might look, feel, and what posture they might adopt. Children are then asked to imagine exactly the same scenario again, but this time to decide that they will just accept that they are going to be soaked, and then to think about how this makes them feel and behave. In this way, children can be helped to understand that although they are not happy that they are wet, they are no more soaked than before, and no less soaked than before, but maybe they are feeling a little better and a little less stressed.

Using this example further, children can be helped to see that a great deal of energy may be used up in trying (however unsuccessfully) not to be wet, and that this energy could be put to a different and more positive use. One adolescent reframed this for herself as the difference between having a monster jumping at her leg and impeding her walking, and carrying the monster in a backpack...it was still there, and still annoying, but seemed to get in the way less!

Using this approach, an exploration of the values children place on aspects of their lives is carried out. These values are unique to the young person in the context of their life, and may involve aspects of school, relationships with family members and social activities with friends. Values are not used as a goal, but they are helpful as a way of motivating and helping the young person to move forward. It can be difficult for children (or anyone) to acknowledge what their values are, and a useful strategy for exploring this is to ask children about someone they admire, someone who is a hero or heroine for them, and then to think about what it is about this person that they would aspire to. Another method for children is to ask them to draw out a network of people in their world, which may include family members, teachers, friends and carers. Some children may choose to draw this as petals of a flower with the child as the centre, or as a football team with the child as captain. Children can then be asked what would be the nicest thing each person would say about them. From discussion of this, children can be helped to explore what is important to how they see themselves and how they would like to be.

Mindfulness techniques are derived from meditation skills and encourage the child to develop an expertise over their body by being aware of sensations and experiences (but not to become preoccupied by them and let them determine what the child is able to do), 'letting pain wash over them'.

Using these techniques, the pain experience is explored, acknowledged, but not given the top priority in treatment. Instead, the child is the focus, with their values and goals being core, and seen in context of their lives. Plans are made collaboratively with the child to augment or develop areas which are likely to increase activities that will improve their quality of life.

6. Skills

Young people and families can be helped to develop their own expertise in living with chronic or recurrent pain conditions, and to adopt self-management strategies that are best tailored to their own needs. One such skill is planning ahead and pacing activities. It is not unusual for young people living with chronic pain to restrict and withdraw from activities to protect themselves from pain. However, at moments when their pain is easier to deal with, young people may 'throw themselves' into high levels of activity. Although they may see themselves as making the best of their situation (and are often praised for doing so by others), the common outcome is for children to exhaust themselves, and find themselves in much higher levels of pain. This can become cyclical, with children then withdrawing even more and becoming even more limited in their response to pain.

Children can learn how to pace their levels of activity, and to make a realistic plan about what is important and possible for them to do in any given day. Being able to organise this plan also requires some forward planning, such as working out how long they can go for a walk or a swim, including the journey time to and from this activity, and how this will impact on their energy resources for the day.

Another skill may be in understanding pain-relieving medication and using it most effectively. It is important that families and children are given appropriate information about how their pain medication works, including how long it may take to build up sufficiently high levels in the body, or how long it takes to work (which could be 30 minutes, for example). It will also be important to be aware of how long the medication will offer pain relief in order that doses are appropriately spaced to ensure effective pain cover. Many children become ambivalent about taking medication, particularly when it has only had limited effect, and are inconsistent in the way they use it. It can be helpful to explore the way in which children take their medicine. If they wait until the pain is intense before they 'give in' and take their medication, this is not the most effective strategy, as the body will be in severe pain and will need time to recover from it, whereas appropriate medical management might keep the pain more under control. Similarly, effective use of pain management tools such as TENS (Transcutaneous Electrical Nerve Stimulation) requires knowledge about where best to place the electrodes, the intensity of the pulse waves to be used and the best timing for using the machine. Families are sometimes uncertain about exploring complementary therapies such as acupuncture or aromatherapy massage, but as long as there is no medical reason not to, families should be encouraged to explore any ways they wish to find a way of coping with pain. Although there is no scientific evidence base for these approaches, they can still be very helpful for children.

MEDICALLY UNEXPLAINED SYMPTOMS (PSYCHOGENIC PAIN)

The process and strategies for managing chronic pain are equally applicable to pain which cannot be attributed to any physical cause, often termed 'psychogenic' or 'non-organic' pain. Psychologists are often asked to assess and offer treatment to children who present with symptoms that have no apparent physical cause, or where the severity of the condition's impact on the child exceeds that which would normally be expected for the medical condition. These symptoms are now usually called 'medically unexplained symptoms' (MUS). The most common types of symptoms in childhood are abdominal pain, headaches and fatigue, but there is often considerable overlap, with many children presenting with a cluster of symptoms. These types of difficulties can be very difficult to manage and require clear communication and liaison between medical and psychosocial teams.

A variety of different terms have been used in the past to describe these types of difficulties, including 'psychosomatic' or 'functional' problems, but the current terminology of medically unexplained symptoms is useful because it is neutral in terms of stating the origin of the symptoms. By contrast, the word 'somatisation', for example, implies that the condition is not physical and has a psychological cause. It is important not to assume automatically that children with these symptoms are presenting emotional and psychological difficulties in a physical way. The term 'MUS' is deliberately non-specific in terms of the cause of the symptoms and is purely descriptive. This makes it more acceptable because it is a term that the child, family, referrer and psychologist can more easily agree on.

Most psychologists working in this field use a biopsychosocial model to understand how physical (biological) symptoms relate to psychological factors and the social presentation of these symptoms (Engel 1977). In a biopsychosocial model, symptoms are explained not just in terms of their biological underpinnings but in terms of the patient's beliefs and presentation of these symptoms, and of how the social context can influence the reporting and impact of such symptoms. By definition, in such a model, there is an interrelationship between body and mind and acceptance that these are linked. However, families or medical teams are often focused on the biological aspects of medical conditions, and these conditions can be hard to understand and frustrating to manage in a more dualist biological model, where any psychological factors are seen as secondary to or separate from physical symptoms.

Some children with medically unexplained symptoms end up having unnecessary investigations or treatments in order to try and find a medical cause. Families of children with these conditions often fear that there has not been enough investigation of the symptoms, and it is difficult for doctors not to respond to parental anxiety about other causes being insufficiently explored. In addition, in tertiary centres where children are referred for second or third opinions, doctors often do see many families in which symptoms caused by rare conditions have not been identified at an early stage, and in this context it can be difficult to feel sure that there are no further investigations that need to be done. As medical knowledge improves, some conditions which might have appeared to have no physical cause only 20 years ago, can now be understood. The symptoms presented may fall under different areas of expertise. For example, a gastroenterologist may see a child for abdominal pain, but a neurologist may then also see the child for investigation of dizziness or headaches. When one specialist is unable to explain the symptoms, they may well refer on and ask for the opinion of another specialist. However, since the child is usually seen separately by each specialist, it can be difficult to share information about the diagnosis and how to manage the child's symptoms.

There have been several epidemiological studies which have shown that MUS are relatively common, more frequent amongst girls than boys, and tend to vary with age (Eminson 2007). Young children are dependent on their parents to report their symptoms, and therefore the parents' representation of their child's symptoms determines help seeking, and also what symptoms are reported. As children get older, they become more able to report independently on their own symptoms, although it is also true that their model of symptoms will have been strongly influenced by their upbringing. There is good evidence that parents who have many unexplained physical symptoms themselves also report and seek help for symptoms in their children (Craig, Cox and Klein 2002), and that parental anxiety and low mood are associated with increasingly seeking help for their child. There is also evidence that children presenting with persistent abdominal pain in childhood are at increased risk of psychiatric disorders in adulthood (Hotopf et al. 1998).

MUS often co-exist with symptoms of anxiety and depression, and there is considerable overlap between these symptoms, with a third to a half of children with MUS meeting the diagnostic criteria for a psychiatric condition (Husain, Browne and Chalder 2007). For example, fatigue is one of the main symptoms of depression, as is withdrawal from normal social activity and loss of enjoyment in activities. Since it is known that there is a lot of overlap between pain and fatigue symptoms, there is likely to be considerable parental influence on which symptoms are seen as 'primary'. There are also cultural differences in how symptoms are described and which ones are seen as 'normal' and 'abnormal'. For example, epidemiological studies have shown that higher rates of headaches are reported among adults in the USA than in China (Wang et al. 1997).

The consequences of MUS mean that children tend to withdraw from typical age-appropriate social activity, especially school attendance, and therefore tend to fall behind in many ways and to be more dependent on their parents than other children of their own age. For some children this then creates a secondary problem, because it makes it hard for them to reintegrate into school and social activities. It is likely that these social and achievement difficulties pre-date the onset of symptoms, but they are often important maintaining factors as well. It is likely that there is a small proportion of children who find the social challenges of school and adolescence overwhelming; who, following a period of illness, find there is some reprieve from these pressures, and whose symptoms on return to school prove quite difficult to manage. This is consistent with frequent clinical reports of children who are achieving extremely well and are apparently very able, who develop prolonged symptoms of fatigue following a viral infection and then have to withdraw from previous activity levels.

CHRONIC FATIGUE SYNDROME AND MYALGIC ENCEPHALOMYELITIS (CFS/ME)

While fatigue is often associated with other MUS, the specific condition of CFS is widely recognised and specialist services have been developed for children and adults presenting with CFS/ME. The diagnosis of CFS/ME includes severe and chronic fatigue for at least three months, accompanied by other persistent symptoms, such as concentration and memory problems, muscle and joint pains, headaches and sleep problems. It is estimated that CFS affects about 0.5 per cent of children aged 11–15 (Viner and Christie 2005). Treatment guidelines which include treatment for children and young people with CFS/ME have been published by the National Institute for Clinical Excellence (NICE 2007). These guidelines clearly emphasise the importance of working with the patient and family in a cooperative way, and the need to acknowledge the reality of the symptoms. The treatment recommended includes CBT, graded exercise therapy and activity management. Some patient groups for CFS/ME have been very critical about the use of CBT for treating CFS/ME (Garralda and Chalder 2005), but the guidelines stress that it should be offered as part of an overall package of care that aims to sustain, and if possible extend, the young person's 'physical, emotional and cognitive capacity'.

ENGAGING THE CHILD AND FAMILY AND MODELS OF CARE

The most important and often the most difficult aspect of working with children with MUS is the initial phase of developing a collaborative therapeutic relationship and reaching a joint understanding of the problem in order to agree a treatment plan. There are many families who do not want to pursue psychological treatment plans and who either do not engage with or drop out of treatment. Many young people with these types of symptoms will actively deny any emotional connection with their symptoms and will resist questions or exploration of these topics. At worst, this backs the young person into a corner where they feel they have to 'prove' the severity of their symptoms. Their parents also can be defensive, and even angry at times.

Working collaboratively with the medical referrer and a multidisciplinary team can greatly enhance the possibility of a rehabilitation programme being accepted and improve the credibility of the treatment plan. This is particularly important in tertiary centres which are likely to see cases where symptoms that have been long-lasting and have had a major impact on the young person's lifestyle are resistant to explanation, and where the parents or child have persisted with seeking a medical explanation. It can be very helpful for the referring practitioner to explain that no further investigation is required and, if appropriate, that it could actually harm the child to continue investigation at that point. It is also important for psychologists and other members of the multidisciplinary team to have developed a model of shared care and mutual trust and to know that they are working in a joint way. It is also essential to convey to the child and family that the team does believe in the reality of their symptoms and in the impact of these symptoms on their life.

Rather than trying to engage the child and family in a psychological model that assumes that the physical symptoms are underpinned by emotional or psychological difficulties, it is better to use a 'rehabilitation model' that combines both physical and psychological elements and which is explicitly focused on improving the child or young person's physical well-being and ability to lead a more normal life (Griffin and Christie 2008). The rehabilitation plan should include both the child or young person and the family. It can be helpful to think of co-constructing a new narrative for the child and family, to enable them to explain the child's symptoms and move on and improve their day-to-day functioning without 'losing face'. Any child or young person who has experienced these sorts of symptoms for a long period of time is likely to have missed out on many developmental opportunities and will therefore have genuine need to find ways of re-integrating. They may well have some weakness or physical deconditioning and need to gradually build up their fitness again.

CBT is often applied to rehabilitation approaches, including activity scheduling, pacing, establishment of a sleep routine, modification of negative and unhelpful thinking, and relapse prevention. However, it is seen as a component of the treatment plan rather than the sole treatment modality.

In addition, the child's parents will need to find ways of letting the child improve, and may find that their own role or functioning has to change considerably as well. The levels of anxiety that prompt parents to persist with investigations and seek an explanation may be entirely resolved by the reassurance that the condition is not caused by any known physical symptoms; but in more persistent and complicated cases this is unlikely, and they may need help to manage the anxiety they continue to experience about their child's well-being.

Part of the plan should include education and a return to full-time school if possible. It is essential to liaise with schools to help develop a sensible, graded recovery plan, and to help the school understand the nature of the problem. Many schools become frustrated with children with poor and sporadic attendance patterns, and as children get older, it becomes harder for them to reintegrate into school, so older teenagers can drift out of education at this point. The involvement of an external agency can help both sides to re-engage, although it is a difficult task.

> Chris had a long history of poor health and had at various times been investigated for abdominal pain. She struggled with the transition to secondary school and her attendance in Year 7 was relatively low, about 85 per cent. When aged 13, in Year 8, she developed headaches that became very disabling. She frequently went to the medical room and was occasionally sent home. On two occasions she vomited at school after her headache started. As well as headaches, Chris felt permanently tired but reported that she was unable to sleep well at night. She became increasingly worried about her symptoms and her attendance at school dropped to less than 60 per cent. Chris's mother had been diagnosed with irritable bowel syndrome and was not working. She herself had had panic attacks a few years previously and had seen a psychologist for CBT, which she had not found helpful. Both Chris and her mother were very anxious about the headaches and had asked for a second opinion because they felt that Chris needed to have an MRI scan in order to rule out an organic cause. Chris was referred to a psychologist but only attended about half the sessions offered. Chris failed to return to school in Year 9 and was then offered home tuition. She was subsequently offered a place at the local tuition centre for children unable to cope with school, and remained there until she completed her formal education at 16.

SAFEGUARDING ISSUES

There are situations in which MUS are considered to be a form of child maltreatment and where it is appropriate to refer to local social care services or a social worker for further assessment. It can be helpful to consider that MUS are a spectrum of conditions, and that at the more severe or persistent end, the child is likely to suffer considerable harm as a consequence of the condition. These conditions are also called 'fabricated or induced illness' (FII). The NICE *Guidance on When to Suspect Child Maltreatment* (2009) gives the following as reasons to consider fabricated or induced illness.

- Despite a definitive clinical opinion being reached, multiple opinions from both primary and secondary care are sought and disputed by the parent or carer and the child continues to be presented for investigation and treatment with a range of signs and symptoms.

- The child's normal daily activities (e.g. school attendance) are limited, or they are using aids to daily living (e.g. wheelchairs) more than expected from any medical condition that the child has.

Psychologists are sometimes involved in the assessment of inpatient observation of children with suspected MUS or FII. These admissions should be undertaken with the help of the local safeguarding children team, and require careful planning. Before the child is admitted it is essential to reach agreement on what is being observed, and how. Admitting a child to hospital just for observation is expensive in terms of resources and therefore it is important to ensure that any admission is set up adequately for observation to take place. It always feels uncomfortable managing these cases because they may involve confronting a family with evidence that does not fit with their presentation of the child's difficulties and this requires high levels of communication skills and confidence. Collaboration with social work colleagues is essential, and it is also essential to ensure that all involved, particularly those who have a lot of contact with the child (e.g. the nursing team) feel clear about what they are required to do, in case their evidence is subsequently needed to help with the diagnosis.

SUMMARY

Chronic pain has a significant impact on the lives of children and their families. It also places big demands on health care resources. There are many good pain assessment measures available, and there have been recent developments, in both acknowledgement and assessment of pain in children who are unable to communicate directly. There is a strong evidence base for using cognitive behavioural strategies to manage pain, and more recently approaches involving acceptance and commitment therapy and mindfulness have been shown to be promising. Any successful pain management programme requires engaging with young people and their family, and a collaborative focus of work in which a shared understanding of the impact of pain on their lives, and an understanding of the values and motivating factors to promote the highest quality of life for the child, are gained. Chronic pain which cannot be explained by medical investigations is one example of a range of presentations of medically unexplained symptoms. An approach for supporting and managing symptoms of explained or unexplained origin was discussed in this chapter.

CHAPTER 7

Promoting Adherence to Treatment

One of the greatest challenges in caring for a child with a chronic illness is how to achieve adherence to treatment plans. Current research estimates that adherence rates for children can be as low as 50 per cent (Rapoff 1999). This has major implications for how effective treatment protocols can be, and makes it much more difficult to evaluate how effective a treatment is. In addition, in some conditions (e.g. HIV infection) problems with adherence lead directly to long-term restrictions in treatment options since, if a medication is not used correctly, it can become ineffective.

'Adherence' is the currently preferred term for the extent to which the patient's behaviour is consistent with the clinician's recommendations. In the past, terminology such as 'compliance' or 'concordance' has been used, but this implied that when a clinician prescribed the treatment, it was then the patient's role to 'comply' with it. The difficulty with this is that it implies that the problem lies with the patient: if only they would do what the doctor recommended, there would be no problem. However, it is important to recognise that the child and his or her parents are not passive recipients of medical advice or recommendations. Therefore there are ways of making it more likely that the child and family will manage the treatment regime successfully. Also, it is clear that adherence is a dimension rather than a category – the child and family may manage to adhere to the treatment regime for some of the time but not all the time, and may adhere to some aspects of treatment but not to some of the more difficult aspects.

It is important to start from the understanding that most of us are not fully 'adherent' in managing our own health. For example, we all know that to maximise our health we should eat five portions of fruit and vegetables a day and exercise at least three times a week, but we do not all follow these recommendations. Many people working in health settings are overweight (despite the health risks associated with obesity) and some smoke (despite the known risks associated with smoking). There is clearly a gap between knowing what is the optimal behaviour for managing health, understanding what we need to do to manage our health, and actually doing these things on a regular basis. This helps us to understand why patients have difficulties adhering to their treatment regimes – it is difficult to maintain health-promoting behaviours on a consistent basis over a long period of time. With many treatment regimes, as with many health-promoting behaviours, there is no immediate benefit or immediate improvement, and therefore it is hard to maintain the behaviour even if you know that in the long term it will be beneficial.

MEASURING ADHERENCE

It can be difficult to get accurate measures of adherence and a lot of research in this area has looked at how to ensure that we get the most accurate measures of adherence from children and families (Quittner *et al.* 2000). There are various ways of measuring adherence, including diary recording, telephone interviews, electronic methods, measuring the amount of medication used or measuring the physiological response (e.g. the level of the medication in blood levels). It can be difficult for children and families to keep an accurate record of their medication regime as this is often seen as an additional burden – and retrospective recall is notoriously unreliable. While in clinical practice we usually rely on written records, most people, and especially children and young people, prefer to use electronic recording devices, which may even be as simple as programming a reminder on a mobile phone. Developments in technology have resulted in more sophisticated means of measuring adherence, such as electronic hand-held devices – personal digital assistants (PDAs) and nebulisers which monitor usage and dose given (Latchford *et al.* 2009). However, in routine clinical practice it is hard to justify the more accurate and patient-friendly but expensive methods. It is important to remember that even these can be misleading – it is possible not to take the medication, even when prompted by an alarm to unscrew the top of a bottle and it is still possible to record having taken a medication when you have not done so.

FACTORS THAT INFLUENCE ADHERENCE

Research studies have highlighted a number of factors that are likely to affect adherence, and we can use this knowledge to help inform how we manage treatment regimes (La Greca and Mackey 2009).

Knowledge and skills relating to the child's condition and treatment are important, but not sufficient for good adherence – while it is important for children and their families to have a good understanding of the condition and the treatment, this does not guarantee they will be able to adhere to treatment plans. However, we know that in most consultations only a minority of the information given is remembered or retained, and therefore it is important to find ways of maximising the amount of information someone can remember from a consultation. This can be done by asking them to explain back what they have understood, which allows any errors to be corrected or any omissions to be addressed. It is also important to give written treatment plans, and the recent change in the NHS to copying families into routine correspondence means that the family routinely receives a written summary of the consultation, which can be helpful in ensuring that they have a good understanding of the condition and treatment plan.

> Anna is a three-year-old girl with severe atopic eczema which is poorly controlled. She had been prescribed emollients and bath products to use regularly, as well as steroid cream for the severe patches. However, her mother found it very difficult to apply the emollients because Anna is a very active and determined girl and it was difficult to get her to cooperate with undressing and dressing to put on the emollients three times a day. Her mother had concerns about the use of steroids, as she felt that these would themselves damage Anna's skin. As a consequence, Anna's skin was very dry and itchy and she found it very hard to sleep at night. Her GP felt that the eczema was getting worse, and Anna was referred to a nurse-led clinic where the use of emollients was demonstrated, a plan for tackling the times when the cream had to be applied was made, and specific strategies for helping manage Anna's behaviour were agreed. The nurse arranged for the mother to make a trial of the steroid cream, as well as providing specific information about the exact amount to use in order to address her fears of using it to excess.

Some social factors, such as low social economic status and other indicators of limited resources, are associated with poor adherence. It is important to remember that these factors are not in themselves deterministic, and it is likely that other factors associated with these, such as higher levels of stress and fewer social supports, make adherence harder for those affected. In general, families who are organised, cohesive and good at problem solving are likely to find it easier to adhere to treatment programmes.

Good communication and trust in the prescribing clinician is important, and is associated with better adherence (Drotar 2009). However, it can also be difficult for parents to talk honestly to their child's doctor about difficulties with adherence. They may feel that they are to blame for not ensuring that their child takes their medication, and may be concerned about letting down their medical team. They may also feel that it is disloyal to their child to talk about difficulties in the presence of people from outside the family, particularly if the difficulties are resulting in high levels of conflict. For this reason, it is important for the clinician routinely to consider how well the child and family are managing the treatment regime, to ask about this and listen to any concerns expressed, and to show willingness to help the family address any issues that arise with managing a treatment regime.

The nature of the treatment regime also influences adherence – it is harder for children and families if the treatment is uncomfortable, complex, time-consuming and intrusive. It is easier if it can be easily fitted into their daily life, is simple and either neutral or gives some immediate benefit. Some conditions such as cystic fibrosis require a range of different treatments (enzyme supplements, nebulisers, physiotherapy, etc.) and a child can be adherent to one aspect of the treatment regime but not others. Over the recent past, treatment regimes have tended to become more complex and are increasingly carried out by families themselves, so this has implications for adherence rates – for example some children in renal failure are taking over 40 tablets a day, as well as food supplements, and are on fluid and dietary restrictions.

One study found that post-traumatic stress disorder (PTSD) symptoms were strongly associated with poor adherence following liver transplant, and attributed the adherence difficulties to avoidance of reminders of the transplant, which were associated with the PTSD symptoms (Shemesh et al. 2000). Children who have had traumatic experiences of medical procedures are likely to find it more difficult to manage subsequent procedures and show high levels of anticipatory anxiety. These symptoms not only cause considerable distress but may lead to ongoing problems with treatment, because the child or parent finds it more difficult to cope with any subsequent necessary treatment. (See Chapter 3 for more on the impact of trauma on children.)

The age of the child is also a very important determinant which affects adherence. For very young children, it is the parents who are wholly responsible for managing their treatment, and parents can control the treatment regime much more effectively. While it can be very challenging to manage a toddler's regime, it is nonetheless possible to control in a very different way from that of a 14-year-old. For young children, it is important for parents to be able to develop and sustain a consistent routine, and they may need help thinking through how to manage this and what might be effective rewards or consequences to use. Given that they may have to sustain the treatment over a long period of time, it is important to pick rewards or consequences that they will be able to follow through, otherwise these are ineffective, and young children pick up very quickly on inconsistency. Young children do respond well to consistent routines, and therefore it is important to help parents find ways to be consistent, because this will help the child accept the need for treatment more easily.

As children grow up, they become more able to be actively involved in their treatment and need gradually to assume responsibility for more and more tasks, and eventually for their own decisions. This process obviously needs to be matched on the part of their parents by gradually allowing the child more responsibility and autonomy, in order for the young person to develop independence (Modi *et al.* 2008). For many young people and parents this leads to high levels of conflict, not just over their medical treatment but also over their lifestyle decisions.

This process can also be exacerbated because we know that even when adults are not fully adherent with their own medication, they tend to be much better at looking after their children than they are at looking after themselves, and will be more likely to ensure that their child takes all their medication. This can become one of the main sources of tension as the child gets older, because young people are unlikely to take as good care of themselves as their parents did, and many parents find it difficult to tolerate this. Conflict may then ensue over who manages the treatment regime and how much freedom and responsibility is given to the young person. In addition, part of the learning process will almost certainly involve the young person taking some risks and making some errors, which understandably parents can find very anxiety-provoking. (See Chapter 10 for further discussion of this.)

For many families these difficulties result in high levels of conflict, which can have a severe impact on relationships in the family. It can also give rise to further problems if the young person begins actively to deceive their parents and the medical team, in order to avoid confrontation.

Examples of this include running water in the bathroom to pretend they are catheterising, and taking tablets just the night before an appointment so that there is some medication in their bloodstream.

MANAGING NON-ADHERENCE

Several different psychological methods of managing adherence to treatment for chronic conditions have been evaluated in research studies. These include behavioural methods, educational programmes and multi-component interventions which combine different methodologies. A recent meta-analysis demonstrated moderate effect sizes for behavioural and multi-component methods, and small effect sizes for educational approaches (Kahana, Drotar and Frazier 2008).

Some problems with adherence are caused by the child not having the necessary skill to manage the treatment, and it can be helpful to think of this in terms of learning any new skill. For example, when children first start taking medication in tablet form, many struggle initially with learning to swallow a tablet. Sometimes they have already had an experience of choking, which makes them fearful of trying this again. It can be helpful to support the child by 'training' them to take tablets, starting off with easy stages or easy techniques and building up to the actual pill they have to swallow. This can include starting with smaller objects to swallow (e.g. small sweets) and gradually increasing to the size and texture of their tablet. Or it can include trying out a variety of techniques for swallowing (e.g. putting the tablet in some 'slippery' food) and finding one the child is comfortable with.

It is important to start from the premise that it is not simple and easy to adhere to a complex treatment programme, and therefore helping children and families manage the demands of their treatment regime should be part of the ongoing review of how treatment is progressing. This means that open discussion about treatment difficulties should be encouraged because this in itself leads to better treatment – for example if a treatment appears not to be effective, it may be because most of the medication is not being taken, and it is more important to try and improve this than to switch to another medication. For example, it can be helpful to have a discussion with the child and family about what they should do if the child forgets to take their medication, and so preparing for this eventuality. There is some evidence that improving communication skills can make consultations more effective and help to normalise difficulties with non-adherence. This enables the child and family to see that this is a joint problem, rather than just their 'fault'.

It is easy for a health care professional to feel forced into a 'directive' style when faced with a young person who is not adhering to a treatment regime and is reluctant to talk it through. It is important that the young person is given the information and that this is done in a way that makes it clear what the medical recommendations are, and also what the consequences are if the young person does not follow the recommendations. However, it can be counterproductive if the whole consultation is experienced as 'telling off', because then it may have the opposite of the desired effect and make the young person dig in their heels, partly because they feel backed into a corner. It is important to try opening up a discussion about what makes it more difficult and what techniques help to improve adherence, and to see this as a joint task.

Managing problems with adherence can be very frustrating for clinicians, who often perceive it as disrespectful of their knowledge and authority if the young person appears to refuse to follow their advice. Many clinicians feel that they have failed if they are unable to ensure that the patient does use their treatment effectively, and do not believe that they should accept a compromise because they know that this is not in the long-term interest of the patient. It may be necessary for the child to be monitored more closely, either by coming to clinic more frequently or, if all else fails, as part of an admission during which the difficulties with adherence can be observed directly and an appropriate routine can be started. In these circumstances it can be helpful to refer on to a psychologist to enable further exploration of the child's and family's difficulties with adherence, but a referral on needs to be handled carefully in order to maximise the probability that the child and family will take up the offer of further help from a psychologist. Despite appearing ambivalent, the adolescent may be concealing high levels of anxiety, and the parents may be feeling guilty and frustrated because of not being able to achieve any change.

In order to discuss these issues and develop a plan to manage non-adherence, it can be helpful to see the parents and the child separately in order to explore why adherence has become more difficult. It can be helpful to talk through strategies with the parents without the child present, and to give them a chance to talk about managing their own frustration. Quite often children will talk more freely when seen alone, particularly when they might otherwise want to protect their parents, or where their views may be in direct conflict with those of their parents. They may also be able to be more honest and reflect more openly on the difficulties they experience without the concern about 'losing face'.

However, it is also important to then develop an agreement with the child or young person and family together, and to reach a consensus about the treatment plan. Behavioural techniques such as incentives and rewards can help in the short term, particularly with young children, who need more immediate rewards for their behaviour. However, behavioural techniques alone are less effective with older children and need to be supplemented by including the whole family and addressing conflict and communication difficulties as well. One example of this sort of approach, behavioural family systems therapy (BFST), has been shown to be more effective for young people with diabetes, compared to education alone or standard care (Wysocki *et al.* 2008).

BFST involves a multifaceted approach to adherence, including interventions in training for problem solving, communication skills, cognitive restructuring and structural family therapy. It also involves the parent simulating living with diabetes for a week, which can be a powerful way of helping them to experience the restrictions of their child's regime. The therapy also includes work with peers and siblings, as well as school when appropriate, and is therefore very intensive. Although this approach has been shown to have benefits in research studies, only about a quarter of those eligible for the study agreed to take part, and therefore these results may not translate to most clinical settings where it is hard to provide such an intensive intervention, and because the types of participants included are likely to be very different from those in the research study.

While most young children can be persuaded to comply with their treatment regime, particularly if they have always had to do this and their parents have set up a consistent routine, many children go through a stage when they become less cooperative and begin to challenge the need for the treatment. This can be partly because of their increased awareness and understanding of being different from their peers, and associated questioning of why this has happened and how unfair it is. Parents understandably find this distressing, not only because it makes it much harder to ensure that the child does take their medication, but also because it may again raise doubts for them about why the child has been affected, and difficulties in managing their own sense of distress over these issues. Even when a child has grown up with a chronic condition, the meaning and impact of the condition will vary over time, depending on their own understanding and its impact on their lives. At these times it can be helpful to review with the child what their understanding is, and if necessary revisit the explanations about what the condition is and how treatments work, to help identify the factors that may be interfering with the management of their condition.

In some circumstances, non-adherence to treatment can also be seen as a way of attempting to block out or deny the reality of the condition and its treatment. Having to take medication is a constant reminder to the child and family of their condition, and by simply ignoring or refusing to participate in this treatment, the young person can avoid these reminders. These difficulties are hard to address directly and are not easily resolved – the young person needs to build up a sufficiently trusting relationship to begin to address their fears and reluctance to 'talk it through'. Occasionally, this is linked to an earlier traumatic experience or is even a sign of being traumatised by the illness and treatment.

> Max had moderate to severe asthma and he and his family had managed this well throughout most of his childhood so that he had not had any hospital admissions for several years. He had always had a good relationship with his GP and paediatrician and had a good understanding of his medication regime. At the age of 15 he suffered an extremely severe episode requiring emergency treatment at A&E and was admitted overnight. Max was frightened by this episode and became quite miserable and withdrawn over the next few months. His parents began to monitor his treatment more closely again, and he found this intrusive and became less cooperative and less communicative with them. Understandably this raised their anxiety and led to considerable conflict at home. At the next clinic appointment, the paediatrician was surprised by the change in Max. He was reluctant to answer questions in the consultation and irritable with his mother. The paediatrician offered to see Max on his own for a while, and was concerned by his degree of hopelessness about the future and sense of lack of control. Max agreed reluctantly to a referral to psychology and was seen for three sessions. The focus of these sessions was on helping Max individually with his sense of frustration at his condition and the long-term implications of this, together with some brief family work focusing on agreeing an appropriate level of supervision and managing conflict.

SAFEGUARDING

Occasionally situations arise when the parent or parents are unable to manage the child's treatment well enough, and this becomes a safeguarding issue because the child's welfare is affected. This usually happens in the context of other concerns about the child's welfare, and it becomes essential to involve a social worker or make a referral to social services. However, many medical teams find it difficult to pursue safeguarding procedures in this context because of the fear that this process may interfere with their relationship with the child and family and make it even harder for them to work cooperatively together. Sometimes the benefit of 'raising the stakes' by identifying that non-adherence has become an issue of safeguarding and involving social work is enough to outweigh concerns about the breakdown in relationships – and in some cases there is no alternative. But in many cases, the outcome of a safeguarding referral will be to improve monitoring and to offer further help to child and family. This should be considered as good practice, and it can be helpful to have the additional input to ensure that the child's best interests are paramount.

MOTIVATIONAL INTERVIEWING

In order to help a young person become more engaged in their treatment plan, it can be helpful to use a technique known as motivational interviewing. Motivational interviewing (MI) is a form of goal-directed, client-centred counselling that helps increase motivation for change (Miller and Rollnick 2002). The philosophy behind MI is that ambivalence to change is normal, and that the therapist's role is to help the patient examine and resolve ambivalence to change by using counselling skills such as empathy and reflective listening. Most of the work with MI has been done with adults, but it can be applied to adolescents and young adults. It is a model specifically aimed at addressing the process of change, and since many adolescents do express ambivalence to change and do not respond to directive change techniques, MI would seem to be particularly relevant for this age group.

Central to this approach is the process of helping the young person separate out how *important* the change is to them, from how *confident* they feel about being able to bring about the change. Frequently psychological approaches such as Cognitive Behavioural Therapy assume that the young person has already accepted the importance of bringing about change, and then the consultation is focused on helping them develop ideas about how to change and what techniques may be helpful to them, and on improving their skills and confidence to bring about change. However, if the young person is not able to commit fully to the importance of change, then they will not be able to make use of specific therapeutic techniques, and this can be a frustrating experience for the young person and therapist alike.

Prochaska and DiClemente's (1982) transtheoretical stages of change model describes a series of five stages which are part of the process of changing a behaviour. These stages are: pre-contemplation, contemplation, preparation, action, and maintenance. This model can be helpful in identifying which stage the young person is operating at, and the most helpful strategy will be tailored to that particular stage. For example, if they are in the 'contemplation' stage, it can be helpful to focus on eliciting talk about change – for example by using questions which highlight the disadvantages of the status quo and the advantages of change:

- What would be the advantages of [...]?

- What differences would you see if you did [...]?

- Who could offer you helpful support in making this change?

If the young person has not yet become convinced of the benefits of change, it is not appropriate to begin developing plans or preparing for change, and this can only be done once they have successfully convinced themselves that they do want to try and change and believe there will be benefits for themselves.

Working with this sort of approach can feel more productive to the therapist than proceeding on the basis that the therapist's role is to convince the adolescent that change may be helpful to them. The term 'roll with resistance' is used to describe techniques for managing the client's expressions of resistance. For example, if the young person says 'It's not that easy – you don't understand how hard it is for me', the technique involves reflecting back that they are finding it difficult, but also suggesting that they sense some frustration about not being able to change, for example: 'It is hard for you because you feel others don't understand. However, I can see you are trying to make some changes and find it frustrating that it is so difficult...'

Channon et al. (2007) carried out a randomised controlled trial (RCT) of MI compared to supportive counselling for young people aged 14–17 with diabetes and the MI group showed benefits both in terms of blood glucose levels and in psychosocial measures. This is one of the very few RCTs of a specific therapeutic intervention in this field and so is a significant piece of evidence for the benefits of this approach. However, given that the study used a selected sample of participants, the results may not generalise to the sorts of cases seen in clinical practice, but this approach can clearly be helpful for some young people.

EXPERT PATIENT PROGRAMME

Many people with chronic illness find it helpful to talk to other people with a similar condition and can draw motivation from identifying with other patients. The expert patient programme has been developed to make use of the expertise that patients have built up through their experience of managing their illness. Groups and workshops are run by trained volunteers who are themselves young people with a chronic illness, in order to attract young people who may benefit from a sense of understanding and belonging. This approach appeals to some young people because they feel it is a more cooperative way of managing their concerns about their condition and treatment, where they are seen as respected authorities in their own right. (See Chapter 9 for further discussion about involving young people in developing services.)

SUMMARY

Problems with adherence are common and it is important to consider these difficulties as part of any long-term treatment programme. A variety of strategies have proved helpful, depending on the age of the child and the reason for non-adherence. These include improving communication with the child and family, behavioural techniques for young children, and motivational interviewing for older young people. Adherence difficulties can result in high levels of stress and conflict in the family and therefore need to be considered whenever a child has a long-term treatment regime. Adolescents present particular challenges with adherence, and this is discussed further in Chapter 10.

CHAPTER 8

Education, School and Peer Relationships

This chapter covers the impact of chronic illness on a child's education, and the services and systems which can be used to help ensure children with medical conditions are able to benefit from education to achieve their potential despite their health problems. This includes both academic skills and promoting achievement, and the social needs of the child, including developing good peer relationships.

School plays a very important part in the life of a child and it is one area which is often disrupted by chronic illness. School is essential not just for learning but also because of its important role in supporting social development and promoting a child's independence. All children should be able to continue with their education despite being unwell, but as each child's needs do vary, it can be hard to find the ideal form of flexible educational support. Illness can disrupt education in several ways. Children may have to miss school for hospital appointments and admissions or because they are too unwell to come to school. Even if a child is well enough to attend school, they may find it harder to access the full curriculum, because of tiredness or physical difficulties. In addition, they may find it more difficult to integrate fully with their peers, especially if it is hard for them physically to join in activities, but also because of discontinuity due to absences, which disrupts friendship groups. Some medical conditions, particularly those which affect the central nervous system (CNS), such as epilepsy, are also associated with increased rates of general or specific learning difficulties. In addition, some treatments can affect the CNS (e.g. some treatments for cancer), and this can result in specific learning difficulties which are quite subtle and difficult to diagnose.

Current education policy aims to support children wherever possible in mainstream education and to promote inclusion, which emphasises the similarities between children rather than the differences between them. *Access to Education for Children and Young People with Medical Needs* (DoH/DfES 2001) states: 'All pupils should continue to have access to as much education as their medical condition allows so that they are able to maintain the momentum of their education and to keep up with their studies.'

All schools are required to have a policy to deal with managing education for children with medical needs. They will usually want to draw up a health care plan for any child whose health care needs affect their day-to-day life at school, and this should cover absences from school. If a child is going to be absent because of medical needs for 15 days or more, the local authority (LA) has to be informed and is obliged to provide education of a 'similar quality and range' to what they would get in school. Creative use of technology, such as the Internet and email, can make it much easier for a child to continue with work set at their own school, even if they are not able to attend school in person. This helps reduce the difficulties which children experience on returning to school following an absence, when they often feel they have missed out on topics and are not able to catch up.

It can be very difficult to find a good balance between encouraging a child to continue education and making allowances because he or she is unwell. All children find it harder to tackle formal learning when they are unwell, and it can be dispiriting for them if they feel they are unable to work as well as before. Many parents find it difficult to enforce school attendance when their child is unwell and it is very easy for children to 'drift' in these circumstances, which can result in long-term attendance problems and increasing social isolation. This is a particularly high risk at secondary school level. However, attendance at school, even if only on a part-time basis, reduces the risk of social isolation because the child stays in contact with friends, classmates and teachers and maintains a sense of natural progression. It becomes increasingly difficult to integrate fully back into school if absence is prolonged and so it is important to keep time off school to a minimum. The best compromise is often to attend school part-time rather than not at all, but this requires flexibility on the part of the school, and also of parents, who may need to be available to bring the child to school and fetch them from school, as well as providing care when the child is not in school. The school may also need advice and input as to how to manage the child's condition during the day so that he or she is not sent home unnecessarily, and it may be helpful to draw up a plan between the child and the school about how to manage symptoms during the day.

The transition between primary and secondary school can be difficult for any child, but it may be particularly significant for children with a medical condition. As the child reaches the end of primary school, they are usually well known by both staff and pupils, and, if all is well, feel settled and confident in their environment. Secondary schools are usually much larger than primary schools, and parents are not as involved in their child's day-to-day school life. Getting to school may involve long journeys, and simply getting around a large secondary school can involve large distances, including stairs. The child will have many different teachers (as well as a key form tutor or equivalent), and will have to get to know them.

> Sarah had missed an increasing amount of school due to her illness. She had attended school for most of Year 4 and some of Year 5, but missed the majority of Year 6. Her family became increasingly concerned about how to get her back to school because she was reluctant to return, and they felt she was not well enough to manage full-time. Sarah was young for her year and also very small for her age due to her ongoing health difficulties.
>
> When the psychologist met the family, it was clear that both Sarah and her parents were reluctant for her to return to school and that the impending move to secondary school looked unrealistic both because of the amount of education she had missed and also her ability to manage the transition. Following a meeting between the primary school Special Educational Needs Coordinator, Sarah and her parents, it was agreed to ask the local authority to let her repeat Year 6 'back-classed'. Sarah gradually returned part-time during the summer term and returned after the summer holidays to repeat Year 6. Despite her initial reluctance, Sarah adjusted to her new year group and gained in confidence during the academic year.

If a child is unable to attend school, there are other options to ensure that they continue with their education. Home tutoring can be very helpful and flexible, and many children build up a good relationship with their home tutor. If a child finds it hard to re-engage with school, home tutors can play an important part in facilitating return to school on a gradual basis, by accompanying the child to school or doing some lessons within the school. However, home tutoring restricts social integration and there are scarce resources for home tutors, so the amount offered to any one child is quite limited (usually only five hours per week), and the range of subjects any one tutor can offer is also reduced.

Some hospitals have their own hospital school, which can provide education for inpatients and sometimes for outpatients or siblings who are unable to attend their own school. The school will have their own admission policy and be regularly inspected by Ofsted, in the same way as any other school. Hospital schools aim to follow the national curriculum and are experienced at adapting work to accommodate the special needs of the child. The children are sometimes taught in small groups within a 'classroom' setting, at their own bedside, or even in an adapted ward school. At the Evelina Children's Hospital's haemodialysis unit, children may need to attend dialysis sessions on 3 school days per week, so it is particularly important to establish continuity in their education. As soon as the children have been started on their dialysis machines, the unit becomes a classroom, where children follow the individual education plan which has been drawn up in conjunction with their home school. A number of children's homes subscribe to an online maths syllabus, which enables children to access the work their peers would be doing at school directly via the internet.

Many children enjoy the education they receive in hospital, partly because it helps create a sense of normality and continuity, but also because it provides a welcome break from medical routines. In addition, they may be able to get more individualised attention, tailored to their own interests and level of ability.

SPECIAL EDUCATIONAL NEEDS (SEN)

The system for providing additional input to children at school who have special educational needs is based on a graduated approach, providing different levels of support to children depending on their needs. While the system is intended to support children and families, many parents find it hard to understand how to access appropriate support for their child and find the system quite daunting. A full explanation of the system suitable for parents can be found in the leaflet *Special Educational Needs – A Guide for Parents and Carers* published by the Department for Children, Schools and Families (2009), which can be downloaded from the teachernet website (see 'Education' in Appendix 1).

All teachers are routinely expected to tailor their lessons to meet the varied learning needs of the children within their class and to differentiate the curriculum in order to do this. If a child has additional needs beyond this, these can be identified by the parent or teacher and the child is placed on the level known as 'school action', where the school monitors their progress and provides additional input from the school internal resources. If further additional help is needed from outside services, or specialist help is required, the child will then be moved to 'school action plus'. As part of the monitoring system when a child has additional needs, the teacher should draw up and record an Individual Education Plan (IEP) for that child. The aim of this plan is to set short-term targets for the child and specify what strategies or provision is required to help the child acquire these targets. These are then reviewed on a minimum six-monthly basis and, if necessary, revised to take account of additional help needed or progress made.

Only those children whose needs cannot be met at 'school action plus' would then be considered for a statutory assessment of special educational needs – often referred to as 'statement of special educational needs' or 'statementing'. Parents can request a statutory assessment themselves (under section 329 of the Education Act 1996) and the LA is required to decide whether to make an assessment within six weeks of receiving a request.

Some children with chronic illness have long-term special educational needs as a consequence of their medical condition or its treatment. The medical condition itself does not give a child special educational needs, but the condition may affect their ability to learn or access educational facilities and so result in greater difficulties in learning than for other children of a comparable age. Psychologists or doctors working within the medical team are sometimes involved in providing information for the school about the needs of the child and, if appropriate, can participate in the assessment process. However, the experts on the local services and options available are the child's teachers, the school Special Educational Needs Coordinator (SENCO) and the local educational psychologist. There is a lot of variation in the types of provision across the country and it can be difficult to give advice without knowledge of the local context. Therefore it is essential that there is good communication and liaison between services in order to ensure that the school has a full understanding of the child's needs. School visits can be an invaluable way of facilitating a direct discussion about the child's needs, including pulling together all sources of information, and although school visits are time-consuming, these can help overcome many barriers. When children are at secondary school and have many different teachers, the SENCO plays a vital role in communicating the child's needs to other staff members.

Some conditions and treatments are known to be associated with very specific cognitive difficulties, and the expertise of the specialist medical team can be very important in helping to guide the assessment process, as well as the sorts of interventions or supports that may make a difference in enabling the child to learn effectively. Sometimes a child's lack of progress at school is attributed to their illness and the amount of time they have had off school, but the child may have subtle cognitive difficulties as a result of their medical condition (e.g. HIV infection), which might not be picked up by routine assessments at school, and which would need more detailed neuropsychological or cognitive testing to identify. These can include some attention and concentration difficulties and problems with executive functioning, which can look like behavioural problems or like a lack of effort on the child's part. In addition, some children with cognitive difficulties have some associated emotional and behavioural difficulties which can affect their ability to progress at school, both academically and socially. These can include social difficulties (including social communication difficulties or autistic spectrum difficulties). Specialist medical teams are more likely to be aware of these difficulties than schools, and can help provide information or assessment for these types of problems.

When providing advice for a statement or for schools, it is essential to phrase any advice to a school in a way that identifies the child's needs, rather than making recommendations for the specific type of input required, because there is a lot of variation in the types of provision that schools and LAs can access. The *Toolkit for the Special Educational Needs Code of Practice*, section 12, 'The role of health professionals' (DCSF 2001), gives specific guidance for health professionals about giving advice for statutory assessments. This recommends that advice should state clearly the likely impact on the child's education of the medical or developmental condition or its treatment. It should include advice on the management of the condition in the school context, including the management of emotional and behavioural difficulties. Schools often find it helpful if any of the child's particular difficulties can be partly explained as a consequence of their medical condition, and especially if there is any research backing this up, which can make it easier for them to access resources.

It can be very easy for parents to get caught up in a battle between their school or LA about provision for their child's special educational needs. Although the explicit policy within education is to support inclusion in mainstream education, many parents report that they have had to struggle with local services to obtain the additional help their child requires. This is a time-consuming task, as well as an emotional one, as most parents are understandably very sensitive about the difficulties their child faces in terms of real, rather than notional, inclusion. The system can be daunting and it can be hard for parents to feel they can participate in it actively. One example of this is that, although parents are included in planning and reviewing IEPs, they often do not know how to influence these or what would or would not make a good target for their child. They are therefore usually dependent on the teacher's advice and may not feel able to challenge this. Parent partnership services act as a support for parents involved with the SEN service and can help parents when they run into any difficulty with the system or are unhappy with the way the school is managing their child's needs (see Appendix 1). However, these services are also very variable and are not always seen as independent from the education system.

Realistically, mainstream schools do not necessarily have access to the ideal resources for all children within the school, and some prioritising does have to happen at the school level. Inclusion is also very dependent on context, and parents with children with mild to moderate difficulties often feel their child's needs are not met because 'they are not the only one with difficulties' and the child is not the neediest in the class. Some children are much happier in a special school, which typically has small class numbers and a high level of teacher support. It is very important to take into account both the child's view and the parents' views and not to presume that one environment will suit all children.

However, there are great variations within the system, and inequalities within the range of services offered. Some schools have excellent provision for SEN but in some areas, there are no real choices of alternative schools. The recent Lamb inquiry into SEN (DCSF 2009) has documented some of the difficulties parents encounter with the system, and advocates many changes to improve the system.

When children are approaching the end of school education and take public exams, they may be entitled to special concessions as a result of their physical condition, including additional time in exams, factoring in time for breaks if needed, sitting exams in a separate room, and using a scribe to write for them. If children are too unwell to sit their exams, their grade can often be prorated from coursework undertaken over the exam syllabus.

Any child who has a statement should have a transition planning meeting in Year 9 to plan for education post-16 and to review their need for ongoing support. The Connexions service should play a key part in assessment and planning for these children.

APPEARANCE DIFFICULTIES AND PEER DIFFICULTIES

There is considerable evidence that children with chronic illness are at higher risk of developing peer relationship difficulties than healthy children (Reiter-Purtill, Waller and Noll 2009). These difficulties are likely to be increased if the child has general developmental difficulties or learning difficulties associated with their condition. This may be because the child is seen as 'different' by their peers, or it may be partly because their skills are also somewhat delayed, which makes it harder for them to 'fit in' with the age-related tasks that their peers are involved with. Social problems may reflect difficulties in participating in normal childhood activities because of either physical limitations or functional disability, or indeed partly because many children who have spent a lot of time away from school or in hospital have become more familiar with interacting with adults than with children. They have spent more time with their parents, and have had to spend more time learning to manage, or at least tolerate, communicating with adult medical and nursing staff.

Children with a chronic illness or medical condition can also look different from their peers – they often have problems with growth and consequently look younger and smaller than their chronological age. They may also have other features that make them look different, such as scars, facial differences, changes in skin and loss of hair. These differences can make them stand out at school, and this can be a source of great distress for many young people. Differences related to physical appearance have also been linked with peer relationship difficulties (Vannatta et al. 2009) and increased incidence of bullying, name-calling and teasing (Rumsey and Harcourt 2007).

Children can also be very sensitive to being treated differently from their peers and having special procedures in place for them, because this can make them feel awkward and self-conscious and remind them that they are different from healthy children. As a result, they may find it harder to adhere to some treatment regimes that require them to do something different from their peers – for example, going to the special needs toilet, even when this has been set up in order to try and help them manage within school.

There is often some benefit in being proactive and helping prepare the child's teacher and classmates if the child has appearance-related difficulties, or is returning to school after a prolonged absence or a treatment that has visible effects. It can be helpful to provide information to the teacher so that he or she can answer any questions from the other children, and indeed, to ensure that teachers are prepared themselves. Several organisations provide useful leaflets for schools to help them with this (CLIC Sargant, Changing Faces, National Eczema Society – see Appendix 1).

Schools play a very important part in creating a culture of tolerating difference and valuing diversity. Schools have become more aware of the importance of tackling bullying and all have anti-bullying policies in place (Olweus 1993). This can make a great difference within the school, and where schools are effective in ensuring that the whole school community is aware of the importance of preventing or reducing bullying, this can genuinely improve acceptance within it. In order to do this, schools have to adopt a positive, inclusive ethos that values diversity, and the anti-bullying policy has to be implemented by all staff. This whole-school approach is an important way of addressing these difficulties which are pervasive throughout our society. O'Dell and Prior (2005) found that school-based interventions to tackle visible differences were effective both for children with visible differences and for other children.

However, children, and adolescents in particular, are very sensitive to differences from the norm. As many as 10 per cent of young people who have no apparent visible difference report that they sometimes do not attend school because of the way they look, and 30 per cent say they do not volunteer in class in order not to draw attention to themselves (Lovegrove and Rumsey 2005). Even providing additional help intended to support a young person can be seen as stigmatising, especially as the child gets older.

Consequently, many children who do have a visible difference find it hard to feel confident about their appearance difficulties, and this can affect their overall self-esteem and cause mood problems. Some young people, who are acutely sensitive in this respect, find it very emotionally demanding to manage the constant staring or comments they receive, become very defensive, and can find it hard to access help. The charity Changing Faces has developed extensive resources for schools, including a leaflet about strategies for managing these situations in ways that go beyond simply ignoring hurtful comments and teasing (Kish and Lansdown 2000).

In order to help children with peer relationship difficulties, it may be appropriate to see them for psychological support either individually or with their parents. If the school is fortunate enough to have counsellors within school, or school-based mental health services, these can also be a valuable resource, especially if they are able to intervene at a systemic level within the school. For children or young people with significant emotional or behavioural difficulties related to appearance or peer relationship problems, it may be essential to address these more intensively away from the school setting, and then liaise with the school (with the agreement of the young person and his or her family) as necessary. Cognitive behavioural techniques and social interaction skills training (SIST) have also been shown to be helpful in both individual and group-based summer camp format (Maddern and Owen 2004, Maddern, Cadogan and Emerson 2006). SIST is based on the premise that many people who have experienced frequent teasing or comments related to their appearance begin to withdraw from social encounters and automatically anticipate a negative reaction from other people. The intervention aims to promote confidence and proficiency in relation to meeting, forming and continuing relationships with other people. However, many young people may lack the confidence to take up these sorts of interventions, and there is a need to develop ways of providing this sort of support on a routine basis and in a way that is more accessible to them.

SUMMARY

It is important for all children with a chronic illness to have the opportunity to benefit from education in the same way as healthy children in order to achieve their full potential. However, the demands of many chronic illnesses make it more difficult for children to attend school at times, and therefore they may need additional support. Hospitals often provide education for children while they are inpatients or if they are attending regular outpatient treatment sessions. The SEN procedure can help children with educational difficulties access additional support, and psychologists or other members of the multidisciplinary team can provide information for schools to help with this. Some children with chronic illnesses also experience social difficulties and schools have an important role to play in promoting tolerance and developing a culture where bullying is not tolerated, for the benefit of all children.

CHAPTER 9

Empowering Young People: Involvement in Decision Making and Developing Health Care Services

In Chapter 7 we looked at promoting adherence, for which engaging young people and promoting their understanding and cooperation with treatment is central to the process. In this chapter we take a more detailed look at effectively engaging with young people, listening to them and understanding their views, so as to involve them appropriately in decision making. We will consider consent for medical treatment as one important example of decision making and look at the factors which impact on decision making, and ways of empowering young people in this process. In the final section of the chapter we will look at engaging with children as part of 'user involvement', using the expertise of children and young people in developing the most effective services for them and promoting child-centred care.

In recent years children's rights have received international recognition in law. The UN Convention on the Rights of the Child (article 12) and the Human Rights Act 1998 both state that children have rights to be given a say in any decision that affects their lives. *The National Service Framework* (NSF) *for Hospital Services* (DoH 2003) states that children should be encouraged to be active partners in decisions about their health and care, and should where possible, be able to exercise choice. This is echoed in the review of the NHS by Lord Darzi (DoH 2008a), and the Department of Health highlights that central to their policy is 'encouraging children and young people to take responsibility for their actions and make informed choices about healthy lifestyles' (DoH 2007). There is evidence that involvement and participation improves quality of service, and increases a young person's self-esteem and sense of responsibility and well-being.

To implement these policies, professionals need to have good communication skills and be able to develop positive relationships with children, such that children can feel confident that their views are respected and valued. There also needs to be a positive and proactive approach from professionals in wanting to involve children and young people, which may involve putting additional time aside for this process and being prepared to take into account new ideas and plans that might require further resources.

Making decisions about medical care and treatment is a central theme in health care. Parents will be expected to make decisions on behalf of younger children, and, in ways that are adapted to the developmental level of their child, to help him or her understand what is going to happen and why. As children progress and develop their knowledge and expertise about their condition and treatment, they will have their own views about treatment and may feel able to express these to people with whom they feel confident. At this point, parents may talk through what needs to happen and involve their child in some aspects of the decision making (with some opportunities for shared decision making). In doing this, it is important to identify the areas in which there is a real choice and an opportunity for their child to express a preference, but also to be honest about areas in which the child may express a view but it will not influence what happens. In this situation it is helpful to convey that the child's view has been listened to, and to explain wherever possible what needs to happen and why.

Even young children can be helped to participate in decisions about their treatment, such as choosing the colour of their plaster cast, or choosing whether to walk or ride to get to the treatment room. Older children may express a preference about whether they receive their medicine in liquid or tablet form, or which site on their arm they have blood drawn from. Other children may work in partnership with their nurse or doctor to plan out the best times to take their medication or carry out self-care routines, so as to fit in most comfortably with school and other activities. As children continue to develop skills and knowledge about their condition, and skills for communicating with health professionals, they will increasingly be involved in decision making, until such time as they jointly make decisions with parents, and eventually make decisions for themselves, ideally with the continued support of their parents and family.

There are different possible levels of involvement in decision making (Royal College of Paediatrics and Child Health 1997), as follows:

1. informing children

2. listening to them

3. taking account of their views so they can influence the decision

4. respecting the competent child as the main decision maker.

The level of involvement may depend on many factors, including assessment of the child's competence and decision making skills; the confidence and experience of the health professional in communicating with children; and how comfortable the child feels with the professional. The child may feel very positive and empowered to be involved in the process, or disinterested and ambivalent, or totally overwhelmed and withdrawn. The context of the decision making is also a key consideration, as children are sensitive to the expectations or pressure exerted on them by professionals to make the 'right' decision.

Research has shown that adults often underestimate children's ability to understand their treatment and its implications for their health (Alderson and Montgomery 1996), and make assumptions about young people's cognitive and emotional maturity and capacity to be involved in decisions. Parents may also feel very protective of their children, and not want them learning information about their condition or treatment that might be upsetting for them. Children who have already experienced illness and medical treatment often have advanced knowledge and maturity in this area in relation to their peers.

In many chronic conditions there is an emphasis on long-term self-care/treatment regimes. Engaging patients successfully in cooperating with treatment is therefore a highly important goal, and this is reliant on developing an effective relationship with them. Positive relationships and joint goals are realised when young people feel that their views have been taken seriously and they are able to voice their questions, worries or views. Through doing this, young people will also have had opportunities to weigh up for themselves the benefits and challenges associated with their treatment option, and will have taken some ownership of the eventual treatment decision, rather than just being told what they have to do. Involvement and 'ownership' of treatment also promotes development of responsibility for self-care and a sense of autonomy, which can be severely compromised by the impact of symptoms and treatment, and can impact on self-efficacy and confidence.

CONSENT

Consent for treatment is one very important area of decision making in health care. There are different levels of a child 'consenting', from 'offering their arm' for a blood test, to signing a form consenting to surgery. For a young person to be able to give informed consent for treatment, a careful assessment of the child's competency may be required. *Legally*, emphasis is placed on the child's cognitive skills and ability to make an 'informed choice'. Within English law, 'Gillick' competence or the 'Fraser ruling' is often used as a way of describing the level of competency required for a child to be able to give informed consent. (Fraser was the presiding judge in the court case brought by Gillick that provides the legal precedent for consent in young people.) *Clinically*, an assessment of the child's capacity to give informed consent is much wider, and incorporates the following areas:

1. The legal rights of the child.

2. The young person's experience of communicating their views or choices and making decisions in any other context (e.g. at home), and family views regarding child's participation in decision making.

3. The specific context and complexity of the decision to be made.

4. The cognitive and developmental capacity of the child.

5. Social and emotional factors and resources.

6. Skills of the professional team.

1. The legal rights of the child

Although best practice is to involve the young person and all those closest to them in making decisions, within English law there is a framework around who can give consent for the child or young person, and when the young person is able to consent for him- or herself.

Anyone over the age of 16 years is deemed competent to give consent for medical treatment, unless there is direct evidence to the contrary. Under the age of 16 years, a child may be regarded as being able to consent to treatment if assessed to be 'Gillick' or 'Fraser' competent, which means that a clinician is confident that the young person can give informed consent and understand the consequences of their decision. Legally, the decision of a child deemed 'competent' to accept treatment cannot be overridden by a person with parental responsibility. If the child is not competent to give consent, then consent can be given by someone with parental responsibility for the child. Parental responsibility is automatically held by the birth mother, and by the father if the parents were married at the time of the child's birth, or (since 2003) if the father jointly registers the birth of the child with the mother. Fathers need to apply for parental responsibility if they were not married to the mother at the time of the child's birth. Only one parent with parental responsibility needs to give consent, even if the other parent does not agree to treatment. In situations where parents and professionals do not agree on treatment, the court may be asked to give a ruling in the best interest of the child.

Children up to 18 years of age can also be assessed to be competent to deny consent for treatment, but this can be overruled 'in the child's best interests' by a parent or by the court. Those with parental responsibility may then consent on the child's behalf for treatment to be given. After 18 years of age, consent cannot be given on the young person's behalf. At this point the Mental Capacity Act comes into force.

2. The child's level of experience

It is helpful to clarify what opportunities have been available to the child or young person to express their views on their condition or treatment, and how they have used this opportunity. Exploration of this area with families can reveal a great deal about communication within the family and also their attitude towards children expressing their views and actively participating in decisions. If a child is expected to follow an adult's instructions or advice without question as a mark of respect, it will clearly be an issue for the family if health care professionals are building up the child as someone able to take a lead in health care decisions. Sensitivity to cultural norms and expectations is therefore important. In order to establish the level of the child's experiences of decision making, it can be helpful to ask about key decisions at home – decisions about the décor of the child's room, how decisions were made about the child's secondary school or the naming of the family pet, for some examples. Older children can be asked about the way decisions were made about academic subjects studied at school, or decisions about how their study time and social time is organised.

3. Context of the decision

This includes the 'weightiness' or seriousness of the decision and, more specifically, the emotional and actual consequences of the decision. Some decisions may be relatively straightforward and have few serious consequences, such as whether the child uses a topical anaesthesia prior to a blood test or tries without. Other medical treatments may be more complex, and without any guarantee of success, such as a young person going on a ketogenic diet (a diet which is high in fat and causes biochemical changes in the body which have been found to be helpful in managing epilepsy) or being offered surgery to straighten their foot. If, once made, the decision is not reversible, such as having surgery to have your jaw reset, or a limb amputation, the decision has even more serious consequences. Some decisions, such as whether or not to have a further course of chemotherapy, or use night-time ventilation when breathing is compromised, may well have life-threatening implications. Children may have confidence and competence to make some decisions, but not all decisions.

Another important dimension of the decision itself is how complex it is. This may be related to the technical complexity of the treatment, and also the number of options and possible outcomes that need to be 'weighed up', with the child having to consider both 'probable' and 'possible' outcomes. The demands and outcomes might be different in the short and long term, further increasing complexity.

> One ten-year-old girl was required to wear a special 'pressure' bandage on her face following severe burns, in order to reduce her scarring. The bandage was uncomfortable and hot, and on a day-to-day basis did not reveal any improvements. She was adamant that she did not care what she looked like or would look like in the future – she did not want this treatment.

The actual treatment process can also be lengthy, with different components over time forming the treatment programme, with the consequent challenge of gaining informed consent from children, as in the following example:

> Surgery involving a bone graft from a child's hip to reconstruct and extend the jaw is the final part of treatment, following several months of orthodontic treatment, for some children born with a cleft lip and

palate. These children will already have undergone essential surgery as infants, and this later treatment is largely cosmetic, to create space in their mouths for their teeth. Due to physical development, optimal time for treatment is around 8–9 years. For successful treatment the child will have to cooperate in having surgery which is usually carried out around a year after orthodontic treatment. It can be difficult to inform the child adequately about the whole treatment sequence, when they do not have prior experience of dental or medical treatment. It may be questionable to give a young child too much detail of surgery so far in advance, as children may become anxious and sensitised to other hospital contact. Parents may be extremely keen for children to have this treatment, as they are able to hold a longer-term perspective of the benefits for the child, and just want the child to be told information gradually, on a 'need to know' basis, in order to build on experience and knowledge and prepare them more gradually for treatment. The whole process (orthodontic treatment and surgery) is required for the child to have any benefits, and although most children may manage the orthodontic procedures well, a number of them may not want surgery. If the treatment process is not completed, the outcome for the child may be worse than having no treatment in the first place.

4. Cognitive skills of the child

When assessing a child's cognitive maturity or skills, it is clearly important to assess their understanding of their illness and treatment. It should be assessed if the child has the skills to be able to:

1. understand choice, options and implications of options

2. weigh up multiple issues/alternatives and be realistic about options

3. consider current and future perspective

4. reason through to conclusion of possible options

5. understand and retain information

6. ask questions to clarify areas or gaps in knowledge

7. listen to and understand different perspectives

8. understand consequences (risks) of all possible options, both current and in the future.

There is no formal assessment package that covers all of these areas. In some services, psychologists may be asked to carry out a screening psychometric assessment to guide clinicians to the cognitive level of the child and what can reasonably be expected of him or her in terms of decision-making skills. It is more common, however, for psychologists to work with the clinician to assess these areas more flexibly, using knowledge of the child, clinically assessing and asking appropriate questions, and listening to the child's experience of other decision-making opportunities.

5. Social and emotional factors and resources

Children's ability to make decisions will also be affected when there are ethical, religious or moral issues involved, or where there is some disagreement between the young person and their family, between family members and the medical team, or among family members themselves. Clearly, making a decision is only part of the process. Being able to cope with the decision and its consequences both for yourself and for your family is also required. Coping with the decision may depend on the emotional resources and maturity of the young person, including their level of anxiety.

> I don't want to be responsible for making decisions, and feel sick at the idea at having to do my own consent forms... Mum has always done that, and I really trust her and the doctors... I don't know enough to sign my consent forms, and I don't want to know...it's too scary...and what if something goes wrong? I'm really scared I will have to do it when I move to adult services. (17-year-old with a chronic condition)

Children also need to be able to limit impulsivity and to make decisions by going through a thinking process that helps them to consider all information and choices. Perceived support to be able to carry through with the decision, either from family members or the professional team, may also impact on decision making.

Children's confidence to offer their views and make decisions will be affected by their perception of what is acceptable or appropriate, and the level of autonomy, perceived or actual, that is appropriate for the responsibility for the decision. Children may be overly compliant in order to please others or may, at the other extreme, take a seemingly perverse stance, believing themselves to be invulnerable and willing to take greater risks.

6. Skills of the professional team

The skills of the health professional team in communicating and working collaboratively with children will be an important influence on the child's ability to make decisions. The team's respect and willingness to involve and support the young person in decision making will also be vital. Involving children in this way will usually require committing more time, possibly including time for the young person to process and discuss information with professionals. The team's effectiveness, both in communicating together and in giving information to the child and family about the proposed treatments and the options available, will clearly underpin the whole process. Informing the child and the family about the process of promoting young people's participation, and even guiding the family in ways of developing these skills, will also be important. The Department of Health publication *Consent – What you Have a Right to Expect. A Guide for Children and Young People* (DoH 2001) is helpful to inform and clarify the process on consent.

Good practice can include enabling children to be directly and actively involved in all clinic appointments by talking to them, and not just their parents. Space can be provided at each appointment for the young person to raise any questions, and these should be responded to and recorded in the child's notes, with an opportunity to revisit these questions at a later appointment to review how they have been resolved. Recording this information can convey to children that their questions have been valued and taken seriously. It is also good practice to copy young people into clinic letters and to ensure that letters are written in an accessible way for young people and their families. This can help young people to understand and feel more in control of their condition and treatment.

USER INVOLVEMENT

It is increasingly acknowledged that many people who have used medical services (particularly those with chronic illness requiring frequent treatment) have expertise arising from their experience, both about the impact and process of treatment and the way services are delivered. In 2002 the NHS launched its *Expert Patient Programme* (EPP) (DoH 2009), which is a self-management programme for people living with chronic conditions to help them to manage their condition more effectively. A more recent development of the EPP is the Staying Positive programme, which is designed for those aged up to 25 years of age and comprises a series of workshops that are facilitated by young people themselves. There are also financial incentives for this, as organisations need to provide evidence of 'patient and public involvement' (PPI) activity and its impact on services when bidding for contracts, and as part of reviewing standards and targets which have been met. Contact a Family (2005) have produced excellent guides for parents and professionals regarding improving services with parent participation (see Appendix 1). In this section, we will focus on involving children.

Action for Sick Children (ASC 2009) has developed a helpful planning tool for health care providers to support them in the process of engaging and involving children and young people in planning and development of health care services (see Figure 9.1).

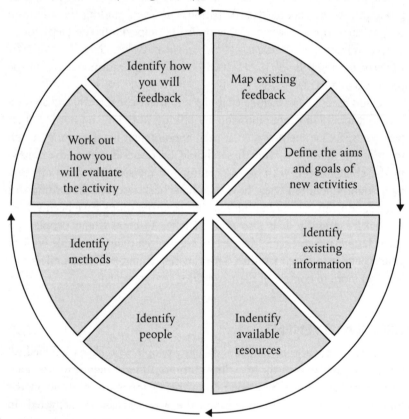

Figure 9.1 User involvement wheel
Source: Action for Sick Children

The first step of the process is for the organisation to carry out an audit or mapping of current activity, and to collate existing examples of good practice of user involvement. It is clearly helpful to learn from previous successful examples and to identify key people with skills in this area. ASC suggest that an audit of good patient and public involvement should involve 'a balance of individual and group activity, proactive and reactive activity, retrospective and real-time activity and direct and indirect activity'.

A key aspect of any effective programme of user involvement activity is being extremely well prepared. This preparatory stage should produce clarity about the objectives and goals for the particular project or work, and how the views of young people will be utilised. The next step is to identify existing information in the particular area under review, in terms of work that has already been done on this area, and to ensure that appropriate policies are being followed.

The next step in the process is to identify available resources, in terms of staff expertise, time, and finances. Guidance from the Department of Health (DoH 2006a) and Royal College of Nursing (RCN 2007a) both suggest reimbursement of travel costs as minimum recompense for people's time and contribution. Providing refreshments during meetings, and even some token of thanks in the form of a book token, or card is a concrete way of thanking and valuing young people. It is helpful to identify the sources of money available for this from the outset, with many trusts writing their own policy or good practice guidelines for PPI.

Identifying which children to involve, in terms of age, level of experience and health status will clearly depend on the nature of the project being undertaken, including the range of methods that would be appropriate to gain the information sought. These might include focus groups, workshops, projects, involving young people on committees or boards, questionnaires and surveys, comment boxes, and eliciting feedback by means of text, blogs or computer programmes. The principle method of gaining children's views may be through verbal discussion, such as in focus groups or workshops; however, role-play or art-based techniques can also be successful. Coad (2007) highlighted the importance of developing nonverbal and art-based techniques in order to access children across the developmental continuum. Children attending hospital may be approached to participate, or contact might be made with local or national support groups to recruit potential participants.

Evaluation of the project needs to take account of the original aims and goals, as well as eliciting the experiences of the young people regarding the whole process of their involvement. Feedback can then be provided to the organisation in terms of informing the relevant area under review. It is also important to monitor the quality and impact of the user involvement in terms of how the information is utilised and how this is fed back to young people. A frequent criticism of user involvement projects concerns the lack of feedback to participants. It can sometimes be difficult to give comprehensive feedback on the piece of user involvement, as this may have been fed into a larger project (which may be more complex) and the final results may take several months to be reported. However, in this case, some interim feedback can be given on the part each participant has played and what has been learned by those working with them. It may also be difficult to let participants know the outcome when their feedback has not been acted on. It can be difficult for young people to fully appreciate the systems in place within health care, and they may need some assurance that their views were valued, even though other needs or information needed to be prioritised. Feedback to young people can be in the form of a report accessible to them, or verbal feedback.

Focus groups

Focus groups are often used as a means of involving young people. These have been defined as 'a carefully planned discussion, designed to obtain perceptions on a defined area of interest in a permissive, non-threatening environment' (Krueger 1994). Essentially focus groups are a form of non-directive group interview, but with the added dimension of interaction and discussion among group members, facilitated by a group moderator, which can add further ideas and thoughts about the topic. The response gained from the group may reflect a range of views or themes for feedback.

As already described, focus groups need to be well prepared, taking into account the resources required, age range of participants, duration of the group (which may depend on the ages or health of group members), timing of the group (day or evening/weekend), location, and environmental factors. A comprehensive review of aspects to consider for effective focus groups can be found in Gibson (2007). The degree of group participants' acquaintance with each other is also an important factor, and this may determine the most appropriate form of 'ice-breaker' to start the session.

In addition to engaging with young people to gain helpful feedback for service developments, their expertise can be utilised in many other creative ways. These include inviting young people to teach at staff training days or conferences. It can be quite daunting for a single person to do this, but an 'expert panel' of young people can be an excellent training resource, with a very powerful message to communicate. Many young people enjoy being able to 'give something back', and recognise the importance of being able to educate health care professionals about the care they deliver. It can also help develop a young person's confidence and self-esteem, as they are able to adopt an important role in sharing their expertise with doctors, who have always been 'experts' to them. It is a valuable experience to add to their curriculum vitae.

Many trusts have developed policies regarding the development of patient resources, such as information leaflets, requiring them to be assessed by representatives of the population that will use the information.

> Within the psychology service at the Evelina Hospital, we worked with a group of adolescents on drawing up an information leaflet for young people about the service. We received some very helpful comments about the 'wordiness' of the leaflet, in terms of the meaning of some words, and too much text which was in a small font. A number of young people were also keen for the leaflet to have a photograph of the team to make the information more real and access to the service less of a worry, as people would have an idea of who they might see.

SUMMARY

Children's involvement and participation in health care decisions has been shown to have positive outcomes for their psychological and medical well-being. It is increasingly recognised that, through their own experiences of receiving health care, children are a valuable resource for informing and shaping health care services that are person-centred and of the highest quality. Involving children and young people appropriately in developing services is an important process, and there is an expectation that all health care trusts are putting this into practice. The 'user involvement wheel' developed by Action for Sick Children is a helpful guide to implementing patient involvement in paediatric health care.

CHAPTER 10

Transition to Adult Services

In recent years there has been a significant emphasis within health services on developing and improving care for young people who are moving from paediatric to adult services. This follows the Children's National Service Framework (DoH 2003b) which sets as one of its core standards 'Growing up into Adulthood', with recommendations for there to be a coordinated plan developed with young people regarding the transition of their care to adult services. A number of key documents have highlighted the gaps in health care provision for adolescents (RCPCH 2003) and evidence of poor health outcomes for young people who have moved to adult services, especially those with complex health needs (*Healthcare for All* 2008c) and those receiving palliative care (ACT 2007). Good practice guidelines (DoH 2006; DoH 2008d) have shown this to be a priority area for improvement within health care, and one that has now seen development in service strategy and provision. In this chapter we look at some of the challenges facing seamless transition between services, and the evidence base for the most effective ways of supporting young people in this process.

Historically, adolescents and young people with chronic illness have received little attention as a specific group with their own set of needs. They have often been placed rather uncomfortably within child or adult services, with limited specific provision of services for adolescents and young people. Adult and paediatric services have traditionally been quite separate in terms of their location and budget and in their philosophy of care, with little effective communication or joint planning in many cases. The age at which young people were moved on to adult services varied between hospitals, between specialities, and sometimes between consultants within these specialities. The timing of transfers might depend on the particular interests of the consultants and the personality of the young person (with suggestions that 'favourite' children remained in paediatric services for longer, while 'difficult' children were transferred as soon as possible!). In addition, many young people with complex conditions would find themselves straddling both adult and child services, with different aspects of their care in either system, and little or no communication between them.

Preparation for the transfer to adult services has often been notably lacking. Young people would receive little notice, let alone preparation, for leaving paediatrics, with some being told at their 'last' paediatric appointment that from now on they would be under the care of the adult service, possibly with little further information as to where this service would actually be, which consultant they would be under, or when their next appointment would be. This has been described as more of a crash landing in adult services than any sort of transition process!

With increasing numbers of young people with chronic medical conditions surviving into adulthood, there are more young people needing to make a transition to adult services. As a result, health care services have been severely challenged to provide appropriate services for this population. Adult health care services have also needed to develop expertise in caring for young people with particular conditions who would previously not have survived during childhood. This has required consultants from adult and child services to collaborate in order to provide specific clinics, such as for adult cystic fibrosis or congenital cardiac conditions.

The most important catalyst for change has been evidence from studies which have showed much poorer than expected health outcomes following transfer to adult services for some groups of young people. Studies have indicated higher rates of non-adherence and loss of transplants (Watson 2000), poorer attendance at clinical appointments (Kipps, Bahu and Ong 2002) and higher mortality rates amongst young people transferred to adult care (Tomlinson and Sugarman 1995 in DoH 2003b; ACT 2007). Negative patient experiences of transfer to an adult service were also regularly described. The NSF (DoH 2003b) formally recognised these challenges and highlighted the importance of ensuring safe and effective transition.

One very important factor which underpins how services are developed is the way transition is conceptualised. Transition is not necessarily a simple transfer of care and responsibility to adult services as a discrete event, but can be defined as '…a purposeful, planned process that addresses the medical, psychosocial and educational/vocational needs of adolescents and young adults with chronic physical and medical conditions as they move from child-centred to adult-orientated health care systems' (Blum, Garell and Hodgman 1993).

The acknowledgement that transition is a process which is planned in the context of the young person's life highlights many needs. These include the need for good communication with young people and an understanding of their psychosocial needs, an effective multidisciplinary approach to transition, and the need for an effective interface between child and adult services. The needs of young people do not finish when they reach adult services. An additional part of the process involves supporting the successful integration into adult services in a way that promotes the most effective utilisation of health care services and also the best health outcomes.

Following the standards set in the NSF (DoH 2003b), hospital trusts are required to have a written transition policy. Tools for hospitals to audit their own policy and procedures in relation to transition, and a template for assessing young people's needs and readiness to move (the transition passport) have been made available (DoH 2008c). Many trusts have appointed a transition coordinator for the hospital or for a particular speciality, to take responsibility for developing and implementing the policy. There is recognition that 'one size does not fit all', and so with individual specialities there may be a cause to adapt the transition programme to fit the needs of their population.

In addition to appointing transition coordinators across hospital trusts, service developments within some hospital trusts have included the establishment of clinical posts which focus specifically on transition or services for young people. These are mainly (but not exclusively) medical, nursing and psychology posts. Although there are still a relatively low number of dedicated adolescent wards or units in health care, there has been an increase in the number of 'teenage and young adult' (TYA) units, particularly in oncology services. There has also been an increase in the number of transition clinics, joint adult and paediatric clinics, young persons' clinics and transition programmes or workshops.

EFFECTIVE COMPONENTS OF A SUCCESSFUL TRANSITION PROGRAMME

There is general agreement about the areas of intervention required for an effective transition programme. These are based on psychoeducational support and psychological principles of responding to developmental needs and appropriately informing and empowering young people. However, there are few systematic studies evaluating the components necessary for a successful transition programme, or their acceptability and utility for both young people and professionals. There is still a need to bridge the gap between research, policy and clinical practice and to evaluate the cost implications of such a programme in terms of time, resources and personnel.

One study evaluating a multidimensional transition programme as part of a multi-centre controlled trial for adolescents with juvenile idiopathic arthritis, has shown some positive initial results (McDonagh, Shaw and Southwood 2006). This programme involved using a transition policy, an individualised transition plan, and extensive information and support resources for young people, families and professionals. A local programme coordinator was appointed to orchestrate the adolescents' care. Initial results indicated improvements in quality of life, satisfaction and knowledge. This study also highlighted some practical issues in implementing such a programme, such as the additional time required by medical teams, and the need to train staff in aspects of adolescent health, including communication and information-giving skills. The role of the local programme coordinator was very positively evaluated.

An effective transition programme includes several components. Each aspect will be considered under the following headings:

- A framework for transition.

- Early preparation.

- Individual transition programmes.

- Supporting transfer and integration into adult services.

A framework for transition

1. It is important to recognise the different perspectives, attitudes and challenges faced by adult and paediatric colleagues in order to establish an effective and manageable transition programme. Within each trust or primary care trust (PCT) it is important to work collaboratively to develop services in order to ensure that the philosophy and value of such services is shared, and that consistency in providing services is possible.

2. An individualised transition plan should be drawn up for each young person.

3. Transition needs to be seen as a process, with inbuilt flexibility to take account of the changing needs of the young person.

4. Transition programmes need to involve both parents and young people, addressing parents' concerns and promoting transfer of responsibility to the young person in the most supportive way.

5. There needs to be good communication between all parts of the system around the young person, including hospital systems, community health, social services and education/vocational services (such as the Connexions service).

6. Information and reviews of an individual's transitional plan should be recorded in the young person's medical notes. Feedback from young people about their experience of this process should be monitored and recorded.

7. Outcome measures should be routinely collected to evaluate the transition programme.

8. Professionals should have access to appropriate training on adolescent health care, including psychosexual issues and mental health. This can be achieved through training courses, workshops and e-learning.

9. Young people and their families should be clearly informed about the transition policies and process within their unit or service, so that they can know what to expect.

10. Information resources tailored to the health, psychosocial and educational needs of adolescents should be made available to young people. This may be through information leaflets or by signposting young people to youth websites. (See Appendix 1 for youth websites on health matters, sexual issues, rights and benefits.) The hospital's Patient Information and Advocacy Service (PALS) may be of particular help in this respect.

Early preparation

One area that is commonly agreed concerns the need to start the preparation phase early. In fact, some would suggest that transition preparation begins at the time of diagnosis, with any promotion of health and self-care being a step towards assuming the responsibility expected within adult health care. There are many ways, throughout children's lives, of giving support to engage and involve young people positively in their health care. If this is successfully carried out throughout the young person's life, it will be of significant benefit, not just in the transition process but for developing the most appropriate adult behaviour for using adult health services effectively, and positive attitudes for healthy living. Strategies for teaching young people the skills for being positively involved in their health care are discussed more fully in Chapters 3 and 7. In the summary which follows, all strategies need to be considered within a developmental framework, which will be unique for each young person.

Throughout the young person's life, they can be helped to develop an appropriate understanding of their condition and treatment, by involving them in conversations about their care, giving information effectively, and listening to their questions and views. An interrelated area involves supporting them in developing the confidence to talk to their doctor and other health care professionals, presenting their concerns and views. Parents play an important role in supporting this by the way they communicate with their children at home and involve them in discussions and decision making within the family. Developing these skills, young people can become increasingly involved in decisions which impact on their health care, and can be engaged in thinking about what they would want to gain from treatment. As young people continue to develop and gain independence, the extent to which they can be involved and take responsibility for their care will increase correspondingly.

More structured preparation for planning may usefully take place following the young person's transition to secondary education. Discussing with the young person how they experienced this educational transition may suggest areas that it is helpful to consider with them in terms of making their transition to adult health services as positive as possible. At this initial stage, preparation is largely about informing young people and families about the transition process and the kinds of areas that are covered within this.

Individual transition programmes

An individual assessment of each young person's needs is a key aspect of this stage in transition planning. A template for a 'transition passport' has been given in a number of documents (DoH 2008c), and this can be tailored to the needs of the young person and the medical setting in which it will be used.

Within the passport, there is a checklist which identifies the skills that are required for functioning in adult services. The checklist includes summaries of the young person's views of transition, their knowledge and skills relating to their treatment, and other key aspects such as confidence, social relationships and school. The aim of the document to be a 'living' assessment continues throughout the transition process and identifies the young person's ongoing and changing needs to confidently integrate into adult services. Although young people can be given this passport to complete themselves, it is more likely to be helpful if this is done jointly with a health professional. The passport can then serve as a structure for talking about health care, rather than a 'yes/no' exercise in which young people may assume they 'know' and answer 'yes' to questions without a clear understanding. In some areas, completion of this passport might be the focus of an annual review for an adolescent; or it might be used as part of a transition clinic assessment. It might also be helpful for the young person to have their own copy of this 'passport', and for another copy to be held in their medical notes, to ensure that the information is not lost.

A range of needs may be identified. These can include the development of skills in communication, decision making, assertiveness, self-care, managing social, educational or vocational opportunities and developing independence in living skills and health care skills. One area of self-care that might be identified is to help the person gain skills to become more independent in managing their medications. There are a number of resources which can be introduced to support young people in safely taking on increased responsibility, such as dosettes (medication boxes which can be filled with a day's or week's medication). Using dosettes can give confidence to young people and also to their parents, who can easily check that medication has been taken. Other resources such as hand-held prompts to take medication, or measures like programming mobile phones, can also be useful. Psychological interventions involving motivational interviewing may help to address any difficulties with adherence flagged up by the assessment. (See Chapter 7 on promoting adherence for more information.)

If young people have a target to gain more independence generally, it may be helpful to review with them what opportunities are available in daily life to achieve this, and to build on these. For example, some parents find it difficult to allow their child to travel independently or go out with friends, and some families may find it helpful to think through ways of moving towards this goal as safely as possible. In addition to ensuring that the young person has, like any other young person, the knowledge and skills to keep themselves safe, the need to communicate information about their medical condition and treatment can be an issue. Most young people have mobile phones, which they might choose to use to carry important medical information such as what condition they have, the treatment they are taking, and who to contact in case of an emergency. Other young people might decide to carry a computer 'memory stick' with this information, while yet others might prefer to wear a medic alert or medical SOS bracelet carrying their information.

With the increasing importance of the peer group in adolescence, another area of need for young people may be developing confidence to talk to friends about aspects of their health care, particularly if knowledge about their condition could help to reduce pressure from peers to become involved in activities which could be unsafe, such as taking drugs or smoking. Even if the young person does not wish to disclose their illness or disability, it might be useful to support the development of assertiveness skills and the self-confidence to resist the urge to conform, or to say 'no' when the group of peers is collectively engaged in a potentially harmful activity.

It is also important to help the young person develop confidence and skills in talking to their doctor without their parent being present for part or all of a consultation. In addition to developing confidence, this can also empower young people to become more involved in their own care, and may highlight areas in which they need more support or information. It is also good practice for young people to be offered some privacy in their medical appointments because they often have questions or concerns that they would prefer not to raise in front of their parents. It might be too difficult, for example, to raise concerns about sexual health with parents present. Opportunities for discussions about changes associated with puberty and any implications of this for their condition should be available, and so should opportunities for questions about sexual health. Sexual health and behaviour may be affected by the physical condition (including impact of pain and medication) and particularly by attitudes, such as acceptance and feelings about intimacy due to body differences. Young people may want to know whether they are fertile and have normal sexual function or whether they could harm themselves during sex or by becoming pregnant. Some young people will have particular concerns relating to continence during sex, or controlling other body movements, such as muscle spasms. Others might need genetic counselling to consider the risks of passing their condition on to their children, and the emotional issues this could raise for them.

Some parents can feel extremely worried that their parenting role is being undermined by doctors if they are not present, and many worry that their child will not be honest, or will not remember information they have been given, which could compromise care. It is therefore important that any goal-setting during transition planning is done with the full participation of the parents and the young person. It is also important for parents to understand that this is about helping their child acquire new skills, rather than their own expertise as parents not being valued. It can be helpful for this goal to be graduated, so that the young person has a short time alone with their doctor at the beginning or end of their consultation, with their parent present for the rest of the time. Parents could otherwise be invited to have a separate appointment with the doctor if they have concerns and their child is being seen alone. It is important to remember that from 16 years of age, the young person has the same right to confidentiality as adults, and so prior thought should be given to any issues that might arise during appointments where the young person is seen alone.

One way of addressing many of the issues relevant at this stage is to hold transition workshops which both parents and young people can be invited to attend. These can include an information component, identification of common themes or areas of difficulty, and solution-focused problem solving and skill sharing that involves parents and young people. One of the most important elements is often the introduction to a supportive peer network and feeling part of a group of young people who may be having similar experiences in adolescence and the lead-up to transferring into adult services. It can also be helpful to invite young adults who have recently made their transition and are prepared to discuss their experiences. It is most appropriate for these workshops to be a joint venture between adult and children's services, with representatives from each being visible and approachable.

The social contact with other young people is an extremely valuable aspect of any transition meeting. This serves many functions, including normalising the concerns that parents and young people may have and identifying and learning helpful strategies from a supportive peer group. This can be a powerful and effective medium for increasing knowledge and adaptation for young people with chronic conditions (Plante *et al.* 2001).

> Transition workshops within cardiology at the Evelina Children's Hospital are organised in conjunction with ECHO (Evelina Children's

Heart Organsiation). These workshops offer an opportunity for patients and families to be updated with specific knowledge about their condition, and to visit the adult department and ward. There is also an opportunity for parents and young people to meet separately to discuss issues and concerns relating to their current situation and the transition process. Young people have a chance to address some of the challenges they commonly encounter with peers. A version of 'tag role-play' has proved popular with young people, in which they can 'tag-in' to a role-play about an issue to offer their ideas about how to deal with the situation being depicted. Issues include disclosing their condition to others and dealing with pressures to smoke or drink. This is demonstrated in a DVD produced by ECHO to support adolescents with cardiac conditions (see Appendix 1).

It is good practice for regular reviews to be held throughout the whole transition process, using the passport as an ongoing tool of assessment to continue to monitor progress and identify any further area of need. Multidisciplinary and multi-system meetings may be required as part of this review for young people with more complex needs, to ensure effective coordination and information exchange.

Supporting transfer and integration into adult services

There is no specified age at which transfer should take place. It is generally agreed that there needs to be some flexibility in this area, in order to take account of the young person's circumstances and developmental and sexual maturity. It is also better for the young person to transfer when their condition is stable or in remission, if at all possible. Being acutely unwell at the time of transition would not be the most comfortable or positive introduction to adult services.

Some services will hold one or more joint adult and paediatric clinics in which the 'hand-over of care' is carried out with the young person in situ, with the adult physician increasingly taking the lead role during the appointment/s. These clinics may take place in the adult environment to help prepare the young person for this aspect. They may involve just adult and children's services, or may be more structured as transition clinics with professionals dedicated to working within the transition framework. Some services will have a young persons' clinic which will continue to provide additional support and monitoring of how the young person is getting on following their transfer to adult services. When this is not in place, it can be helpful for the young person to visit the adult service and meet their new team before moving in to this service, as this allows time for 'troubleshooting' of any predicted difficulties to occur.

CHALLENGES TO SEAMLESS TRANSITION

Although an agreed policy on transition can go a long way to overcome challenges with transition, there are still difficulties which need to be addressed. For example, there are differences, and indeed inequities, in provision between children's and adult services. Even when young people are well prepared, some may still perceive a loss as they move to an adult environment and focus.

> 'They don't have games or anything to do in the [adult] ward, and there's nowhere for Mum to stay… I don't want to go there!' (One young person following a visit to the adult ward)

The strong relationships which many young people have established with members of the paediatric health care team, some over their whole life, are not easy to recreate in adult services. Adult teams are likely to be treating larger numbers of patients and therefore have less time and flexibility to be available to young people.

> 'I have been to the adult clinic three times and seen three different doctors. It's really frustrating to have to keep telling people about my history.' (Young person who had recently moved to adult services)

Another area of difference is that paediatric services are organised around a multidisciplinary framework, which is less often the case in adult services. This can be a particular challenge for young people with complex conditions, where their care is provided across many specialities and coordinated by their general paediatrician. In some cases, there is no equivalent medical lead in adult services who can coordinate care in the same way, and so service delivery can feel much more fragmented. This particular challenge is heightened for young people with complex conditions and learning difficulties. Within paediatrics, the 'team around the child' encompassing health, education and social services is often seen as very protective and supportive to families, and the absence of this team approach can be perceived as a significant loss. Good practice guidelines (DoH 2008c) have been specifically developed to address transition for young people with complex medical conditions and disability, and also for young people receiving palliative care (ACT 2007), who are acknowledged to be particularly vulnerable in the transition process.

A further challenge is for young people who are being cared for in tertiary paediatric or specialist hospitals and who will need be transferred to a local hospital or community team for their adult care. In these situations, the young person is moving to a totally different service and team, and may find the adjustment to a less specialised service difficult. Communication between systems is vital for this transition to work and for young people to have confidence in their new team. One young person commented that she had three medical files full of her very complex medical history, and had little confidence that her new team would read and know all of that, so prepared herself to inform them of particular aspects of her care.

Many professionals within paediatrics are acutely aware of some of the differences in adult health care provision and the challenges associated with transition, and can feel very protective of young people and their families leaving paediatric care. Although there may be organisational aspects of this which are outside their control, being able to take a proactive and positive stance in helping a young person develop the skills to cope in adult care can help professionals frame this transition more positively, in the knowledge that an effective transition process can improve health outcomes. Moving on to adult services can be an extremely positive experience for many young people, some of whom relish being respected as the one to make decisions and talk directly to doctors. Some may have other reasons to be happy to leave sometimes very unhappy and traumatic paediatric experiences behind them and feel positive about starting afresh in an adult service. As one young man said, 'I haven't had much of a childhood, and now I just want to get on with my life as an adult.'

SUMMARY

Transition is a process which needs to take account of medical, psychosocial and educational/vocational aspects of a young person's life. A well planned transition can improve clinical, educational and social outcomes. There are several models for providing transition services, but to date there has been little systematic review to indicate which is the most effective. Any evaluation of transition programmes would need to involve both satisfaction measures and health care outcomes. Currently, outcome measures for successful transition to adult services include short-term health indicators, or measures of optimal uptake of adult medical services, such as records of attendance (or non-attendance) at adult appointments. More detailed, long-term follow-up involving attitudes to health care and longer-term use of services and health outcomes would be beneficial.

Palliative Care and Bereavement

Palliative care for children and young people with life-limiting conditions is defined as:

> An active and total approach to care, from the point of diagnosis or recognition, throughout the child's life, death and beyond. It embraces physical, emotional, social and spiritual elements and focuses on the enhancement of quality of life for the child/young person and support for the family. It includes the management of distressing symptoms, provision of short breaks and care through death and bereavement. (Association for Children's Palliative Care (ACT) 2009)

Department of Health figures estimate that 18,000 children and young people are likely to require access to palliative care services annually in England, which equates to 16 per 10,000 population (DoH 2007). If neonatal deaths are included in this figure, the estimate rises to 21,000. The DoH statistics indicate that approximately three-quarters of children (74%) who receive palliative care die in hospital, with around 19 per cent of children dying at home and just over 4 per cent in a hospice. The average number of hospital admissions in the last twelve months of life was 2.4, with the majority (78%) having one admission and 13 per cent having three or more admissions. This indicates the importance for the family of having positive and supportive relationships with both hospital and community teams, and of good communication and continuity of care between hospital and home-based services.

Most young people requiring palliative care will fall into one of the following clinical groups:

1. Young people with life-threatening conditions for which there may be a possibility of curative treatment, but where treatment may

not always be successful. Palliative care may be necessary during phases of the condition in which the prognosis is uncertain, or if treatment is not successful. Examples of this would be cancer and irreversible organ failure (liver, kidney and heart failure).

2. Young people with life-limiting conditions often involving periods of intensive treatment which may help to prolong life and quality of life, but where an early death is inevitable. An example of this is cystic fibrosis.

3. Young people with progressive conditions without curative treatment options, where treatment is exclusively palliative and may commonly extend over many years. An example of this is degenerative neuromuscular conditions, such as Duchenne Muscular Dystophy, and many metabolic conditions.

4. Young people with severe neurological disability which may lead to health complications and premature death. Deterioration may be unpredictable and not usually progressive. Examples include severe multiple disabilities following brain or spinal cord injuries, and severe cerebral palsy.

Palliative care and end-of-life care are often used as synonymous terms; however, this is not the case. End-of-life care specifically refers to preparation for an anticipated death and managing the last stage of a condition, including around the time of death and after death, whereas palliative care may extend for many years. Palliative treatment (such as symptom management) may co-exist with curative treatments at particular phases of some conditions, but will become increasingly important as the main focus of treatment as there cease to be any curative options – the transition from 'cure to care'. For other life-limiting conditions, death is the final phase of the condition or illness, and palliative care has been the treatment focus throughout.

When end of life is recognised, the Association for Children's Palliative Care (ACT) (2007) advocates that professionals should be open and honest with families. They recommend that a written end-of-life plan is drawn up between relevant professionals and family members, reflecting the needs and goals of both the young person and their family. ACT suggests that this care plan needs to include decisions about the level of medical intervention to be carried out – for example the method and extent of resuscitation. This plan should be communicated to the whole care system around the child, including emergency services, who might otherwise carry out medical interventions which the child and family have decided they do not want. Built in to any care plan is the need for review and revision to take account of any changes.

In reality, the transition from active treatment to symptom management or end-of-life care can be extremely challenging for health care professionals and for families, and there may be delays or avoidance of naming or recognising it as such. Many studies have indicated that parents find it difficult to initiate this discussion and have waited for their doctor to raise this. In addition, doctors may be reluctant to 'give up' on possible treatments options, leading to a rather unclear focus of care at the end of the child's life. The consequences of these delays can impact on whether the young person is appropriately involved in decisions about their care and can also impact on the most effective symptom control. Acknowledging the child's impending death can allow more effective communication between family members and between the family and professional network. Wherever appropriate, it can also enable the young person and their family to be involved in the development of a care plan which is most helpful and respectful of their needs and wishes.

SYMPTOMS AT THE END OF LIFE

The physical symptoms most commonly seen in children at the end of their life include pain, fatigue, seizures, breathlessness, nausea, vomiting and constipation (ACT 2007; Hongo et al. 2003; Theunissen et al. 2007). Fewer studies have discussed the psychological symptoms reported by children and their families. The study by Theunissen et al. (2007) observed the physical, psychological and social symptoms reported by children receiving palliative care for cancer and their parents. Psychological symptoms for children included sadness, difficulty talking about feelings relating to their illness and death, fear of being alone, loss of perspective and loss of independence. Parents' greatest fears related to physical symptoms and fears of their child's death. The social aspects addressed in the study involved school and holidays. Half the children did not attend school or any other enjoyable activities during the palliative phase of their condition. The authors concluded that health professionals tend to focus more on physical symptoms and are less able to acknowledge the psychological symptoms of children or their parents.

This relatively restricted understanding and acknowledgement of psychological and spiritual factors may impact on successful symptom management. For example, the same study by Theunissen et al. indicated that pain was not managed as successfully as hoped for in the final stages of illness. It may be difficult to separate out physical, psychological and spiritual pain when a young person is so ill and emotionally overwhelmed by the enormity of their situation, and so care in all of these domains is important.

CHILDREN'S AWARENESS AND UNDERSTANDING OF DEATH

Children's understanding of death is often described as a developmental progression growing from simple ideas, such as death being a reversible process not unlike sleep, to a more comprehensive understanding, with a move from concrete to more abstract and complex constructs. By the age of eight or nine most children will have the cognitive skills to develop a fully comprehensive concept of death (Kane 1979; Lansdown and Benjamin 1985; Oltjenbruns 2001).

Kane (1979) identified nine components that contribute to a fully comprehensive understanding of death. These include:

1. realisation – an awareness of death

2. separation – a physical separation from loved ones

3. immobility – a dead person cannot move around

4. irrevocability – once a person is dead he or she cannot come back to life

5. causality – there is a physical cause to death

6. dysfunctionality – there is a cessation of bodily functions, i.e. the person is not breathing, seeing, hearing or requiring food

7. universality – every living organism dies at some point

8. insensitivity – a dead person cannot feel anything

9. appearance – a dead body looks different from a living person.

Although a developmental framework can be helpful, it can never be assumed that children of a certain age or developmental stage have acquired a particular understanding. It is clear that a number of factors will influence children's awareness and understanding, including their own unique experiences with illness and death, what they have been told or have picked up from other sources (such as books, films, other children), and their ethnic and cultural background. Direct experiences of knowing another child who has died will undoubtedly focus or even advance a child's knowledge of death when compared with their peers who do not have this experience. Children's expressed views or understanding of death will also be affected by their verbal abilities, their emotional state (including the level of denial or anxiety about death) and also the context of the discussion, including their perceived 'permission' to talk openly about death.

Although Kane (1979) indicated the age by which she expected children to have achieved each of these concepts, we now see children's understanding as being more fluid and affected by all the factors described above. Children's questions or comments will indicate which concepts they may have grasped and which ones they are still trying to make sense of. Children may also ask questions repeatedly in an effort to make sense of things.

Even very young children may have an awareness of death, even if they have little understanding of it. They are likely to be particularly affected by the emotional distress around them and any change in care-giving routine. In pre-school children, death is often confused with sleep, and children are unlikely to be able to grasp the finality and irreversible nature of death. This may well be reflected in their conversation, where they can appear to have grasped some understanding of death and can tell you, say, that their sister has died, but then reveal their immature level of understanding by suggesting she will be coming back home from the hospital 'another day'. Children may well be sensitive to the sadness around them surrounding this death, but will not necessarily be distressed themselves in the same way, as they may not have understood that the dead person has really gone for ever.

In primary school (between five and eleven years), children will be developing a greater understanding of the irreversibility and 'forever' aspect of death. They can be fascinated by the physical aspects of death or the rituals surrounding it and might act out these rituals in their play. Children are also more likely to believe that their thoughts and feelings and actions make things happen, which is often termed 'magical thinking'. Children may worry that they themselves have caused the death by something they have said, and may also worry about the dead person being lonely, hungry or sad. As children's thinking progresses, they are able to realise that everyone dies.

Young children tend to develop a concrete idea of being in a place and doing things after death, and many of their questions will reflect their thoughts about this. During adolescence young people develop a more comprehensive and mature concept of death, which might include grappling with a spiritual existence or even a concept of 'not existing'.

TALKING TO CHILDREN ABOUT DYING

Worst of all was the agony
Of not knowing
What you knew.

(Poem by Mrs. Mulholland 1973, cited in Lansdown and Benjamin 1985)

Many professionals and parents express anxiety about being 'put on the spot' by children asking them difficult questions about death, for fear of saying the 'wrong thing' or worrying that they might upset the child or feel too upset to have this conversation. It can therefore be very helpful to talk this through carefully within the family and professional system to explore concerns and prepare the way.

It is helpful to consider what children may want or need to know, who is best placed to tell them, and when is the best time to begin this process of information-giving. Central to any planning is having an understanding of, and respect for, the family system around the child, and for there to be good communication between the family and professional system. Parents may not be in agreement with each other about what their child needs or wants to know, and professionals within the health care team may also disagree about the best way of managing this. Some parents and professionals feel it is extremely important that children are properly informed, in the hope that they come to some sort of acceptance and resolution about their life. Others are very opposed to this view, feeling that children should be protected from such emotive information, as they do not have the emotional resources to cope with it, or that they will in effect 'give up' and hasten towards their death.

We know that generally children will make their own sense of their experiences with whatever information or resources they have available, and that simply not talking to children about dying does not mean that they will not be aware, thinking or worrying about it, (Bluebond-Langner 1978; Hilden, Watterson and Chrastek 2000; Spinetta 1974). For example, Bluebond-Langner's work (1996, 1978) with dying children in a cancer centre suggested that children as young as three had awareness of death. Hongo *et al.* (2003) studied medical notes of 28 children with cancer who had died, and reported that just over 30 per cent of them (the youngest being five years of age) were able to verbally indicate awareness and fear, or even acceptance, of death. When children are aware of the seriousness of the situation but adults around them are denying this, there can be incongruence between a child's inner experience and reality and the external context, leaving the child feeling more isolated, confused and frustrated.

> One mother reported that following a sudden deterioration in her adolescent son's condition while on the intensive care ward, he had become increasingly agitated when she tried to comfort him by telling him he was going to be alright, he was getting better and did not need to worry. She recognised that he was much better comforted when she acknowledged that he was very sick, but that she would be right there with him throughout everything. Although this young man died before it was possible to talk openly about dying, his mother felt that her comments had led to an implicit understanding between her and her son about what was happening, which validated his experience. This became a source of great comfort to her following her child's death.

The guidelines *Improving Outcomes for Children and Young People with Cancer* (NICE 2005) have advocated open communication with young people and opportunities for them to be involved in decisions about their care. Research has highlighted the psychological consequence for parents in being open in communication about death. Kreicbergs *et al.* (2004) studied parents' views about telling or not talking to their child about death, using a questionnaire for bereaved parents. Thirty-four per cent of parents (147) reported talking about death with their children, and none of them regretted having done so. However, 27 per cent of parents who had *not* talked with their child about death expressed regrets, particularly those who sensed that their child had some awareness of dying. Parents who regretted not having talked about death had a higher level of anxiety at follow-up than other parents.

Although the NICE guidance highlights the importance of being open with children, in reality only a minority of parents feel comfortable talking to their children about dying. The age of a child may impact on how a parent feels about this. For example, parents may feel able to 'contain' a very young child's anxiety by giving reassurances, such as there being 'no more pain', or going to a place where they will be looked after by someone safe and meaningful for the child. However, older children with much more sophisticated understanding may raise feelings that the parents themselves also have, around issues such as the unfairness and injustice of facing death or questioning their faith. Young people may no longer be helped by simplistic reassurances as they have greater anxieties regarding the uncertainties surrounding death.

It is important for parents to feel supported, to be able to think through how best to care for their child, to be well informed as to how children might experience this phase of their illness, and to be able to anticipate their child's needs and questions. An excellent resource to support parents in talking with their child facing death is the booklet *Facing the Death of your Child* by Edwards and Palmer (2008).

In talking to children who may be dying, the following principles are generally accepted as good practice. It is expected that all of these principles will be considered in the context of the family's own belief system.

1. Follow the cues of the child.

2. Show the child that you appreciate their thoughts and questions and have taken them seriously.

3. Answer the child's questions in a straightforward, honest and reassuring way.

4. Always check what the child already knows or thinks about what they have asked you. If a child has formulated a question, they have already been thinking about the subject, and may already have some ideas or possible solutions to their questions.

5. Create opportunities for children to communicate in a variety of ways, including through play, pictures, poetry and stories.

6. Ensure that all adults caring for the child are in good communication about what children have been told, to ensure consistent information.

7. Give children the opportunity to revisit this conversation and build on their knowledge over time.

Following the principles above, it is clearly important to listen carefully to children's questions and to take their cues as to what information they are seeking. Sometimes this will not be immediately clear, as with the child who asks 'How does this treatment work?' The child may just want to know about the practicalities or the biological explanations about the treatment. It may also be that the child is initiating a conversation about whether this treatment will be successful and what would happen if it did not work. It is therefore important to go slowly in giving information to the child, checking out what he or she already knows, and wants to know.

Children may have some very practical and concrete questions about dying and what happens afterwards. In this situation it is helpful to acknowledge to the child that they have asked a very good question, which they have clearly been thinking about already. It might be helpful to acknowledge to children that people often have good ideas and beliefs about what happens when someone dies, but that no one can really know, so that the child's idea and beliefs are just as valid as those of anyone else. If a child has a safe, containing and reassuring picture of what will happen to them after death, it makes good sense to value and build on this picture, rather than offer something that might be quite contradictory to the child. It might only be when the child has a frightening or worrying image that, in cooperation with the parents, you might help them develop a more reassuring picture.

Older children may have deeper and more spiritual questions about death, including whether they will be remembered and the meaning their life has had. Talking to young people facing death can be extremely moving, and yet it is also a tremendous privilege to be able to think through their life with them, and how they have impacted on the lives of others. The expression 'footprints in your soul' seems to convey this so well.

Some young people may need to vent their anger, frustration and sorrow about how unfair life has been to them. It is not helpful to expect that all children and young people can reach a point of resolution or acceptance of their fate, but you can give them the opportunity to have their thoughts and feelings listened to and taken seriously.

The work carried out by Kübler-Ross (1969) in talking to dying children has assisted the development of some helpful metaphors to share with children to help them understand death and dying. One such metaphor is the caterpillar, which during its life-cycle develops into a cocoon and eventually sheds this casing to emerge as a beautiful butterfly. The sick child's body can be likened to the cocoon, which is no longer needed when the child dies and their spirit (the butterfly) emerges.

Edwards and Palmer (2007) suggest a number of other images which may be comforting for the child, including a child sailing away in a boat towards the horizon, with their loved ones on shore watching them, waving and loving them. The image continues that although the boat sails out of sight, you know they are there, and this image can be extended to suggest that people on the opposite shore will be waiting to welcome them. They also suggest a more active metaphor to which some children may relate better, of a rocket going up into space, disengaging from the parts it no longer needs until it is just a bright trail in the sky. In time, this trail becomes invisible to the human eye, even though the rocket is still there. There are some very helpful books which can be used with dying and bereaved children to help questions and feelings to be aired. (See Appendix 2.)

Doctors may feel challenged by a child's questions about what it is like to die. Some doctors have likened it to falling more and more deeply asleep. Although this may be extremely comforting to some children, others have then become fearful of falling asleep in case they die. If this explanation is offered, it may be helpful to tell the child that you will let them know when the time for dying is getting close, so that the child is not anticipating this all the time. One beautiful description used by a palliative care consultant at GOSH (Craig 2010) is that it might feel like the sensation you have as a young child falling asleep in the back of the car after a lovely and exhausting day out with your family. You have the subtle awareness of your loved ones around you, but you are dozing and falling more and more asleep. The example continues that dying and 'finding yourself in a different place' could be like being so soundly asleep that you are unaware of being carried out of the car and into bed.

SUPPORTING DYING CHILDREN AND THEIR FAMILIES

This is a profoundly emotional time for family and friends, and a time in which the positive relationships established with the health care team are most valued. Supporting the families of dying children is often seen as a huge privilege by staff, but it can also be extremely challenging and distressing. Good leadership and communication between members of the health care team is essential for effective teamworking. Strong feelings and desires to help in some way can create be a tendency for staff to become too involved or to take on too much responsibility. Good leadership of the team can help identify the role each team member should play (either directly or indirectly) vis à vis the family. (See Chapter 12, 'Staff Support and Caring for the Carers', for more information.)

Good liaison with school can be very supportive for the child and family. Children may feel isolated and detached from schoolfriends if they have not attended school regularly for a while, and may not feel well enough to want to see them. Schools can help by organising cards, audios and videos of classmates, to help the young person feel linked in to a peer network and valued, in the knowledge that people have made this effort to wish them well.

SUPPORTING CHILDREN WHO ARE NOT ASKING QUESTIONS

It is important to offer an open invitation for children to ask questions or share concerns or thoughts about what is happening to them. It is also important to respect a child's wish not to talk about death – and important for the team around the child to be aware of possible reasons why the child might feel awkward about talking. For example, children may not feel comfortable talking to certain people (it may be too difficult, initially, to talk to family members or to the doctor who has been treating them for many years), and the timing and environment need to feel right for the child. Conversations may take place more naturally in the course of an activity than in a more structured 'talking' session, and so opportunities need to be created for time when the young person does not feel under any pressure to talk, but has the time and privacy to do this with an adult.

Some children may indicate they do not want to know any information, and may never openly acknowledge that they know they are dying, although they may demonstrate this knowledge in other ways.

> One adolescent girl was adamant that she did not want to know what was going to happen, when her treatment was clearly not working. She remained positive and cheerful to the end with her parents, apparently oblivious or in total denial of her situation. Following her death, it was evident that she had been preparing herself in her own way, and had organised presents for all members of her family to show them how much she loved them.

> One young eight-year-old boy with a brain tumour repeatedly indicated both to his parents and the medical team that he had no questions and did not want to talk about what was happening to him. He came from a large family that lived some distance from the hospital and his parents visited as often as they could. One day he disclosed that he was upset that his rabbit had died, as his family had been too busy to care for it. This gave an opening to talk with him about the death of his rabbit, including where his rabbit had gone and, building on the child's

comments, adding some reassurance that it was now safe and cared for in heaven. Only later, in talking to his parents, was it discovered that this young boy did not actually have a rabbit at all! His family was initially mystified as to why he had made up such a story about this rabbit. Although they were never able to talk to their son about his impending death, they were able to spend much more time caring for him when he was transferred to a local hospice.

SUPPORTING PARENTS WHO DO NOT WANT INFORMATION SHARED WITH THEIR CHILDREN

At all times it is important to be respectful of parents' views, beliefs and wishes. It is not uncommon for members of the health care team to feel very frustrated with parents who are seen to be withholding necessary information from their children. However, the frustrations of a team valuing openness with the child and wishing to provide the best care for the child need always to be balanced with respecting the wishes of the family and considering the family's experience, both with their child when alive, and also after their child's death.

If parents are adamant that they do not want their child to know that he or she is dying, it is important to understand the beliefs that underpin this view, and to be able to support them in thinking through the implications of telling or not telling. It may be, for example, that parents feel so overwhelmed and unable to cope with their own feelings that they feel powerless to manage the anticipated questions or emotional distress of their child. It may be that culturally it would not be acceptable to 'burden a child' with such information.

> One father refused to let doctors tell his 16-year-old son that his heart was failing and that he might die soon. He believed that if you were told you were going to die, then your spirit just 'gave up'. He had been told earlier in his son's life that his child might not survive surgery, and yet he had survived, which the father believed was due to his son's (and his own) positivity and will to live. This reinforced his belief that it would be harmful for the doctors to share their current concerns with his son. The medical team felt uncomfortable with this, as they felt this young man had a right to know what was happening to his body. The agreement reached between the consultant and the father involved the medical team not volunteering any information to this young man, but being clear that they would answer honestly any direct questions that he asked about his prognosis. He did not ask any questions, and following discharge from the ward, he survived for a further year.

SUPPORTING OTHER FAMILY MEMBERS

The exhausting physical demands of treatment and the powerful and profound emotional demands of having a very sick child can sometimes leave little in reserve either physically or emotionally for supporting other members of the family. Siblings may feel displaced and estranged from their family, often being placed with other family or friends, or suffering disruptions to their schooling and other normal routines.

A good model of care for siblings involves:

1. recognising the emotional needs of siblings

2. keeping siblings as involved as possible in the care process

3. keeping routines as normal, familiar and predictable

4. informing children effectively and keeping channels of communication open

5. informing other adults (e.g. at school) so that understanding and support can be offered.

There are many ways in which siblings can be involved. If siblings are present (with the sick child in hospital, at home or in the hospice), there may be some aspects of care they could be invited to help with, such as providing relief and entertainment by reading to the sick sibling or helping to choose music or films to watch and listen to, or being involved in certain aspects of physical care. When siblings are not physically present for much of the time, they can still be involved by sending letters and cards or making pictures. If siblings are living away from their families for extended periods, they can be invited to keep their own diary of this time, in order to share their experiences more fully with their families. In the diaries kept about the sick child, it is helpful to make regular references to siblings who are not present, such as to noting how pleased people were with their card or telephone call, or news about what they were doing. In later months, these diaries can be a very positive way of bringing siblings' experiences and the importance of their role in the whole process into focus.

SUPPORTING BEREAVED CHILDREN

There are many organisations that offer excellent information for families and professionals, both in written form and via telephone helplines. These include the child bereavement charity Winston's Wish, the Child Death Helpline, Child Bereavement Trust, and Cruse. (See Appendix 1.)

Bereaved parents may feel so preoccupied with their own grief and the unfamiliarity of the situation they are confronting that they feel undermined in their capacity to support their other children. It is helpful to reassure parents that there is no single right way of supporting their bereaved child or children and no 'right way' to grieve. Children's responses will be particular to their own unique circumstances, according to their age, personality, understanding of death, and relationships with others. A very helpful guide for parents and carers at this time is provided by Winston's Wish (see Appendix 1).

Children of all ages need opportunities to voice questions, talk about the sibling who has died and express their thoughts and worries. They may experience a range of emotions following the death of their sibling, and these may be manifest in different ways, from tantrums, denial, guilt and irritability, to being unusually good, quiet or withdrawn. Some children show anxiety and are more clingy, and they may have raised concerns about other people they love dying. Some children feel guilty about having fun and will need reassurance that it is alright to get on with their lives.

Some parents may be concerned that their young child is not showing distress in the way they would expect – that the child is not 'grieving', or even that the child appears not to care about their sibling who has died. It can be helpful to normalise this response for parents. For example, if young children have not understood the irreversible aspect of death, they are unlikely to be experiencing the same level of distress as other people, since they anticipate the return of the dead person. Even if children have grasped this concept, they are unlikely to be able to experience intense emotions for as long as adults. The term 'puddles of despair' has been coined to suggest how a child might be inconsolable one minute in their grief, and playing happily on their bike the next.

Parents are often unsure as to whether children should see the body or attend the funeral of their sibling. General advice is that if parents feel it is appropriate, and children can be prepared for, and supported in, the experience they are likely to have, then it can be helpful for the child in accepting the reality and finality of death and saying goodbye. It is important to invite the child to do these things and give them an opportunity to change their minds if it feels too difficult for them. In terms of preparation to attend a funeral, it might be helpful to say that this is a time for everyone to say goodbye, and that people may show that they are very sad and cry. It is also helpful to give a practical explanation of what will happen and why. It is also helpful for another adult to be present to support the child during the service, so that if the child is unable to stay for the whole time, someone is there to attend to his or her needs.

The burial or cremation may well provoke some questions about what is happening to the body, so it will be important to reinforce for children that bodies cannot feel pain, heat or cold. It might also be helpful to clarify that when the 'body' is buried, we mean *all* of the person.

If it is not appropriate or possible for the child to attend the funeral service, there are many other ways of 'saying goodbye', including visiting the grave, or a place that was special for the child who has died, and holding their own 'service' there, which might include singing favourite songs, leaving a present or letter written for the child, lighting a special candle, or releasing balloons in memory of them.

Practical ways of supporting grieving children include making a memory box or memory book relating to their sibling, story books which cover death and associated feelings, and activity books (such as the 'Good Grief' series) which prompt the child (supported by an adult) to carry out practical exercises to help work through aspects of bereavement. The Child Bereavement Network have produced some lovely postcards which carry some very simple prompts for children, parents and carers about supporting a child following bereavement. There are also websites such as Winston's Wish, which have some practical interactive web pages suitable for children of all ages (see Appendix 1).

SUPPORTING BEREAVED CHILDREN WITH LEARNING AND SENSORY IMPAIRMENTS

For children with learning difficulties, the same good practice guidelines are relevant as for all children, in that they should be informed, involved and supported as much as possible in what is happening. They may need much more time to assimilate the information, and may need more concrete information broken down into more manageable parts and repeated as many times as necessary to help them to understand. There are some helpful workbooks suitable for young people with learning difficulties, and 'Seesaw' has also produced some useful resources for schools to help in supporting bereaved children (see Appendix 2).

SUPPORTING THE WARD SYSTEM WHEN A CHILD DIES ON THE WARD

The death of a child on the ward, especially one who is well known by other patients and their families, will clearly have a significant emotional impact on the whole hospital system, including the health care professionals. (See Chapter 12 for guidance on supporting staff.)

In the past, children who died on the ward were removed as discreetly as possible without informing other patients. However, we now have a greater understanding of the impact of trying to 'protect' children in this way, and can recognise the occasion as one in which to sensitively inform and support children as they experience this loss. The challenge can often be in ensuring appropriate respect and privacy for the grieving family, as well as implementing good practice for informing and supporting other families.

The knowledge of a fellow patient's death is likely to create anxieties for other children about their own vulnerability, particularly if they identify to some extent with the child who has died.

> One young man became very anxious about his heart, as he heard his friend had died from a heart attack. His own heart was being routinely monitored on an annual basis, and there were no current medical concerns about his heart. However, this young man reasoned that if his heart was being monitored, then he could also have a problem, and might have a heart attack and die too.

This can be intensified further for children being treated on an illness-specific ward such as an oncology unit, and may trigger questions about whether they are having a similar treatment, and if so, what if it does not work for them either?

If children are resident on the ward or attend the ward regularly for treatment, they can be invited to work within their family group or within a small patient group to create a memory book or memory box about the child who has died. Hospital teachers and play specialists may take a lead in supporting children in this activity, the aim of which would be to enable children to engage in a fun activity where they can talk about the deceased child and raise any questions or thoughts they may have. Parents may also appreciate some support and guidance for talking to their children about this death, and so participating in this activity together can be a way of helping parents too. It is very much more reassuring for a child to see that when someone dies they are remembered and treasured by other families and by the staff caring for them, than it is to hear people talking in hushed tones about the death, in an environment where no-one talks about the deceased child, as if he or she had never existed.

It can be more challenging to support children and families who will be deeply affected by another child's death, but who are not involved as inpatients at the hospital. In this case, the health care team will need to make a decision about contacting families before their next hospital appointment, as well as providing some additional time and space to talk through the news and its impact on family members.

> In an outpatient adolescent support group run by one of the authors for young people with chronic and life-limiting conditions, a protocol has been developed for supporting the group following the death of a group member. Following a young person's death, a phone call is made to each group member and their parents to break the news. An opportunity to talk further, either on the phone or face-to-face, is then offered to each member. The (monthly) youth group meeting has not itself been used as a forum for support in relation to the member who has died, as there are always newer members of the group who have not necessarily known this individual, and others who would not wish to be involved in talking and supporting others in these circumstances, since this monthly meeting is often valued as a time to have fun with others. Instead, a separate group meeting is offered for those who want time to talk about the person and the impact their loss has had on them. What has often been discussed by the adolescents at such times is their concern about the bereaved family, and their desire to collectively show their support by sending them cards and photographs. Photographs of the group member are available to view in the group photograph album. The group facilitators are careful to monitor how young people feel in the groups which follow, and sensitively provide opportunities for group members to approach them to talk if needed.

SUMMARY

Palliative care involves psychological, social and spiritual elements of care. When working within a developmental framework it is important to be mindful of the goals and aspirations of young people and to help them achieve the highest possible quality of life. Open communication, which shows respect for the needs and wishes of the young person and gives them a voice in understanding what they want, underpins quality care and the emotional support which can be so valuable for young people, their family and carers.

CHAPTER 12

Staff Support and Caring for the Carers

The importance of a well managed and well supported health professional team cannot be underestimated, because of the implications for the quality of care for families, as well as for the health and well-being of staff. The links between staff well-being and families' experience of care have been highlighted by the Care Quality Commission, with self-reported stress being associated with poorer patient experience (NHS Employers 2009).

Stress also has significant financial implications in terms of staff sickness and retention of staff in posts. Research has shown that prolonged stress is linked to psychological conditions such as anxiety and depression, as well as to physical conditions such as heart disease, back pain and headache. Work-related stress is the main cause of absence and illness in the health sector. NHS Employers (2009) report that stress is responsible for 30 per cent of sickness absence in the NHS in England, costing the service an estimated £300–£400 million each year. Stress related to workload demands was also reported as a major reason for nurses leaving their current post (RCN 2007b).

Working with sick children is an emotionally and physically demanding role, and one which often attracts staff who are highly motivated to help others and make a difference in their lives. There are great rewards in this type of work, and many staff feel that their work is worthwhile and highly valued. However, there are also many stresses associated with the work, which need to be addressed at a personal as well as an organisational level.

Clinical psychologists working in paediatrics are often seen as a resource for medical teams in terms of managing stress, particularly for nursing staff. However, it is important to remember that psychologists are also carers, and that they need to put into place systems and structures to enable them to manage the stress that they experience themselves. Professionally, psychologists are required to 'understand the importance of maintaining their own health' and 'be able to manage the physical, psychological and emotional impact of their practice' (Health Professional Council 2009). Psychologists use clinical supervision structures as their primary resource for reflective practice, but it is important to remember that they may also need to use the full range of systems discussed in this chapter, and should be able to recognise their own needs as well as the needs of others.

STRESS MANAGEMENT STANDARDS

There are legal requirements for organisations to carry out stress risk assessments as part of health and safety legislation. Important documents promoting the practical implementation of best practice include NICE guidance *Promoting Mental Wellbeing at Work* (2009) and the Royal College of Nursing good practice guide on managing work-related stress (RCN 2009). Both sets of guidelines acknowledge the stress management standards developed by the Health and Safety Executive (HSE 2007) as being helpful in the assessment of workplace stress. The standards are based around six dimensions and highlight the areas which may be potential areas of stress if not adequately managed.

Demands

This standard covers issues such as workload, working patterns and the work environment. To achieve this standard, employees need to feel that they are able to cope with the demands of their job, have the requisite skills and abilities, and that the demands placed on them are achievable within their agreed working hours.

Control

This standard covers the extent to which individuals can control the way they do their work. It is important for staff to be consulted and have a say over aspects of work practice, and to be encouraged to use and develop their skills.

Support

This involves the level of organisational support, for both management and peers, and requires systems to be in place for providing adequate support and addressing individual concerns.

Relationships

This standard includes promoting positive working between staff, and dealing with conflict and unacceptable behaviour. The organisation is required to have policies and procedures to prevent or resolve these issues and systems for managing unacceptable behaviour such as harassment or bullying.

Role

This standard is concerned with people's understanding of their role in the organisation and avoidance of role conflict. Clarity is required in the roles and responsibilities of staff.

Change

This standard involves the management and communication of organisational change, and requires that staff are prepared, informed and supported in change.

It is good practice for organisations to have a policy for promoting well-being and managing work-related stress in staff. Putting in place mechanisms to manage stress in the workplace involves an organisational response, in terms of an acknowledgement of stress and allocation of resources, and for managers to be informed and supportive, for example by providing time to attend sessions to address work concerns and stresses.

Clinical psychologists working within paediatrics often take a key role in supporting staff caring for children and families, through consulting either to individual staff or to staff teams about clinical work, facilitating meetings to help support staff (support/reflective/debrief meetings), and running stress management programmes. A key aspect of this role is understanding and communicating about what stress is, identifying factors that are causing or maintaining high levels of stress, and identifying more adaptive or effective stress management strategies.

SYMPTOMS OF STRESS

Stress can be defined as a mismatch between an individual's perceptions of the demands being made on them and their perception of their capacity to meet those demands (McVicar 2003).

Common indicators of stress

Stress can present through emotional, cognitive, behavioural and physiological manifestations.

- *Physical stress.* A range of somatic complaints can be stress-related or exacerbated by stress. Examples include fatigue, nausea, dizziness, chest pain, headache, raised heart rate and blood pressure, feeling tense and unable to relax, muscle tremors and aches, excessive sleeping or difficulties sleeping, digestive upsets, including heartburn or lack of appetite.

- *Cognitive presentation of stress.* This can include difficulty in a range of executive or higher cognitive skills such as decision making, prioritising and planning, and problem solving, and difficulties initiating or following through on tasks. Poor attention and concentration, memory impairment, and either heightened or lowered alertness are also common symptoms.

- *Emotional states* can include extremes of mood and loss of emotional control, characterised by impulsivity, frustration, anxiety, depression, tearfulness, irritability, loss of confidence and self-esteem. Some people describe waking with a sense of apprehension or panic.

- *Behavioural changes* can vary, from becoming withdrawn and feeling less connected to friends or peers, to being highly extro-vert and active, keeping busy and socialising heavily. This often involves increased alcohol consumption, overeating or binge eating. Some people feel they have lost their sense of humour and describe their conversation as being problem-focused. Many feel they are less able to communicate effectively.

The term 'burnout' is often used to describe the effects of chronically high levels of stress which result in exhaustion, feelings of cynicism and detachment from the job, and a sense of ineffectiveness and lack of accomplishment (Maslach, Schaufeli and Leiter 2002).

IMPACT OF STRESS ON WORK PERFORMANCE

An individual's stress may impact on their quality of work, in terms of being less able to engage and relate to children and families. It can also affect relationships with colleagues, who are often a good source of peer support in dealing with work stress. Working less effectively or needing time off work often requires other team members to cover or take on additional work, which can lead to frustration and fatigue in others. Stress within teams can lead to poor cohesion, poor communication, and difficulties in relationships between team members. Low staff morale can lead to a de-motivated team or part of a team, with an increased sense of isolation and lower job satisfaction. This has implications for staff retention, resulting in a workforce in constant flux due to frequent changes.

A team experiencing high or chronic levels of stress will find it difficult to deliver the quality of care that is expected. The atmosphere within a team is often noticed by children and families, and when the team is functioning well many families comment on the warm and friendly atmosphere on wards, which is often characterised by the humorous banter between staff, and between staff and families. There can be a perceptibly different atmosphere in a setting where staff are feeling overwhelmed or deeply dissatisfied with their work. Parents are also very aware of staff who are feeling upset or frustrated. Although parents can often be very supportive of staff, this can confound professional roles and boundaries, and result in confusion about who is caring for whom. Families will quickly lose confidence in professional carers if they perceive them to be preoccupied, or if there are communication difficulties and inconsistencies in the way care is provided.

UNDERSTANDING WORKPLACE STRESS

Staff report many different types of stresses. Drawing on our own experiences of supporting staff, we have highlighted a number of themes relating to the nature of the work and communication and relationship issues.

Emotional burden of work

The rewards of caring for families of children with serious medical conditions are immense. However, children who are distressed, in pain or very sick can evoke very powerful and protective feelings in carers, who want to make everything better or 'rescue' the child. These situations can be painful for staff, because there are times when this cannot be achieved and staff have to face their own personal and professional limitations. Personal needs, professional roles and boundaries can become blurred, with the danger of becoming over-involved emotionally. The challenge is to be able to empathise with and acknowledge suffering, without feeling so overwhelmed emotionally that this leads to being over-detached and distant from the human element and suffering that is present.

One theme which recurs for staff is the lack of feedback about particular children who have caused concern for staff when those children have left the hospital. Hospital-based staff (particularly those in specialist centres) often see children in their most acute stages of illness and distress, and seldom see those who have made a good recovery as they will have moved on to more local units or have returned home. It can be helpful to set up systems to convey feedback about how a family is getting on. Information from outreach nursing staff, or community staff, or a phone call or card received from a parent, can be recorded in a 'communication book' and left for staff to read in their rest room.

Communication issues

Staff work with children and families from diverse cultural, religious, ethnic, educational, class and socioeconomic backgrounds. Understanding and respecting diversity is integral to quality health care, but can present challenges in terms of staff feeling confident that they have sufficient understanding to demonstrate respect for an individual's needs, beliefs and expectations. There can also be concerns about providing equitable care for families who, being unable to speak English, rely either on family members to interpret for them, or on a hospital interpreting service. In urgent situations, telephone interpreters are used, and however excellent they are, the direct personal aspects of support can feel compromised.

Although direct contact and relationships with children and families are often an extremely positive part of the health professional's role, there can be notable exceptions to this. It is important for staff to have the opportunity to reflect on their own responses to difficult or challenging situations, in order to ensure that they retain the highest professional standards of care. The focus of clinical care should always be on providing the best care and service for the child, and therefore staff must have ways of recognising and managing situations where this is a challenge for them. For example, parents who are highly stressed themselves may find it difficult to tolerate some aspects of care, such as waiting for tests or test results, or waiting for doctors who are seeing other children as a higher priority. There may also be challenges for parents in understanding or accepting treatment decisions or the way care is being delivered. Professionals are very understanding of the stresses for parents and cope very well with parents' behaviour at these times. However, some staff can feel undermined by an assertive and angry parent, and some feel very wary or even scared of family members being abusive or physically intimidating, or of those who are openly critical of care and threaten to make complaints about their competence. Family members can also be in conflict with each other and 'split' the professional team, resulting in the staff team mirroring the dynamics within the family system. This can raise significant problems for the staff team in being able to work effectively with all family members.

'Expert parents' can also appear challenging to staff. Many parents have developed high levels of expertise about their child's condition, and it can be difficult for them to hand over aspects of their child's care when they are in hospital, especially if they perceive the nursing or medical staff to be less expert in managing their child's condition than they are. Hospital staff have to follow protocols and manage the care of all the children on the ward. This can seem inflexible to parents who are used to providing care for their child. Professionals may experience family members as critical or pedantic in the way they expect their child's care to be carried out, and can also feel undermined when parents refuse to let less experienced staff care for their child.

Interpersonal communication is key to developing a supportive working environment. However, it is not unusual for disagreements and conflicts to arise within one's own professional group or multidisciplinary team. These differences of opinion can be extremely helpful, promoting debate and advancing thinking or practice. However, they can also be very challenging. Conflict might arise due to attitudes shown to others, inappropriate behaviour which needs to be challenged, or professional disagreements about treatment decisions or the way these are being carried out. Junior staff may feel unsupported in the level of responsibility expected of them by senior staff. Other junior staff feel well supported themselves, but concerned about support for their senior staff, and feel unable to ask or provide support to their lead. Clearly, as one progresses and becomes more senior in the workforce, there are fewer peers available to give support, and also increased expectations of being able both to cope and to support the junior workforce.

WAYS OF DELIVERING SUPPORT

Support can be provided both formally and informally. It might involve holding extra meetings specifically focused around supporting staff, or it might be a component of an existing professional activity, such as a ward meeting or psychosocial meeting. It is important to remind staff of all the different sources of support that they can use, including occupational health, in-house counselling services and their own GP.

Psychosocial team meetings

Many wards, units and clinics hold regular psychosocial meetings attended by the multi-professional team members involved in caring for children and families. These meetings are an opportunity to share concerns about families and to pass on information that might get lost in the medical handovers and notes. They are also an opportunity to plan more holistic care as a team, considering both the needs of the child and family and those of the wider professional group and junior staff. These meetings can provide support in the form of an opportunity to talk about managing any difficulties, and as a means of providing consultation about cases.

Debrief meetings or focused support meetings

Debrief or focused support meetings are often requested following a difficult incident, such as the death of a child or an event which has affected a group of staff. There are different types of debriefing meetings. For example, some focus primarily on the medical aspects of care and look in more detail at the process of medical treatment in an attempt to learn from the situation. Others are more holistic, and consider other aspects of the child's care and treatment. These may be described as 'psychological debriefing'. Although these meetings are often requested, they have not been well researched and their effectiveness has been difficult to establish. There have been some concerns raised about 'debriefing' (British Psychological Society 2002) in terms of sensitising people by raising distressing feelings, without giving them the resources to cope with these feelings. It is therefore important to be clear, when responding to requests for debriefing, about the context for this work, including what you are intending and expected to provide and what further resources are available to staff who are experiencing high levels of psychological distress.

> The aims of psychological debriefing are twofold. Firstly, to promote normal recovery, resilience and personal growth. Secondly, within the organisation

or community to provide a means of enhancing social cohesion and group understanding.

(British Psychological Society 2002)

Organising or facilitating this type of more focused meeting in response to a particular situation clearly needs to take account of the specific context and needs of the professional group. The session may involve staff from a particular profession, or even a specific grade within this professional group. The whole multidisciplinary team may be involved, which could be unit- or ward-specific or could involve a wider range of professionals. It may be that these meetings are offered regularly over a period of time, or repeated regularly to enable maximum numbers of staff to attend (taking into account shift patterns), or they may just be 'one-off' meetings.

It is important to establish a clear remit for what is expected from running such a meeting, to ensure that there is managerial support and practical support for releasing staff to attend the meeting, and then to communicate in a timely and effective manner to all staff where and when the meeting will occur. As the meeting takes place, it is important to re-establish with group participants what they are expecting or hoping for, and to clarify 'ground rules' for the meeting. It is also important to clarify the timings for the session and to prepare for the ending of the meeting. From our experience, it is helpful to allow some time at the end of a group for staff to have a short break in which to compose themselves before getting back to their work.

Co-memorating groups

Staff may find it helpful to have a protected space in which to meet together to remember and talk about children who have died. Staff 'support' groups can have negative associations for some people, and a 'co-memorating' group meeting, which offers an opportunity to talk through connections and memories of the child, can feel more positive than a support group. These meetings have been well described by Fredman (1997). The membership of this group is open to all who wish to attend, and may involve staff from community or other hospital services. A facilitator (usually someone not involved with the child's care) invites participants to 'tell their story' about their connection with the child. This produces a collective piecing together of different aspects of the child's life in a way that helps make sense of the child's experiences and can enable the team to build up a shared memory of the child. The role of the facilitator is to ensure that space is available to everyone who wishes to share, and that each contribution is valued. With the intense and often powerful feelings experienced, it can be difficult for some to acknowledge the extent of the role and connection felt by other people.

Supervision/reflective staff groups

Peer group supervision/reflection can be an invaluable way of learning from each other and can be extremely important when the members of the peer group do not have many opportunities to work together regularly, or if they only meet to hand over patient information at the change of shift. There can be limited opportunities to feel part of a group that can share experiences and strategies for dealing with difficulties, as well as to be creative in developing initiatives within the workplace. These might be regular groups, which happen as part of professional 'away days', or could happen regularly as an independent supportive activity. It can be helpful to have a model of reflective practice which illustrates the reflective practice process, to facilitate a structured way in which the group can operate – for example, the model based on experiential learning (described by O'Curry 2009). This process involves getting group members to describe their experience and then to reflect on the feelings and thoughts arising from experience. It can be helpful to develop a hypothesis about the factors that were particularly relevant in a given case, and to make a plan about how to respond in a similar situation. This can be done by exploring what could have been done differently and what might have led to a more positive outcome. Over time the group can build up a repertoire of shared reflections and helpful strategies.

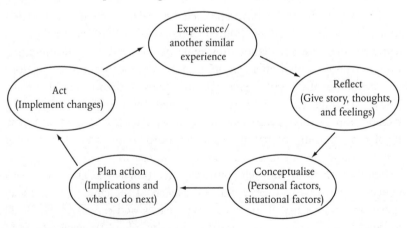

Figure 12.1 Reflective Practice Model
Source: O'Curry 2009

In addition to providing a positive structure for addressing and problem-solving their own issues, many staff have valued the experience of this model in terms of understanding a little more about the role of the psychologist or counsellor in their work with families. This can have additional positive benefits as staff introduce the role and benefits of referral on to these services.

In some units attendance at ongoing groups based on reflective practice is a compulsory or expected part of ongoing professional development or support. In most places, attendance is optional and dependent on the support of senior managers. While managers may support the development of such groups in theory, practical difficulties such as short staffing on the ward, or the need to get other tasks done, can prevent them from allowing staff time to attend such meetings.

Even when staff have been invited, or have offered, to attend these meetings, it can be difficult for them to allow themselves to attend, particularly when the unit is busy and they are aware of the additional pressure this will place on other staff who are covering their patients. It can be difficult, in any respect, to change suddenly from an active and 'doing' role to a more reflective, thoughtful stance, and to prioritise something that can feel somewhat 'indulgent' over patient care, especially if staff are not feeling particularly in need of support at that particular time. Senior staff may be very positive about their junior staff attending such a group, but may not feel able to make time to go themselves. Although they may genuinely feel that they are facilitating others to go, it can generate an interesting dynamic on the unit as to who thinks who should attend these meetings, and may perpetuate a model of certain staff being strong and coping, and of others as needing support. Many staff are extremely valuing of groups being available to them; however, sometimes it appears that it is sufficient just to know that there is an ongoing group as a 'safety net', and staff do not necessarily feel that they need to attend regularly.

It can also be problematic maintaining continuity between groups, because of the way shift patterns work. With different staff attending, it can be hard for the group to develop the model of supervision practice in that group. When staff do not know each other well, they are not always confident enough to 'expose' themselves to others' reflections on their work, and until the group has built up sufficient cohesion, it is difficult to engender a sense of trust and respect for each other.

Informal support

A number of staff will not access or use formal support systems. This could be because of pressure on time (real or perceived), or a worry about being seen as not able to cope if they attend such a session, or concern about becoming distressed during a session. Some staff are more receptive when the person in the key support role (often the psychologist, counsellor, social worker or chaplain) is around as a presence on the ward, and available for a short time to talk. It can be difficult to prioritise this rather unstructured use of time, but when there is high stress on the wards, it is often very much appreciated by staff.

It is important for an organisation to be able to offer varied and flexible ways of supporting staff, to acknowledge the different personalities and needs across the staff teams. One way is through organised social events. At the Evelina Children's Hospital, particular nurses on each ward take on a special responsibility for particular aspects of care and link up with other nurses in the same role across the hospital. For example, the intensive care ward has a social events coordinator, who helps promote and organise social events for staff, and after shifts on different wards, staff may go out for supper or drinks together. Some units and wards have supper groups, for staff to eat together before starting their night shift. These are examples of opportunities for staff to get to know each other and develop positive relationships in a more relaxed way, and can have a positive effect on the way they support each other at work.

Mentoring programmes

Many hospitals have mentoring programmes in place for nursing staff. Training is available for senior nurses to take on this mentoring role. These programmes can be very helpful in providing space to discuss work and the impact of work with an experienced colleague. Peer mentoring is another opportunity for staff.

Training

Stress management workshops which encompass a psycho-educational approach to understanding work-related stress can help at both an organisational and an individual level. Workshops aim to normalise and destigmatise experiences of stress, and to enable people to identify their own stress and evaluate strategies which they have found helpful (or not helpful) in the past to manage it. It can also be helpful for staff to identify how colleagues may present when they are stressed, as this enables staff to support each other better. Staff can consider their own 'first aid for stress plan' and communicate this to colleagues, to let them know how they can be most helpful and supportive. Continually asking 'Are you ok?!' is often considered the least helpful response, but sharing a smile or a knowing look, or joining someone in an activity and just 'being with them' are often suggested as being the most helpful immediate ways of helping.

Staff are not always aware that some of the ways they have been feeling or behaving are linked with stress, and they can be helped to 'tune in' to their bodies and anticipate situations and events where they need to take even more care of themselves. This may involve practical care such as taking adequate breaks during shifts, healthy eating and drinking, and good sleep hygiene. There is a helpful document from the Royal College of Nursing on managing stress that can be a helpful resource for nurses and provides a useful structure for developing these workshops (RCN 2005).

Workshops may identify a need for further and specific training on aspects of work that are commonly associated with staff stress. This might include training on subjects such as communication skills, bereavement support, managing children's behaviour, procedural distress and conflict resolution.

SUMMARY

In order to develop high quality care, it is important for the workforce to feel valued and supported. Although it can be extremely rewarding to care for sick children, this work can be extremely challenging, and staff can easily lose perspective on their own needs in the context of overwhelming needs and demands from children and families. There is little systematic evaluation of staff support methods to indicate the most effective way of delivering support. However, access to support is positively valued by nursing staff and other professional groups. It is important, when organising and delivering support, to have a good understanding of the organisational and local context of work, and to have a clear remit for what is required. Agreement and support from senior staff within the organisation to deliver this service is essential. There is scope for psychologists to be more involved in staff training for stress management, and in other areas highlighted by staff that are stressful for them.

Concluding Remarks

It is very encouraging to see how psychological care for children with a chronic illness has improved and expanded over recent years. At both a policy level and in clinical practice, the psychological needs of children are increasingly recognised as important influences on outcome, and improving psychological well-being is valued in its own right.

The experience of childhood illness continues to change as medical knowledge and expertise advance, and the types of difficulties which children and families encounter have changed considerably. There is increasing prevalence of some conditions (such as obesity and diabetes), increased survival rates for many conditions (such as cystic fibrosis), and more children are surviving thanks to intensive medical treatments, which have a long-term impact on the child and their family. We are likely to see new challenges arising, but also, we hope, improved quality of life for many children and their families.

Advances in technology also bring new opportunities of finding creative ways of bringing psychological approaches to a wider range of children and families, via the use of the Internet and computer technology. The amount of information available to children and families has increased dramatically, and while this has some negative aspects at times, it does mean that patients are able to be better informed than ever before, but need to develop skills for making the best use of the information available in making decisions about their health care. In other areas of psychology, standardised treatment packages are available on CD or online (e.g. Cognitive Behavioural Therapy for depression), and these may prove to be attractive, particularly to children who are confident and familiar with using computer technology on a daily basis.

Within psychology, the evidence base for interventions that can be useful for children with medical conditions has evolved and become stronger, although there is still a long way to go. One difficulty with the current evidence base is the division between the demands of rigorous research and the reality of clinical practice. In order to conduct research, it is necessary to use standardised treatment protocols and to ensure that criteria for inclusion are uniform, but in most areas of clinical practice, even within the larger treatment centres, the clinical group comes from a diverse range of backgrounds and presents with a range of difficulties, and the numbers are relatively small, which makes it hard to conduct high-quality research. At the same time, scarce resources have made it even more important to be able to demonstrate not just that treatments are effective, but also that they contribute to health outcomes in a cost-effective way.

Many psychologists work within specialist clinical areas because of the way that funding for posts has emerged, and they may be active in collaborative research with other members of the team working with these conditions. It is true that there are issues that are specific to particular conditions, and it is important for psychologists to become familiar with the issues that are relevant for the speciality within which they work. However, there are also themes that cut across many conditions, such as difficulties with adherence, and coping with visible differences, and it is important to continue to communicate effectively across speciality groups to learn from each other's experiences. In particular, there is now a lot more research on conditions such as diabetes, cancer and cystic fibrosis, and psychologists working with children with rare conditions can apply much that has been learnt in other groups to their own speciality.

Web Resources

There are many websites specific to particular medical conditions, which can provide valuable information about the condition itself as well as information about support for children and families affected by the condition. We have only listed websites for specific conditions which have been referred to in the text of this book. To identify relevant sites for a specific condition, please refer to the Contact a Family website (www.cafamily.org.uk). This has an alphabetical listing of an extensive range of medical conditions which provides links to the key organisations or support groups for those conditions. Medikidz (www.medikidz.com) has a range of information about medical conditions and procedures as well as comic books presented in professional cartoon type style which can be ordered from this site.

ADOLESCENTS/YOUNG PEOPLE

after16.org.uk
www.after16.org.uk
Provides advice on opportunities and services available for young people when they leave school.

Brook
www.brook.org.uk
This provides free and confidential sexual health advice for young people.

Connexions
www.connexions-direct.com
Connexions is for you if you are 13–19 years, living in England and wanting advice on getting where you want to be in life. It also provides support up to the age of 25 years for young people who have learning difficulties or disabilities (or both).

jimmyteenstv
www.jimmyteenstv.com
An online forum for young people to share their experiences of having cancer, through using video diaries and animation.

like it is

www.likeitis.org.uk

Gives young people access to information about all aspects of sex education and teenage life and is part of the Marie Stopes charity.

Teen Growth

www.teengrowth.com

An American site which provides information for teenagers on topics that typically concern them, such as health, bullying, sexuality and drugs.

Teenage Cancer Trust

www.teenagecancertrust.org

Teenage Cancer Trust is a national charity which supports teenagers and young adults with cancer through education, research and provision of specialist TYA units.

Teenage Health Freak

www.teenagehealthfreak.org

Delivers information for teens on bullying, body changes, alcohol, drugs, accidents, moods, sex and not feeling well. Options are available to talk to doctors, with answers to a 'zillion questions' available.

Transition Info Network

www.transitioninfonetwork.org.uk

Provides guidance on the transition to adulthood for parents, carers and young disabled people, including information about policy, employment and education.

BEREAVEMENT

The Child Bereavement Charity

www.childbereavement.org.uk

Provides separate sections for families, young people, school and professionals on how to support children following a bereavement. Tel. 01494 446648.

Child Bereavement Network

www.childbereavementnetwork.org.uk

Provides resources for bereaved families, including the I Can…You Can postcards, which can be used by bereaved children to alert their parent/carer, friend or teacher to how best to support them.

Cruse Bereavement Care

www.cruse.org.uk

RD4U is the branch of Cruse Bereavement Care for children and young people aged 12–18 years.

Grief Encounter

www.griefencounter.com

Offers support to children who have suffered a bereavement. With separate sections for adults and children, the website allows individuals to access help and support following a death and to share thoughts with other bereaved children and families.

Seesaw

www.seesaw.org.uk

This is a charity based in Oxford that provides information and advice for parents and professionals about bereavement. 'Hand in hand' by Seesaw is a resource pack for schools for supporting children and young people with learning difficulties through the experience of bereavement.

Winston's Wish

www.winstonswish.org.uk

Offers a telephone helpline and a range of informative and interactive web pages designed for children who have suffered a significant bereavement, and those supporting and caring for them. Tel. 08452 03 04 05.

BULLYING

Beatbullying

www.beatbullying.org

The UK's leading bullying prevention charity. The focus is to empower young people to lead anti-bullying campaigns in their schools and local communities, and build the capacity of local communities to sustain the work. It assists and supports young people who are being bullied, and re-educates and changes the behaviour of young people who bully, in schools and communities across the UK.

Kidscape

www.kidscape.co.uk

A UK-wide charity for prevention of bullying and child abuse that works with children and young people under the age of 16, their parents/carers, and those who work with them. It provides individuals and organisations with practical skills and resources necessary to keep children safe from harm.

CANCER

CCLG

www.cclg.org.uk

Provides a good range of literature and information about cancer in children for children, families and professionals.

Cancer and Leukaemia in Children Sargent Charity
www.clicsargent.org.uk
Works with children with cancer and their families and funds posts for specialists working with children with cancer. The website provides general information and has a good range of publications for use with children, families and schools.

Macmillan
www.macmillan.org.uk
Provides general information and support for people affected by cancer but also has a specialist section (www.click4tic.org.uk) for teenagers affected by cancer.

The Royal Marsden Cancer Campaign
www.royalmarsden.org
The adventures of Captain Chemo and Chemo command – an animated interactive site about childhood cancer treatment. It is not about what cancer is as such, but about chemotherapy, radiotherapy and their side effects.

CONTINENCE

ERIC (Education and Resources for Improving Childhood Continence)
www.eric.org.uk
ERIC operates an interactive website for children and young people and also provides a telephone helpline offering information and support to children, young people, parents and professionals on all aspects of children's continence. Tel 0845 370 8008.

EDUCATION

BBC
www.bbc.co.uk/schools/revision
Contains bite-size revision for children and young people. Revision help is available for Key Stages 1–3, GCSE, Scottish Standard Grade and Scottish Highers. Many subjects are covered, with additional sections on how to prepare for revision and stay healthy while revising.

Direct
www.direct.gov.uk
Provides information and links to key websites for information about special educational needs.

Easy Health
www.easyhealth.org.uk
Provides a range of accessible health information for people with learning disabilities. Functions include leaflets and short films, as well as information for health professionals on how to improve their work with this group.

Parent Partnership
www.parentpartnership.org.uk
This is the organisation which provides advice and support to parents about the SEN process and can provide information about the local parent partnership service.

Skill: National Bureau for Students with Disabilities
www.skill.org.uk
Promotes opportunities for young people and adults with any kind of disability in post-16 education, training and employment across the UK.

TeacherNet
Special Educational Needs (SEN) A Guide for Parents and Carers (Download from www.teachernet.gov.uk.)
Users can choose to view or download relevant publications and order copies (paper-based, CDs, videos, etc.), and receive email alerts to the latest documents.

LIFESTYLE

AbilityNet
www.abilitynet.co.uk
Offers a range of services to help disabled adults and children make the most effective use of computer technology.

Aidis Trust
www.aidis.org
Helps people with disabilities make the best use of information and communication technology by giving information, help and support on all aspects of disability computing.

Artsline
www.artsline.org.uk
Disability access information service for access to theatre, cinemas, galleries, clubs and music venues in London.

DisabledGo
www.disabledgo.com
Provides free, detailed information for people who are disabled on which hotels, cinemas, restaurants, tourist attractions, pubs, train stations, leisure centres, shops and other services are accessible with their particular need across the UK.

Get Kids Going
www.getkidsgoing.com
Gives children and young people with disabilities the opportunity to participate in sport.

MENTAL HEALTH

YoungMinds

www.youngminds.org.uk

A charity dedicated to improving the emotional health and well-being of children and young people, as well as empowering them, their parents and carers. There is a helpline for parents and anyone concerned about the emotional well-being of a young person, and a range of useful and accessible publications.

Youth in Mind

www.youthinmind.co.uk

Provides a summary of resources for mental health conditions, and has a geographical search facility to help find local child mental health services.

PAIN

Action on Pain

www.action-on-pain.co.uk

Provides support and advice for people affected by chronic pain, including a range of helpful leaflets giving advice for carers.

PARENTS AND FAMILIES

Carers UK

www.carersuk.org

Provides information, advice and support to families caring for someone with an illness or disability.

Parent Line Plus

www.parentlineplus.org.uk

Provides information and support for parenting issues as well as a free telephone helpline for further advice.

Relate

www.relate.org.uk

Provides information about relationship difficulties as well as a geographical search facility to find local support services.

Young Carers

www.youngcarers.org.uk

Provides information and support to young people caring for a family member.

RELAXATION

Relax Kids

www.relaxkids.com

Resources for relaxation sessions with children. This is a good website to help children relax and tackles issues such as stress, anxiety and sleeping problems.

VISIBLE DIFFERENCE

Changing Faces

www.changingfaces.org.uk

This charity supports and represents people who have disfigurements of the face or body from any cause. The charity delivers information and guidance about disfigurements to enable all pupils to feel aware and included. A number of booklets and DVDs are available.

Climb (Children Living with Inherited Metabolic Diseases)

www.climb.org.uk

A website for children living with inherited metabolic conditions – provides information for children and their families, along with guidance for families on how to support young people.

Eczema

www.eczema.org

Provides information about eczema and its treatment and also has a helpful section on talking to schools about managing appearance-related difficulties.

UK Psoriasis Help

www.psoriasis-help.org.uk

Dedicated to helping people suffering from the chronic skin disease psoriasis. This site contains information about treatments, tips for living with psoriasis, and other topics.

WISH-GRANTING CHARITIES

Dreams Come True

www.dctc.org.uk

A national charity serving the whole of the UK with the mission of bringing joy to children who are seriously or terminally ill.

Make-A-Wish Foundation

www.make-a-wish.org.uk

A UK charity granting wishes of children and young people aged 3–17 living with life-threatening illnesses.

Rays of Sunshine

www.raysofsunshine.org.uk

Rays of Sunshine Children's Charity was formed in 2004 to help children aged 3–18 living with serious or life-limiting illnesses, across the United Kingdom.

Starlight Children's Foundation

www.startlight.org.uk

Grants wishes for seriously ill children and provides stimulating programmes in hospital.

OTHER

Action for Sick Children

www.actionforsickchildren.org

Campaigns to improve health care for children and has a range of information for young people, parents and professionals.

Children First for Health

www.childrenfirst.nhs.uk

'Children First for Health' website by Great Ormond Street Hospital, aimed at 7–11-year-olds. Various sections, including 'Health and Body' (teaches all about the body and illnesses, eating smart, and real stories from children about their illnesses) and 'Hospital Life' (advice on different hospitals, what to expect from your stay in hospital, and what it's really like inside).

Contact a Family

www.cafamily.org.uk

'Contact a Family' is a website for parents of disabled children, providing advice, information and support. The charity has a helpline and a wide range of information for families and professionals. Tel. 0808 808 3555.

Diabetes UK

www.diabetes.org.uk

Contains a wealth of information for people with diabetes, aimed particularly at children. The website promotes diabetes education and information on treatment and health, living with diabetes, and recipe tips and ideas.

Department of Health

www.doh.gov.uk/integratedchildrenssystem/involvingchildren

This website lists publications and resources for enabling children to be involved in planning and consultation within the NHS.

ECHO Evelina

www.echo-evelina.org.uk

This is a website for families and children with congenital heart problems who receive their care at the Evelina Children's Hospital (Guy's and St Thomas' Foundation Trust). Amongst other helpful information, this website gives access to two DVDs to support young people with cardiac conditions: 'Eddie ECHO's Heartbeat' (for younger children) and 'ECHO Teen Club… You ask the questions' (for adolescents).

Epilepsy Action
www.epilepsy.org.uk
Information aimed at young people with epilepsy and related worries and concerns (e.g. alcohol, going out, sex, etc.).

Great Ormond Street Hospital for Children
www.gosh.nhs.uk
Contains a range of information about staying in Great Ormond Street Hospital, the services and facilities available, how to get referred and what the stay will be like for children. Downloadable documents are available in a range of languages. The website also contains information for children and families on a range of conditions, treatments and tests.

Guy's and St Thomas' Hospital
www.guysandstthomas.nhs.uk/services/childrens/mri/jacks/jacks-mri.aspx
This site for the Evelina Children's Hospital (part of Guy's and St Thomas' Foundation Trust) provides preparation material for a young person requiring an MRI scan, including a video of a child having a scan ('Jack's MRI adventure') and a sequence of photographs and 'sound bites' of the MRI scan for older children.

KidsHealth
www.kidshealth.org/kid
Has separate web sections for parents, kids and teenagers and provides information about a range of medical conditions. Information is also available on a range of topics from 'How the body works' and 'Staying safe' to 'Movies and games'.

Little Hearts Matter
www.lhm.org.uk
This website provides an excellent preparation booklet for a child going into hospital for cardiac surgery, which can be downloaded from the site. The booklet also recommends toys and books to use with children.

National Centre for Young People with Epilepsy
www.ncype.org.uk
This website provides a useful literature review as well as charts for monitoring seizures. The diary resource 'Day by Day by Me' is available from this website.

National Deaf Children's Society
www.ndcs.org.uk
Provides information and support for deaf children and their families, including details of weekend events for young people.

Paediatric Psychology Network

www.ppnuk.org

This website, which is a subsystem of the Faculty of Children and Young People within the British Psychological Society. Psychologists working with children and young people with a chronic illness can use this to access information and relevant publications and to link with other psychologists working in similar fields.

Right Health

www.righthealth.com

This website gives anatomical information about the kidneys, what they do and how. It has links to articles about kidneys, medical journals, patient experiences and news articles. It also has links to videos, including kidney dialysis and the anatomy of the kidney.

Sibs

www.sibs.org.uk

A website especially for people who grow up with a brother or sister with any disability, long-term chronic illness or life-limiting condition. Separate sections are available for young and adult siblings, and for parents and professionals supporting siblings and families.

Staying Positive

www.staying-positive.co.uk

This website is maintained by young people and offers other young people information about workshops on managing their condition and treatment. This has developed from the 'Expert Patients Programme'.

Transplant Kids

www.transplantkids.co.uk

An interactive website for children who have had a transplant, and for parents/carers, friends and relatives of a child who has received a transplant. There is child-friendly information on receiving a transplant, a forum to speak with other young people who have received transplants, success stories and links to other useful resources.

Books for Children, Adolescents and Young People

A helpful website which lists books covering a wide range of physical health, life events and emotional issues for children is www.healthybooks.org.uk. The Wellbeing Collection also provides a list of books dealing with feelings and life situations for younger and older children and their families: www.rbkc.go.uk/libraries/bibliotherapy. National charities often have detailed booklists for their specific condition or focus of support (e.g. www.ncype.org.uk/epilepsy/book-reviews/for-children for helpful guides to children's books on epilepsy). One section of the Scope website (www.childreninthepicture.org.uk) features stories involving children with different disabilities available to view and download. The following list details books and resources with particular significance for children with chronic and life-threatening conditions.

BEREAVEMENT/SERIOUS ILLNESS

Braithwaite, A. (1982) *When Uncle Bob Died.* Miami: Parkwest Publications.
This storybook offers a starting point for discussing death and children's own thoughts about the subject.

Courtauld, S. *My Brother and Me.* (Only available from the Child Bereavement Charity www.childbereavement.org.uk.)
This book (appropriate for children aged 4–10 years) deals with issues surrounding a sibling's serious illness and admissions to hospital.

Edwards, L. and Palmer, J. (2007) *Facing the Death of Your Child – Suggestions and Help for Families, Before and Afterwards.* London: Children's Cancer and Leukaemia Group and the Royal Marsden. Download from www.childcancer.org.uk.

Geisel, T. and McKie, R. (1969) *My Book About Me.* New York: Random House Books for Young Readers. An activity book for children. Available from the Child Bereavement Charity (www.childbereavement.org.uk).

Hanson, W. (1997) *The Next Place.* Singapore: Mission Publishing.
A beautifully illustrated book that approaches the subject of death sensitively and explains what death means.

Harper, A. (1994) *Remembering Michael.* London: SANDS (Stillbirth and Neonatal Death society).
A book for children about the death of a baby sibling.

Heegard, M. (1991) *When Someone has a Very Serious Illness.* Minneapolis: Woodland Press.

Heegard, M. (1991) *When Someone Very Special Dies.* Minneapolis: Woodland Press.
These are non-directive workbooks, where children can illustrate the book with their own personal story. These books are suitable for using with children with learning disabilities.

Hollins, S. and Sireling, L. (2004) *When Mum Died.* London: Books Beyond Words, The Royal College of Psychiatrists.
This picture book tells a story about death and bereavement without using words.

Hughes, J. (1988) *Will My Rabbit Go to Heaven?* Oxford: Lion Hudson Publications Corporation.
This book suggests answers for difficult questions asked by children about death and heaven, amongst other things.

Kelley, A. (2005) *The Burying Beetle.* Edinburgh: Luath Press.
This book tells the story of a child who is waiting for a heart transplant.

Maple, M. (1992) *On the Wings of a Butterfly.* Seattle: Parenting Press.
This is based on the true story of a young girl with cancer.

Mills, J. (2003) *Gentle Willow (A Story for Children About Dying).* Washington DC: Magination Press, second revised edition.
This book is written for children who may not survive their illness or for the children who know them, addressing difficult feelings with love and compassion.

Stickney, D. (2004) *Water Bugs and Dragonflies.* Boston: Pilgrim Press.
This storybook uses metaphors of transformation to assist children's understanding of death, including why people who die cannot come back to us.

Sims, A. (1986) *Am I Still a Sister?* Washington: Big A and Company.
A story book about an 11-year-old girl who loses her 13-month-old brother. For young children.

Sunderland, M. and Armstrong, N. (2003) *The Day the Sea Went Out and Never Came Back.* Oxford: Speedmark Publishing.
A story for children who have lost someone they love, dealing with feelings of loss from the perspective of a sand dragon that misses the sea.

Varley, S. (1992) *Badger's Parting Gifts.* London: Collins Picture Lions New Ed.
This is a story of an old badger that dies, but is fondly remembered by all his friends for the special skills and times he shared with them.

Weiss, L. (1996) *My Book about Our Baby that Died.* Greenfield Newport: Greenfields Publishing.
A workbook for young children when a baby brother or sister dies at, or soon after, birth. It aims to guide parents and gives ways to encourage their children to express their feelings.

Wells, R. (1988) *Helping Children Cope With Grief.* London: Sheldon Press.
A book for carers and children to help address children's questions and feelings about grief.

Wilhelm, H (1985) *I'll Always Love You.* New York: Victoria Publications.
The story of a young boy growing up with his dog and his gradual realisation that his best friend will not be there forever.

Winston's Wish (2000) *Muddles, Puddles and Sunshine: An Activity Book to Help When Someone has Died.* Gloucestershire: Hawthorn Press.

FEELINGS/SELF-EXPLORATION

Brownjohn, E. (2003) *All Kinds of Feelings.* London: Tango Books Ltd.
A 'lift the flap book' for children to explore their feelings in a fun way.

Ironside, V. (2004) *The Huge Bag of Worries.* London: Hodder Children's Books.
A story book about worrying for children and their families.

Milne, A.A. (1995) *Winnie the Pooh: All About You.* London: Reeds Children's Books.
An activity book for children to record a story about their daily lives.

Pincus, D. (1990) *Feeling Good about Yourself.* California: Good Apple, Frank Schaffer Publications.
An activity book designed to build self-confidence and encourage expression through art, speech and written tasks.

Silver, N. (1999) *Temper Temper.* London: Hodder Weyland.
A fun and engaging way of managing tantrums. Tells the story of a boy called Jonathan who isn't very good at not getting his own way – until a hairy monster called Temper Temper arrives!

Striker, S. and Kimmel, E. (1978) *The Anti-Colouring Book.* London: Scholastic Ltd.
An activity book for children, encouraging them to use their imagination and think about their feelings in a creative way.

Sunderland, M. and Armstrong, N. (2003) *Ruby and the Rubbish Bin.* Oxford: Speechmark.
A book to help children with low self-esteem. Tells the story of Ruby, who everyone thinks of as 'rubbish', and describes how she overcomes these comments and grows in confidence.

Watt, M. (2007) *Scaredy Squirrel.* Toronto: Kids Can Press Ltd.
A fun story book in which a squirrel addresses fear of the unknown.

ILLNESS/DISABILITY/PAIN

Braithwaite, A. (1989) *I Have Cancer.* Surrey: Dinosaur Publications Ltd.
Braithwaite, A. (1982) *I Have Diabetes.* Surrey: Dinosaur Publications Ltd.
Braithwaite, A. (1987) *I Have Epilepsy.* Surrey: Dinosaur Publications Ltd.
Braithwaite, A. (1983) *I Use a Wheelchair.* Surrey: Dinosaur Publications Ltd.
These books have a simple storyline and describe how life might be with the conditions mentioned.

Broome, A. and Jellicoe, H. (1987) *Living with Your Pain: A Self-Help Guide to Managing Pain.* London: British Psychological Society.
Suitable for adolescents and young people.

Chilman-Blair, K. and Taddeo, J. (2009) *What's Up with Wendy?* London: Medikidz Publishing
A comic-style book for 10–15-year-olds about dealing with epilepsy. (Available from www.kidzcomics. com.)

DeBode, A. and Broene, R. (1997) *Tomorrow I Will Feel Better.* London: Evans Brothers Publishing.
The story of a young girl going into hospital for a heart transplant.

Hynsley, D. (1996) *A Day with Sam.* London: Arthritis Care.
This book is suitable for children aged up to seven years who have arthritis, and helps siblings and friends to understand the challenges of living with arthritis.

Kish, V. (1998) *What Happened to You?*
Kish, V. (1998) *Do Looks Count?*
Kish, V. (1998) *Looking Good, Feeling Different.*
These are a selection of books available from Changing Faces: www.changingfaces.org.uk, a UK-based charity giving support and information to people with disfigurements to the face, hands or body, and their families.

Laird, E. (1998) *Me and My Electric.* Pennsylvania: Mammoth Press.
Each chapter in this book is written by a young person with a different condition or disability.

Matthews, N. (2006) *Rory and Stella Save the Earth* (available from www.childreninthepicture.org.uk).
This short story is about a young boy and his adventures with his little sister. The boy uses a wheelchair and alternative forms of communication.

McGrath, P., Finley, G.A., Ritchie, J. and Dowden, S. (2003) *Pain, Pain, Go Away: Helping Children with Pain* (second edition). London: Association for the Care of Children's Health.
This resource suggests a range of pain relief techniques which are appropriate for use with children of all ages.

Minaki, C. (2007) *Zoe's Extraordinary Holiday Adventures.* Toronto: Second Story Press.
This is a story about a young girl who uses a wheelchair, and her struggles and adventures with school friends and at home.

Mooney, I. and Roscoe, S. (2007) *The Sleepover.* (Available from www.kidspremiership.com.)
Tells the story of a group of friends who overcome the challenge of having a friend who cannot climb stairs to a sleepover, in a humorous way.

Regan, P. and Hollomby, D. (2003) *Epilepsy: The Detective's Story.*
Available from the National Society for Epilepsy (www. nse.org.uk) and recommended for children between four and ten years.

Silkstone, J. and Hague, A. (1989) *When Your Brother or Sister Has a Tumour.* Manchester: Regional Oncology Support Service.

Waddell, M. (2003) *Hi Harry!* London: Walker Books.
The moving story of how one slow tortoise slowly made a friend.

Westcott, P. (2002) *Living with Leukaemia*. London: Hodder Weyland.
Through four different case studies, readers learn about living with leukaemia.

TOILETTING/BEDWETTING

Gomi, T. (1993) *Everybody Poos*. London: Kane/Miller Book Publishers.
This children's book has a straightforward approach to children's bodily functions, encouraging them not to be ashamed about potty training.

Mills, J.C. and Crowley, R.J. (1988) *Sammy the Elephant and Mr Camel*. New York: Magination Press.
The story of Sammy, a little elephant who keeps spilling his buckets of water, helps children overcome bedwetting, while also enhancing personal self-esteem.

Ross, T. (1988) *I Want My Potty*. London: Kane/Miller Book Publishers.
This is a humorous account of potty training which aims to amuse young children and help their parents.

Willis, J. and Jossen, P. (2001) *Do Little Mermaids Wet Their Beds?* Illinois: Albert Whitman & Company.
This is a reassuring story for children who wet the bed, aiming to take the worry out of the problem.

SLEEPING

Waddell, M. and Firth, B. (2001) *Can't You Sleep, Little Bear?* London: Walker Books Ltd.
A story about a little bear who is frightened of the dark, even with the biggest lantern of them all at his bedside.

Wineman-Marcus, I. and Marcus, P. (1991) *Scary Night Visitors*. Washington DC: Magination Press.
A story for children with bedtime fears.

BOOKS FOR SIBLINGS/WHEN SOMEBODY ELSE IS ILL

Clarke, G. (2002) *Betty's Not Well Today*. London: Andersen Press Ltd.
A young girl considers all the things she could be doing if she (or her doll, Betty) were not feeling unwell.

Diggon Shields, C. (1988) *I Wish My Brother was a Dog*. London: Chard Books.
This book deals with the mixed feelings of jealousy and love children might have towards their siblings, using the voice of a child who wishes his baby brother was a dog.

Graham, B. (2000) *Brand New Baby*. London: Walker Books Ltd.
A child-friendly account of the birth of a new sibling.

Lamount, S. (1988) *Ewen's Little Brother*. Singapore: Victoria Publications.
A simple story for very young children that explains the loss of a younger sibling through illness

Shulman, D. (1994) *Dora's New Brother*. London: Red Fox Picture Books.
This book tells the story of Dora, who is experiencing the excitement and jealousy that having a new baby brother can bring.

Peterkin, A. (1992) *What About Me? When Brothers and Sisters get Sick*. New York: Magination Press.
This story deals with the many complicated feelings a child may experience when their sibling has a serious illness.

Siegel, I.M. (1989) *Hey, I'm Here Too!* London: The Muscular Dystrophy Group.

GOING INTO HOSPITAL/PREPARATION FOR PROCEDURES

Bond, M. (2001) *Paddington Goes to Hospital*. New York: HarperCollins Publishers.
This book describes the amusing misunderstandings and adventures of Paddington as he goes into hospital, and is good for children who may be apprehensive, or merely curious, about what goes on inside a hospital.

Braithwaite, A. (1986) *Going Into Hospital*. Miami: Parkwest Publications.

Moon, T. and Stachini, V. (2009) *Jack's MRI Adventure*. Guy's and St Thomas' Foundation Trust (only available through www.guysandstthomas.nhs.uk).
A photo story book of a young boy having an MRI at the Evelina Hospital.

Wade, B. and Fairclough, C. (1981) *Linda Goes To Hospital*. London: A & C Black.

RELAXATION

Allen, J.S. and Klein, R.J. (1996) *Ready…Set…R.E.L.A.X* (A Research Based Program of Relaxation, Learning and Self-Esteem for Children). Wisconsin: Inner Coaching.

Thompson, L. (2005) *Harry the Hypno-Potamus: Metaphorical Tales for the Treatment of Children*. Norwalk, CT: Crown House Publishing Company.

Viegas, M. (2004) *Relax Kids: The Wishing Star*. Winchester: O Books.
This book uses guided meditations based around traditional stories to introduce older children to meditation and relaxation.

Williams, M.L. (1996) *Cool Cats: Calm Kids, Relaxation and Stress Management for Young People*. Atascadero, CA: Impact Publishers.
This book uses a cat behaviour analogy to teach children good ways of managing stressful situations.

References

ACT (2007) *The Transition Care Pathway (A framework for the development of integrated multi-agency care pathways for young people with long term and life limiting conditions)* www.act.org.uk.

ACT (2009) *How Many Children Have Palliative Care Needs?* www.act.org.uk.

Alderson, P. and Montgomery, J. (1996) *Health Care Choices: Making Decisions with Children.* London: Institute for Public Policy Research.

Andrews, J., Scharff, L. and Moses, L. (2002) 'The influence of illustrations in children's storybooks.' *Reading Psychology 23,* 4, 323–330.

Austin, J.K. and Caplan, R. (2007) 'Behavioural and psychiatric co-morbidities in paediatric epilepsy: toward an integrative model.' *Epilepsia 48,* 1639–1651.

Barakat, L., Alderfer, M.A. and Kazak, A.E. (2006) 'Posttraumatic growth in adolescent survivors of cancer and their mothers and fathers.' *Journal of Pediatric Psychology 31,* 413–419.

Barrera, M., Chung, J. and Fleming C. (2004) 'A group intervention for siblings of pediatric cancer patients.' *Journal of Psychosocial Oncology 22,* 21–39.

Bauchner, H., Vinci, R. and Waring, C. (1989) 'Pediatric procedures: do parents want to watch?' *Pediatrics 84,* 907–909.

Bauchner, H., Vinci, R. and May, A. (1994) 'Teaching parents how to comfort their children during common medical procedures.' *Archives of Disease in Childhood 70,* 548–550.

Beales, J.G., Holt, P.L.J., Keen, J.H. and Mellor, V.P. (1983) 'Children with chronic arthritis: Their beliefs about their illness and therapy.' *Annals of Rheumatic Disease 42,* 483–486.

Beresford, B. (1994) 'Resources and strategies: How parents cope with the care of a disabled child.' *Journal of Child Psychology and Psychiatry 35,* 171–209.

Berge, J.M., Patterson, J.M. and Reuter, M. (2006) 'Marital satisfaction and mental health of couples with children with chronic health conditions.' *Families, Systems and Health 24,* 267–285.

Blount, R.L., Piira, T. and Cohen, L.L. (2003) 'Management of Pediatric Pain and Distress Due to Medical Procedures.' In M.C. Roberts (Ed) *Handbook of Pediatric Psychology* (216–233). New York: Guilford Press.

Bluebond-Langner, M. (1978*) The Private Worlds of Dying Children.* Princeton, NJ: Princeton University Press.

Bluebond-Langner, M. (1996) 'In the Shadow of Illness.' *Parents and Siblings of the Chronically Ill Child.* Princeton, NJ: Princeton University Press.

Blum, R.W., Garell, D. and Hodgman, C. (1993) 'Transitions from child-centred to adult health care systems for adolscents with chronic conditions – a position paper of the Society for Adolescent Medicine.' *Journal of Adolescent Health 14,* 570–576.

Breau, L.M., McGrath, P.J., Camfield, G. and Finley, A. (2002) 'Properties of the non-communicating children's pain checklist-revised.' *Pain 99,* 349–357.

Breau, L.M., Camfield, C.S. and McGrath, P.J. (2003) 'The incidence of pain in children with severe cognitive impairments.' *Archives of Paediatrics and Adolescent Medicine 157,* 12, 1219–1226.

British Psychological Society (2002) *Psychological Debriefing: Professional Practice Board Working Party.* Leicester: BPS.

Broome, M.E., Bates, T.A., Lillis, P.P. and McGahee, T.W. (1994). 'Children's medical fears, coping behaviour patterns and pain perceptions during a lumbar puncture.' *European Journal of Cancer Care 3,* 31–38.

Brown, R.T., Wiener, L., Kupst, M.J., Brennan, T. *et al.* (2008) 'Single parents of children with chronic illness: An understudied phenomenon.' *Journal of Pediatric Psychology 33,* 4, 408–421.

Cadman, D., Boyle, N., Szatmari, G. and Offord, D. (1987) 'Chronic illness, disability and mental and social wellbeing: Findings from the Ontario Child Health Study.' *Pediatrics 79,* 705–712.

Channon, S.J., Huws-Thomas, M.V., Rollnick, S., Hood, K. *et al.* (2007) 'A multicenter randomised controlled trial of motivational interviewing in teenager with diabetes.' *Diabetes Care 30,* 1390–1395.

Christie, D. and Wilson, C. (2004) 'CBT in paediatric and adolescent health settings: A review of practice-based evidence.' *Paediatric Rehabilitation 8,* 4, 241–247.

Clay, R. and Knibbs, J. and Joseph, S. (2009) 'Measurement of posttraumatic growth in young people: A review.' *Clinical Child Psychology and Psychiatry 14,* 3, 411–422.

Coad, J. (2007) Using art-based techniques in engaging children and young people in health care consultations and/or research. *Journal of Research in Nursing 12*, 5, 487–497.

Cohen, L., Blount, R.L., Cohen, R.J., Schaen, E.R. and Zaff, J.F. (1999). A comparison study of distraction versus topical anesthesia for pediatric pain management during immunizations, *Health Psychology 18*, 591–598.

Cohen, L., La Greca, A.M., Blount, R.L., Kazak, A.E., Holmbeck, G.N. and Lemanek, K.L. (2008) 'Introduction to special issue: Evidence-based assessment in pediatric psychology' *Journal of Pediatric Psychology 33*, 911–915.

Cohen, L., Lemanek, K., Blount, R., Dahlquist, L. *et al.* (2008) 'Evidence-based assessment of pediatric pain.' *Journal of Pediatric Psychology 33*, 939–955.

Connelly, M. Rapott, M.A. and Tompdon, N. (2006) 'Headstrong: A pilot study of a CD-ROM intervention for current paediatric headache.' *Journal of Pediatric Pain 31*, 7, 737–747.

Contact a Family (2005) Parent participation guide. Available at www.cafamily.org.uk/pdfs/ParentParticipationGuide.pdf, accessed on 2 July 2010.

Craig, T.K.J., Cox, A. and Klein, K. (2002) 'Intergenerational transmission of somatization behaviour: A study of chronic somatizers and their children.' *Psychological Medicine 32*, 805–816.

Craig, Dr. Finella (2010) Personal communication. Consultant in Palliative Care at Great Ormond Street Hospital.

Curle, C., Bradford, J., Thompson, J. and Cawthron, P. (2005) 'Users' views of a group therapy intervention for chronically ill or disabled children and their parents: Towards a meaningful assessment of therapeutic effectiveness.' *Clinical Child Psychology and Psychiatry 10*, 509–527.

Currie J. (2006) 'Management of chronic pain in children.' *Archives of Disease in Childhood Educational Practice 91*, 111–114.

Dahlquist, L.M., Gil, K.M., Armstron, F.D., DeLawyer, D.D., Greene, P. and Wuori, D. (1986) 'Preparing children for medical examinations: The importance of previous medical experience.' *Health Psychology 5*, 249–259.

Dahlquist, L.M., Pendley, J.S., Landtrip, D.S., Jones, C.L. and Steuber, C.P. (2002) 'Distraction interventions for preschoolers undergoing intramuscular injections and subcutaneous port access.' *Health Psychology 21*, 94–99.

Deiros-Collado, M. (2010) The experience of attending a social support group for young people with multiple chronic health conditions (submitted as part of Doctoral Research Thesis). UCL.

Department for Children, Schools and Families (2001) *Toolkit for the Special Educational Needs Code of Practice.* London: The Stationery Office.

Department for Children, Schools and Families (2009) *Lamb Inquiry: Special Educational Needs and Parental Confidence.* London: The Stationery Office.

Department for Education and Skills (2002) *Together from the Start: Practical Guidance for Professionals Working with Disabled Children and Their Families.* London: The Stationery Office.

Department of Health (1993) *Guidance on Permissible Forms of Control in Children's Residential Care.* London: The Stationery Office.

Department of Health (2000) *The NHS Plan: A Plan for Investment, a Plan for Reform.* London: The Stationery Office.

Department of Health, Department for Education and Skills (2001) *Access to Education for Children and Young People with Medical Needs: Statutory Guidance.* London: The Stationery Office.

Department of Health (2003a) *Keeping the NHS Local: A New Direction of Travel.* London: The Stationery Office.

Department of Health (2003b) *Getting the Right Start: National Service Framework for Children – Standard 7: Services for Children and Young People in Hospital.* London: The Stationery Office.

Department of Health (2006a) 'Reward and Recognition: The principles and practice of service user payment and reimbursement in health and social care'. *A Guide for Service Providers. Service Users and Carers.* London: The Stationery Office.

Department of Health (2006b) *Transition. Getting it Right for Young People.* London: The Stationery Office

Department of Health (2007) *Palliative Care Statistics for Children and Young Adults.* London: The Stationery Office.

Department of Health (2008a) *Better Care: Better Lives. Improving Outcomes and Experiences for Children, Young People and Their Families Living with Life-limiting and Life-threatening Conditions.* London: The Stationery Office.

Department of Health (2008b) *High Quality Care for All.* Lord Darzi Report. London: The Stationery Office.

Department of Health (2008c) *Healthcare for All. Report of the Independent Enquiry into Access to Healthcare for People with Learning Difficulties.* London: The Stationery Office

Department of Health (2008d) *Transition. Moving on Well.* London: The Stationery Office.

Department of Health (2009) *The Expert Patients Programme.* London: The Stationery Office

Drotar, D. (2009) 'Physician behavior in the care of pediatric chronic illness: Association with health outcomes and treatment adherence.' *Journal of Developmental and Behavioral Pediatrics 30*, 3, 246–254.

Duff, A.J.A. (2003) 'Incorporating psychological approaches into routine paediatric venepuncture.' *Archives of Disease in Childhood 88*, 931–937.

Duff, A.J.A. and Bryon, M. (2005) 'Consultation to paediatric teams.' *Clinical Child Psychology and Psychiatry 10*, 102–111.

Duff, A.J.A. and Bliss, A.K. (2005) 'Reducing stress during venepuncture.' In T.J. David (Ed.) *Recent Advances in Paediatrics 22*, 149–157. London: Royal Society of Medicine.

Eccleston, C., Morley, S., Williams, A., Yorle, L. and Mastroyannopoulou, K. (2002) 'Systemic review of randomised controlled trials of psychological therapy for chronic pain in children and adolescents, with a subset meta-analysis of pain relief.' *Pain 99*, 157–165.

Eccleston, C., Jordan, A.L. and Crombez, G. (2006) 'The impact of pain on adolescents: A review of previously used measures.' *Journal of Pediatric Psychology 31*, 684–697.

Edwards, L. and Palmer, J. (2007) *Facing the Death of Your Child – Suggestions and Help for Families, Before and Afterwards*. London: Children's Cancer and Leukaemia Group (CCLG) and The Royal Marsden.

Eiser, C. (1993) *Growing Up with a Chronic Disease: The Impact on Children and Their Families*. London: Jessica Kingsley Publishers.

Eiser, C. (1989) 'Children's understanding of illness: A critique of the "stage" approach.' *Psychology and Health 7*, 249–257.

Eiser, C. and Jenney, M. (2007) 'Measuring quality of life.' *Archives of Disease in Childhood 92*, 348–350.

Eminson, D.M. (2007) 'Medically unexplained symptoms in children and adolescents.' *Clinical Psychology Review 2*, 7, 855–871.

Engel, G.L. (1977) 'The need for a new medical model.' *Science 196*, 129–136.

Fredman, G. (1997) *Death Talk*. London: Karnac Books.

Gaffney, A. and Dunne, E. (1986) 'Developmental aspects of children's definitions of pain.' *Pain 26*, 1, 105–117.

Gaffney, A. and Dunne, E. (1987) 'Children's understanding of the causality of pain.' *Pain 29*, 1, 91–104.

Garralda, M.E. and Chalder, T. (2005) 'Practitioner review: Chronic fatigue syndrome in childhood.' *Journal of Child Psychology and Psychiatry 46*, 1143–1151.

Gessler, S., Low, J., Daniells, E., Williams, R. *et al.* (2008) 'Screening for distress in cancer patients: is the distress thermometer a valid measure in the UK and does it measure change over time? A prospective validation study.' *Psycho-Oncology, 17*, 538–547.

Gibson, F. (2007) Conducting focus groups with children and young people: strategies for success. *Journal of Research in Nursing, 12*, 5, 473–483).

Glasscoe, C., Lancaster, G.A., Smyth, R.L. and Hill, J. (2007) 'Parental depression following the early diagnosis of cystic fibrosis: a matched, prospective study.' *Journal of Pediatrics 150*, 2, 185–191.

Glazebrook, C., Hollis, C., Heussler, H., Goodman, R. and Coates, L. (2003) 'Detecting emotional and behavioural problems in paediatric clinics.' *Child: Care, Health and Development 29*, 141–149.

Goodenough, B. Warwick, T.G. Champion, D., Perrott, D. *et al.* (1999) 'Unravelling age effects and sex differences in needle pain: ratings of sensory intensity and unpleasantness of venepuncture pain by children and their parents.' *Pain 80*, 1–2, 179–190.

Goodman, R. (1997) 'The Strengths and Difficulties Questionnaire: A research note.' *Journal of Child Psychology and Psychiatry 38*, 581–586.

Griffin, A. and Christie, D. (2008) 'Taking the psycho out of psychosomatic: Using systemic approaches in a paediatric setting for the treatment of adolescents with unexplained physical symptoms.' *Clinical Child Psychology and Psychiatry 13*, 4, 531–542.

Grinyer, A. (2007) *Young People Living with Cancer – Implications for Policy and Practice*. London: Open University Press.

Harvey, A. and Morton, N. (2007) 'Management of procedural pain in children.' *Archives Disease in Childhood. Educational Practice 92*, 20–26.

Health Professions Council (2009) *Standards of Proficiency for Practitioner Psychologists*. London: HPC.

Health and Safety Executive (2007) *Managing the Causes of Work Related Stress*. Sudbury: HSE Books.

Hilden, J.M., Watterson, J. and Chrastek, J. (2000) 'Tell the children.' *Journal of Clinical Oncology 8*, 3193–3195.

Hirschfield, D.R., Rosenbaum, J., Biederman, J., Bolduc, E.A. *et al.* (1992) 'Stable behavioural inhibition and its association with anxiety disorder.' *Journal of the American Academy of Child and Adolescent Psychiatry 31*, 103–111.

Holmbeck, G.N., Gorey-Ferguson, L., Hudson, T., Sefeldt, T. *et al.* (1997) 'Maternal, paternal, and marital functioning in families of preadolescents with spina bifida.' *Journal of Pediatric Psychology 22*, 2, 167–181.

Hongo, T., Watanabe, C., Okada, S., Inoue, N. *et al.* (2003) 'Analysis of the circumstances at the end of life in children with cancer: Symptoms, suffering and acceptance.' *Paediatric International 45*, 60–64.

Hotopf, M., Carr, S., Mayou, R., Wadsworth, M. and Wessely, S. (1998) 'Why do children have chronic abdominal pain and what happens to them when they grow up? Population based cohort study.' *British Medical Journal 316*, 1196–1200.

Houghton, J. (2005) 'Paediatric psychology in the twenty-first century: Forward together?' *Clinical Child Psychology and Psychiatry 10*, 112–115.

Hunt, A., Goldman, A., Seers, K., Crichton, N. *et al.* (2002) 'Clinical validation of the Paediatric Pain Profile.' *Developmental Medicine and Child Neurology 46*, 9–18.

Husain, K., Browne, T. and Chalder, T. (2007) 'A review of psychological models and interventions for medically unexplained somatic symptoms in children.' *Child and Adolescent Mental Health 12*, 2–7.

Jaaniste, T., Hayes, B., and Von Bayer, C.L. (2007) 'Providing children with information about forthcoming medical procedures: A review and synthesis.' *Clinical Psychology: Science and Practice 14*, 124–143.

Jay, S.M., Ozolins, M., Elliott, C.H. and Caldwell, S. (1983) 'Assessment of children's distress during painful medical procedures.' *Health Psychology 2*, 133–147.

Judd, D. (1995) *Give Sorrow Words. Working with a Dying Child.* London: Whurr Publishers Ltd.

Kahana, S., Drotar, D. and Frazier, T. (2008) 'Meta-analysis of psychological interventions to promote adherence to treatment in pediatric chronic health conditions.' *Journal of Pediatric Psychology 33*, 590–611.

Kain, Z.N., Mayers, L.C., Wang, S.M., Caramico, L.A., Krivutza, D.M. and Hofstadler, M.B. (2000) 'Parental presence and a sedative premedication for children undergoing surgery: A hierarchical study.' *Anaesthesiology 92*, 939–946.

Kane, B. (1979) 'Children's concept of death.' *Journal of Genetic Psychology 134*, 141–153.

Kazak, A.E. (1989) 'Families of chronically ill children: A systems and social-ecological model of adaptation and challenge.' *Journal of Consulting and Clinical Psychology 57*, 25–30.

Kazak, A. (2006) 'Pediatric Psychosocial Preventative Health Model (PPPHM): Research, practice and collaboration in pediatric family systems medicine.' *Families, Systems and Health 24*, 381–395.

Kazak, A.E., Kassam-Adams, N., Schneider, S., Zelikovsky, N., Alderfer, M.A. and Rourke, M. (2006) 'An integrative model of pediatric medical traumatic stress.' *Journal of Pediatric Psychology 31*, 343–355.

Kazak, A.E., Penati, B., Boyer, B.A., Himelstein, B. *et al.* (1996) 'A randomised controlled prospective study of a psychological and pharmacological intervention protocol for procedural distress in pediatric leukaemia.' *Journal of Pediatric Psychology 21*, 615–631.

Kazak, A.E., Schneider, S. and Kassam-Adams, N. (2009) 'Pediatric Medical Traumatic Stress.' In M.C. Roberts and R.G. Steele (eds) *Handbook of Pediatric Psychology* (4th edition). London: Guilford Press.

Kingsley, E.P. (1981) *Welcome to Holland.* From 'Kids like these' CBS-TV Movie of the Week, Nexus Productions.

Kipps, S., Bahu, T. and Ong, K. (2002) 'Current methods of transfer of young people with type I diabetes to adult services.' *Diabetic Medicine 19*, 8, 649–654.

Kish, V. and Lansdown, R. (2000) 'Meeting the psychosocial impact of facial disfigurement: Developing a clinical service for children and families.' *Clinical Child Psychology and Psychiatry 5*, 497–512.

Kleiber, C., Schutte, D., McCarthy, A., Floira-Santos, M., Murray, J. and Hanrahan, K. (2007) 'Predictors of topical anaesthesia effectiveness in children.' *Journal of Pain 8*, 168–174.

Kraemer, S. (2009) 'The menace of psychiatry: does it still ring a bell?' *Archives of Disease in Childhood 94*, 570–572.

Kreicsbergs, U., Valdimarsdottir, U., Onelov, E., Henter, J.I. and Steineck., G (2004) 'Talking about death with children who have severe malignant disease.' *New England Journal of Medicine 12*, 351, 1175–1186.

Krueger, R.A. (1994) *Focus Groups: A Practical Guide for Applied Research* (2nd edition). Thousand Oaks, CA: Sage Publications.

Kübler-Ross, E. (1969) *On Death and Dying.* New York: Macmillan.

LaGreca, A.M. and Mackey, E. (2009) 'Adherence to Pediatric Treatment Regimes.' In M.C. Roberts and R.G. Steele (eds) *Handbook of Pediatric Psychology* (4th edition). London: Guilford Press.

Laming, W.H. (2003) *The Victoria Climbié Inquiry.* London: Department of Health.

Lansdown, R. and Benjamin, G. (1985) 'The development of the concept of death in children aged 5–9 years.' *Child: Care, Health and Development 11*, 13–20.

Lansdown, R. and Sokel, B. (1993) 'Commissioned review: Approaches to pain management in children.' *Association of Child Psychology and Psychiatry Review and Newsletter 15*, 105–111.

Latchford, G., Duff, A., Quinn, J., Conway, S. and Conner, M. (2009) 'Adherence to nebulised antibiotics in cystic fibrosis.' *Patient Education and Counselling 75*, 141–144.

Lavigne, J.V. and Faier-Routman, J. (1992) 'Psychological adjustment to pediatric physical disorder: A meta analytic review.' *Journal of Pediatric Psychology 17*, 133–157.

Lazarus, J.V. and Folkman, S. (1984) *Stress, Appraisal and Coping.* New York: Springer.

Lewis-Jones, M.S. and Finlay, A.Y. (1995) 'The Children's Dermatology Life Quality Index (CDLQI): Initial validation and practical use.' *British Journal of Dermatology 132*, 942–949.

Liossi, C L., White, P., Franck, L. and Hatira, P. (2007) 'Parental pain expectancy as a mediator between child expected and experienced procedure–related pain intensity during painful medical procedures.' *Clinical Journal Pain 23*, 5, 392–399.

Lovegrove, E. and Rumsey, N. (2005) 'Ignoring it doesn't make it stop: Adolescents, appearance and bullying.' *Cleft Palate-Craniofacial Journal 42*, 33–43.

McDaniel, S., Hepworth, J. and Doherty W. (1992) *Medical Family Therapy.* New York: Basic Books.

McDonagh, J.E., Shaw, K.L. and Southwood, T.R. (2006) 'Growing up and moving on in rheumatology: Development and preliminary evaluation of a transitional care programme for a multicentre cohort of adolescents with juvenile ideopathic arthritis.' *Journal of Child Health Care 10*, 1, 22–42.

McDowell, E., Davidson, S. and Titman, P. (2010) 'Parents' experiences one year on from their child's haematopoietic stem cell transplant for congenital immunodeficiency.' *Journal of Health Psychology* (in press).

McGrath, P., Rice, L., Berde, C.B., Steward, D.J. *et al.* (1993) 'Psychologic perspectives on pediatric pain.' *Journal of Paediatrics 122*, 5, 41–46.

McGrath, P., Rosmus, C., Campbell, M.A. and Hennigar, A. (1998) 'Behaviours caregivers use to determine pain in nonverbal, cognitively impaired individuals.' *Developmental Medicine and Child Neurology 40*, 340–343.

McVicar, A. (2003) 'Workplace stress in nursing: A literature review.' *Journal of Advanced Nursing 44*, 6, 633–642.

Macleod, K.D., Whitsett, S.F., Mash, E.J. and Pelletier, W. (2003) 'Pediatric sibling donors of successful and unsuccessful hematopoietic stem cell transplants (HSCT): A qualitative study of their psychosocial experience.' *Journal of Pediatric Psychology 28*, 223–230.

Maddern, L., Cadogan, J.C., Emerson, M. (2006) 'Outlook: A psychosocial service for children with a different appearance.' *Clinical Child Psychology and Psychiatry 11*, 3, 431–443.

Maddern, L. and Owen, T. (2004) 'The Outlook summer group: A social skills workshop for children with a different appearance who are transferring to secondary school.' *Clinical Psychology 33*, 25–29.

Maslach, C., Schaufeli, W.B. and Leiter, M.P. (2002) 'Job Burnout.' In S.T. Fiske, D.L. Schacter, Zahn-Waxler, C. (eds) *Annual Review of Psychology 52*, 397–422.

Melamed, B.G. and Siegal, L.J. (1975) 'Reduction of anxiety in children facing hospitalization and surgery by use of filmed modeling.' *Journal of Consulting and Clinical Psychology 43*, 4, 511–521

Meltzer, L.J. and Moore, M. (2008) 'Sleep disruptions in parents of children and adolescents with chronic illnesses: Prevalence, cause. and consequences.' *Journal of Pediatric Psychology 33*, 279–291.

Meltzer, H., Gatward, R., Goodman, R. and Ford, T. (2000) *Mental Health of Children and Adolescents in Great Britain.* London: The Stationery Office.

Melzac, R. and Wall, P.D. (1965) 'Pain mechanisms – a new theory.' *Science 150*, 971–979.

Melzac, R. and Wall, P.D. (1982) *The Challenge of Pain.* New York: Basic Books.

Miller, W.R. and Rollnick, S. (2002) *Motivational Interviewing: Preparing People to Change Addictive Behaviour* (second edition). New York: Guilford Press.

Modi, A.C., Marciel, K.K., Slater, S.K., Drotar, D. and Quittner, A.L. (2008) 'The influence of parental supervision on medical adherence in adolescents with cystic fibrosis: Developmental shifts from pre to late adolescence.' *Children's Health Care 37*, 78–92.

Moon, T. and Stachini, V. (2009) *An Audit of the Impact of Play Preparation for Children Undergoing MRI Scan...* Poster presentation at Guy's and St Thomas' Hospital.

Morgan, D. (2009) 'Caring for dying children – assessing the needs of the pediatric palliative care nurse.' *Paediatric Nurse 35* (2), 86–90.

National Deaf Children's Society (2004) Deaf children and young people in hospital: A guide for professionals. *Care Guideline.* www.ndcs.org.uk

National Health Services Employers (2009) Staff Engagement: Healthcare Commission Research. Available from www.nhsemployers.org.

NICE (2005) *Improving Outcomes for Children and Young People with Cancer: Needs Assessment.* London: National Institute for Health and Clinical Excellence.

NICE (2007) *Chronic Fatigue Syndrome/Myalgic Encephalomyelitis (or Encephalopathy): Diagnosis and Management.* London: National Institute for Health and Clinical Excellence.

NICE (2009a) *Promoting Mental Wellbeing at Work.* London: National Institute for Health and Clinical Excellence.

NICE (2009b) *Guidance on When to Suspect Child Maltreatment.* London: National Institute for Health and Clinical Excellence.

NICE (2009c) *Medicines Adherence: Involving Patients in Decisions about Prescribed Medicine and Supporting Adherence.* London: National Institute for Health and Clinical Excellence.

Nolan, T., Zvagulis, I. and Pless, B. (1987) 'Controlled Trial of Social Work on Childhood Illness.' *The Lancet 2*, 411–415.

O'Curry, S. (2009) 'Staff support in a medical setting.' Paper presented at the Paediatric Psychology Study Day, Leeds, UK.

O'Dell, L. and Prior, J. (2005) 'Evaluating a school's service for children with a facial disfigurement: The views of teaching and support staff.' *Support for Learning 20*, 2, 35–40.

Oltjenbruns, K.A. (2001) 'Developmental Context of Childhood Grief: Grief and regrief phenomena.' In M.S. Strobe, R.O. Hansson, W. Stroebe and H. Schut (eds). *Handbook of Bereavement Research: Consequences Coping Care.* Washington, DC: American Psychological Society.

Olweus D. (1993) *Bullying in School: What We Know and What We Can Do.* Oxford: Blackwell.

Moon, T. and Stachnini (2009) An Audit of the Impact of Play Preparation on the MR Images of Paediatric Patients at ECH. (poster presented at GSTFT study day).

Packman, W.L. (1999) 'Psychosocial impact of pediatric BMT on siblings.' *Bone Marrow Transplant 24*, 701–706.

Palermo, T.M., Long, A.C., Lewandowski, A.S., Drotar, D., Quittner, A.L. and Walker L.S. (2008) 'Evidence-based assessment of health-related quality of life and functional impairment in pediatric psychology.' *Journal of Pediatric Psychology 33*, 983–996.

Paediatric Psychology Network (2008) *A Guide to Commissioning Paediatric Clinical Psychology Services in the UK Briefing Paper.* London: PPN.

Paediatric Psychology Network (2010) *Good Practice Guidelines for the Management of Invasive and/or Distressing Procedures with Children.* London: British Psychological Society.

Pate, J.T., Blount, R.L., Cohen, L. and Smith, A. (1996) 'Childhood medical experience and temperament as predictors of adult functioning in medical situations.' *Children's Health Care 25*, 4, 281–298.

Penguin, C.W., Hunfield, J.A.M. and Harzbrock-Kampschreur, A.A.J.M. (2001) 'Insights in the use of health care services in chronic benign pain in childhood and adolescence.' *Pain 94*, 2, 205–213.

Phipps, S., Dunavant, M., Garvie, P., Lensing, S. and Rai, S.N. (2002) 'Acute health-related quality of life in children undergoing stem cell transplant: I. Descriptive outcomes.' *Bone Marrow Transplantation 29*, 425–434.

Phipps, S., Dunavant, M., Lensing, S. and Rai, S.N. (2002) 'Acute health-related quality of life in children undergoing stem cell transplant: II. Medical and demographic determinants.' *Bone Marrow Transplantation 29*, 435–442.

Phipps, S., Dunavant, M., Lensing, S. and Rai, S.N. (2005) 'Psychosocial predictors of distress in parents of children undergoing stem cell or bone marrow transplantation.' *Journal of Pediatric Psychology 30*, 2, 139–153.

Piira, T., Sugiura, T., Champion, G.D., Donnelly, N. and Cole, A.S.J. (2005) 'The role of parental presence in the context of children's medical procedures: A systematic review.' *Child: Care, Health and Development 31*, 233–243.

Plante, W.A., Lobato, D. and Engel, R. (2001) 'Review of group interventions of pediatric chronic conditions.' *Journal of Pediatric Psychology. 26*, 7, 435–454.

Pless, I.B. (1984) 'Clinical assessment: Physical and psychological functioning.' *Pediatric Clinics of North America 31*, 33–46

Prochaska, J.O. and Di Clemente, C.C. (1982) 'Transtheoretical therapy: Toward a more integrative model of change.' *Psychotherapy: Theory Research and Practice 19*, 276–288.

Quittner, A.L., Buu, A., Messer, M.A., Modi, A.C. and Watrous, M. (2005) 'Development and validation of the Cystic Fibrosis Questionnaire in the United States: A health related quality of life measure for cystic fibrosis.' *Chest 128*, 4, 2347–2354.

Quittner, A.L., Espelage, D.L., Ievers-Landis, C.E. and Drotar, D. (2000) 'Measuring adherence to medical treatments in childhood chronic illness: Considering multiple methods and sources of information.' *Journal of Clinical Psychology in Medical Settings 7*, 41–54.

Quittner, A., Espelage, D.L., Opipari, L.C., Carter, B., Eid, N. and Eigen, H. (1998) 'Role strain in couples with and without a child with chronic illness: Associations with marital satisfaction, intimacy and daily mood.' *Health Psychology 17*, 112–124.

Ranger, M. and Campbell-Yeo, M. (2008) Temperament and pain response:a review of the literature. *Pain Management Nursing 9*, 1, 2–9.

Rapoff, M.A. (1999) *Adherence to Pediatric Medical Regimens.* New York: Kluwer Academic/Plenum Publishers.

Reaney, R. (2007) 'Assessing pain in children.' *Anaesthesia and Intensive Care Medicine 8*, 5, 180–183.

Reder, P. and Fredman, G. 'The relationship to help: Interacting beliefs about the treatment process.' *Clinical Child Psychology and Psychiatry 3*, 1, 457–467.

Reiter-Purtill, J. Waller, J.M. and Noll, R.B. (2009) 'Empirical and theoretical perspectives on the peer relationships of children with chronic conditions.' Chapter 45 in M.C. Roberts and R.G. Steele (eds) *Handbook of Pediatric Psychology* (4th edition). London: Guilford Press.

Rennick, J., Johnston, C., Dougherty, G., Platt, R. and Ritchie, J. (2002) 'Children's psychological responses to illness and exposure to invasive technology.' *Developmental and Behavioral Pediatrics 23*, 133–144.

Retsch-Bogart, G.Z., Burns, J.L., Otto, K.L., Liou, T.G. *et al.* (2008) 'A phase 2 study of aztreonam lysine for inhalation to treat patients with cystic fibrosis and Pseudomanas aeruginosa infection.' *Pediatric pulmonology 43*, 47–58.

Rolland, J.S. (1987) 'Chronic illness and the life cycle: A conceptual framework.' *Family Process 26*, 203–221.

Royal College of Paediatrics and Child Health (1997) *Withholding and Withdrawing Life Saving Treatment in Children: A Framework for Practice* (second edition). www.rcpch.ac.uk.

Royal College of Paediatrics and Child Health (2003) *Bridging the Gaps: Healthcare for Adolescents.* Accessed from www.rcph.ac.uk

Royal College of Nursing (2005) *Managing Your Stress: A Guide For Nurses.* www.rcn.org.uk.

Royal College of Nursing (2007a) *Guidance on User Involvement in Research by Nurses.* www.rcn.org.uk.

Royal College of Nursing (2007b) *Holding On: Nurses' Employment and Morale in 2007.* London: RCN.

Royal College of Nursing (2009) *Work-Related Stress. A Good Practice Guide for RCN Representatives.* London: RCN.

Rumsey, N. and Harcourt, D. (2007) 'Visible difference amongst children and adolescents: Issues and interventions.' *Developmental Neurorehabilitation 10,* 113–123.

Russell, P. (2003) *Bridging the Gap: Developing Policy and Practice in Child Care Options for Disabled Children and Their Families.* London: Council for Disabled Children.

Sabbeth, B.F. and Leventhal, J.M. (1984) 'Marital adjustment to chronic childhood illness.' *Pediatrics 73,* 762–768.

Sanders, M.R. (1999) 'Triple P Positive Parenting Program: Towards an empirically validated multilevel parenting and family support strategy for the prevention of behavior and emotional problems in children.' *Clinical Child and Family Psychology Review 2,* 71–90.

Schechter, N.L., Blankson, V., Pachter, L.M., Sullivan, C.M. and Costa, L. (1997) 'Ouchless place. No pain, children's gain.' *Pediatrics 99,* 890–894.

Scope (1994) *Right From The Start Report: The Template.* Right from the Start Working Group.

Sharpe, D. and Rossiter, L. 'Siblings of children with a chronic illness: A meta-analysis.' *Journal of Pediatric Psychology 27,* 699–710.

Shemesh, E., Lune, S., Stuber, M.L., Emre, S. *et al.* (2000) 'A pilot-study of post traumatic stress and non-adherence in pediatric liver transplant patients. *Pediatrics 105,* e29.

Sleed, M., Eccleston, C., Beecham T., Knapp, M. and Jordan, A. (2005) 'The economic impact of chronic pain in adolescence: Methodological considerations and a preliminary costs-of-illness study.' *Pain 119,* 183–190.

Sloper, P. (2000) 'Predictors of distress in parents of children with cancer: a prospective study.' *Journal of Pediatric Psychology 25,* 79–91.

Sloper, T. and Beresford, B. (2006) 'Families with disabled children.' *British Medical Journal 333,* 928–929.

Spinetta, J.J. (1974) 'The dying child's awareness of death: A review.' *Psychology Bulletin 81,* 256–260.

Spirito, A. and Kazak, A. (2006) *Effective and Emerging Treatments in Pediatric Psychology.* New York: Oxford University Press.

Stallard, P. (2002a) 'Brief report: Behaviors identified by caregivers to detect pain in noncommunicating children.' *Journal of Pediatric Psychology 27,* 209–214.

Stallard, P. (2002b) *Think Good Feel Good: A Cognitive Behavioural Therapy Workbook for Children and Young People.* Chichester: Wiley.

Stehl, M.L., Kazak, A.E., Alderfer, M., Rodriguez, A. *et al.* 'Conducting a randomised clinical trial of a psychological intervention for parents/caregivers of children with cancer shortly after diagnosis.' *Journal of Pediatric Psychology 34,* 803–816.

Stoneman, Z. and Gavidia-Payne, S. (2006) 'Marital adjustment in families of young children with disabilities: Associations with daily hassles and problem-focused coping.' *American Journal of Mental Retardation 111,* 1–14.

Suls, J. and Wan, C.K. (1989) 'The effects of sensory and procedural information on coping with stressful medical procedures and pain: A meta-analysis.' *Journal of Consulting and Clinical Psychology 57,* 372–379.

Tedeschi, R.G. and Calhoun, L.G. (1996) 'The posttraumatic growth inventory: Measuring the positive legacy of trauma.' *Journal of Traumatic Stress 9,* 455–472.

Theunissen, J.M.J., Hoogerbrugge, P.M., van Achterberg, T., Prins, J.B., Vernooij-Dassen, M.J. and van den Ende, C.H. (2007) 'Symptoms in the palliative phase of children with cancer.' *Pediatric Blood Cancer 49,* 160–165.

Tomlinson, P. and Sugarman, I.D. (1995) 'Complications with shunts in adults with spina bifida.' *British Medical Journal 311,* 7000, 286–287.

Turner, J. (2006) 'Representations of illness, injury and health in children's picture books.' *Children's Health Care 35,* 2, 179–189.

Uman, L.S., Chambers, C.T., McGrath, P.J. and Kisely, S. (2008) 'A systematic review of randomised controlled trials examining psychological interventions for needle-related procedural pain and distress in children and adolescents: An abbreviated Cochrane Review.' *Journal of Pediatric Psychology 33,* 842–854.

Vannatta, K., Gartstein, M.A., Zeller, M. and Noll, R.B. (2009) 'Peer acceptance and social behavior during childhood and adolescence: How important are appearance, athleticism, and academic competence?' *International Journal of Behavioral Development 33,* 303–311.

Varni, J.W., Thompson, K.L. and Hanson, V. (1987) 'The Varni-Thompson Pediatric Pain Questionnaire 1. Chronic musculoskeletal pain in juvenile rheumatoid arthritis.' *Pain 28,* 27–38.

Varni, J.W., Rapoff, M.A., Waldron, S.A., Gragg, R.A., Bernstein, B.H. and Hindsley, C.B. (1996) 'Chronic pain and emotional distress in children and adolescents.' *Developmental and Behavioral Pediatrics 17,* 154–161.

Varni, J.W., Seid, M. and Kurtin, P.S. (2001) 'PedsQL 4.0: Reliability and validity of the Pediatric Quality of Life Inventory version 4.0 generic core scales in healthy and patient populations.' *Medical Care 39,* 800–812.

Viner, R. and Christie, D. (2005) 'Fatigue and somatic symptoms.' *British Medical Journal 330*, 1012–1015.

Voepel-Lewis, T., Merkel, S., Tait, A.R., Trzcinka, A. and Malviya, S. (2002) 'The reliability and validity of the Face, Legs, Activity, Cry, Consolability observational tool as a measure of pain in children with cognitive impairment.' *Anesthesia and Analgesia 95*, 1224–1229.

Vrijmoet-Wiersma, C.M.J., van Klink, J., Kolk, A.M., Koopman, H.M., Ball, L.M. and R. Maarten Egeler, R.M. (2008) 'Assessment of parental psychological stress in pediatric cancer: A review.' *Journal of Pediatric Psychology 33*, 694–706.

Wallander, J.L. and Varni, J.W. (1995) 'Appraisal, coping and adjustment in adolescents with a physical disability.' *Adolescent Health Problems: Behavioural Perspectives*, 209–231.

Wallander, J.L. and Varni, J.W. (1998) 'Effects of pediatric chronic physical illness on children and family adjustment.' *Journal of Child Psychology and Psychiatry 39*, 29–46.

Wang, S.J., Liu, H.C., Fuh, J.L., Liu, C.Y. *et al.* (1997) 'Prevalence of headaches in a Chinese elderly population in Kinmen: Age and gender effect and cross-cultural comparisons.' *Neurology 49*, 195–200.

Waseem, M. and Ryan, M. (2003) 'Parental presence during invasive procedures in children. What is the physician's perspective?' *Southern Medical Journal 96*, 884–887.

Warson, A.R. (2000) 'Non-compliance and transfer from paediatric to adult transplant unit.' *Pediatric Nephrology 14, 6*, 469–472.

Webster-Stratton, C. (2005) *The Incredible Years: A Trouble Shooting Guide for Parents of Children Aged 2–8 Years.* Seattle, WA: The Incredible Years.

Wechsler, D. (2003) *Wechsler Preschool and Primary Intelligence* (third edition). San Antonio, TX: The Psychological Corporation.

Wechsler, D. (2004) *Wechsler Intelligence Scale for Children* (fourth edition). San Antonio, TX: Psychological Corporation.

Weisman, S., Bernstein, B. and Schechter, N. (1998) 'Consequences of inadequate analgesia during painful procedures in children.' *Archives Pediatric Adolescent Medicine 152*, 147–149.

Weiss, D.S. and Marmar, C.R. (1997) 'The Impact of Event Scale.' Revised in J.L. Wilson and T.M. Keane (eds) *Assessing Psychological Trauma and PTSD* (pp 399–411) New York: Guilford Press.

Woolfram, R.W., Turner, E.D. and Philpur, C. (1997) 'Effects of parental presence during young children's venipuncture.' *Paediatric Emergency Care 13*, 325–328.

Wong, D. and Baher, C. (1988) 'Pain in children: Comparison of assessment scales.' *Pediatric Nursing 14*, 19–17.

Wright, B., Aldridge, J., Wurr, K., Sloper, T., Tomlinson, H. and Miller, M. (2009) 'Clinical dilemmas in children with life-limiting illness.' *Palliative Medicine 23*, 3, 238–247.

Wysocki, T., Harris, M.A., Buckloh, L.M., Mertlich, D., Lochrie, A.S. and Taylor, A. (2008) 'Randomised controlled trial of behavioural family systems therapy for diabetes: Maintenance and generalisation of effects on parent-adolescent communication.' *Behavior Therapy 39*, 33–46.

Subject Index

Author Index